The Green Buddha

Christopher Titmuss

edited by Gill Farrer-Halls

Whosoever sees the Dharma sees the Buddha.
Whosoever sees the Buddha sees the Dharma.
The Buddha

Insight Books (Totnes)

Insight Books (Totnes)
c/o Gaia House
Denbury
near Newton Abbot
Devon. TQ12 6DY
England.

tel: 0803 865436
tel: 0803 813188

Distributors:
Wisdom Publications
402 Hoe Street
London E17 9AA
England.

tel: 081 520 5588

Layout and design by Lewis Taylor

Cover design by Rick Lawrence

Cover photo by Glenn McKay of the ascetic Buddha,
Chiang Mai, Thailand

Insight Books is grateful to Micky Karlholm for his support in financing the printing of this book.

ISBN 1-899289-00-3

A catalogue record for this book is available from the British Library.

Printed and bound in Great Britain by
Cromwell Press, Melksham, Wilts.

Dedicated to the welfare, happiness and liberation of all beings.

The Head of the Roman Catholic Church: POPE JOHN PAUL II
Buddhism offers a "doctrine of salvation" that seems increasingly to fascinate many westerners.... It is necessary to pay special attention to Buddhism.

The Author, H.G.WELLS
Buddhism has done more for the advance of world civilization than any other influence in the chronicles of mankind.

The Economist, E.F. SCHUMACHER
From the economist's point of view, the marvel of the Buddhist way of life is the utter rationality of its patterns.

The Fashion Magazine, HARPERS BAZAAR
One might venture that Buddhism, or at least the Buddhist outlook on man and the universe, is becoming more and more the widely accepted world view.

The Nobel Prize Winner, THE DALAI LAMA
My religion is kindness.

The Philosopher, ARTHUR SCHOPENHAUER
If I am to take the results of my study as the standard of truth, I should be obliged to concede to Buddhism the pre-eminence over the rest.

The Poet, T.S. ELIOT
I am not a Buddhist but some of the early Buddhist scriptures affect me as parts of the Old Testament do.

The Non-Violent Activist, MAHATMA GANDHI
Buddha fearlessly ... brought down on its knees an arrogant priesthood. Both [the Buddha and Christ] were for intensely direct action.

The Political Leader, JAWAHARLAL NEHRU
It is essentially through the message of the Buddha that the individual, national and international problems of today can be looked at from the right perspective.

The Psychologist, CARL JUNG
As a student of comparative religion, I believe that Buddhism is the most perfect one the world has seen.

The Scientist, ALBERT EINSTEIN
The religion in the future will be a cosmic religion. It should transcend a personal God and avoid dogma and theology. Buddhism answers this description. If there is any religion that would cope with modern scientific needs, it would be Buddhism.

The Social Commentator, ERICH FROMM
The main ethical goals of Judaism and Christianity—overcoming greed and hate—cannot be realised without another factor that is central in Buddhism: ... penetrating the surface and grasping reality.

The Thinker, ALDOUS HUXLEY
I shall say again and again, that between Buddhism and modern science there exists a close intellectual bond.

Table of Contents

Table of Contents

Acknowledgements

I wish to express appreciation to The Buddha, the 2500 year-old Buddhist tradition and all those that express wisdom and compassion. I wish to express gratitude to Ajahn Dhammadharo (1914–) and Ajahn Buddhadassa (1907-1993) of Thailand. They were pillars of support during my six years as a Buddhist monk in Thailand and India.

I would like to thank the numerous people world wide who continue to give me support in countless ways.

I wish to express gratitude to my daughter, Nshorna Titmuss, the mother of our daughter, Gwanwyn Williams of Totnes, and my mother.

I have benefited from contact with or from the writings and communications of various people world wide. These include Amaravati Monastery, Amnesty, Stuart Anderson, Maurice Ash, Awake, James Baraz, The Barn, Stephen and Martine Batchelor, BBC, Tony Benn, The Beatles, Bergonzi family, Jerusalem Bible, R.H. Blyth, Bodhi Farm, Bodh Gaya, British Rail, Lester R. Brown, Buddhist Peace Fellowship, Buddhist Publishing Group, Wat Chai Na, Channel 4, Noam Chomsky, Edward Conze, the cooks, Dana, Rose Deiss, Christina Feldman, Findhorn Community, Gaia House Carlos Gil, Ven. Maha Ghosananda, Goenka, Joseph Goldstein, Greenline, Chris Gudmensen, Bede Griffiths, Sir Edward Heath, Siva's Hotel, Simeon Hughes, International Network of Engaged Buddhists, Insight Tapes, Michael Jeffries, Jesus, Ken Jones, Paul Koppler, Wat Kow Tham, Joanna Macy, Isabel Marto, Eoin Meades, Milarepa, Mudita, Nyanaponika, R.D. Laing, Trevor Ling, James Lovelock, Mary Lightfoot, Stanislav Menshikov, Thai Monastery, Corrado Pensa. John Pilger, Sutta Pitika, Yanai Posternik, Jack Kornfield, Prajna Vihar School, Resurgence, Self-Heal Association, staff of retreat centres, Root Institute, Larry Rosenberg, Rick Petersson, Poonja, Jose Reissig, Alan Scott-Henderson, Sharda, Sharpham Community, chai shops, Piers Smith, Sobhana, Helen Southern, Anthony Steen, Wat Suanmoke, Ajahn Sumedho, Tricycle, Nanananda, Triple Gem, Turning Wheel, Utne Reader, Varanasi, Steve Verge, Vimalo, Russell Walker, Roger Walsh, Vaughan Williams, the 1930's poets and alternative Totnes. Many of those not listed here are named in my previous book *The Profound and the Profane*.

Special thanks to my editor, Gill Farrer-Halls, who read through the various drafts. Her assistance was invaluable. Thanks also to Amy Ayres who carefully polished one draft and made several helpful suggestions. Many thanks to Gill Farrer-Halls, Micky Karlholm, Rick Lawrence, Dick St. Ruth and Lewis Taylor who form the small team enabling publication and distribution of Insight Books. Thanks also to numerous people and places who have given me support through the years.

May all beings live in peace
May all beings live in harmony
May all beings be liberated.

Introduction

Rain soddens what is kept wrapped up. Uncover then
what is concealed, lest it be soddened by the rain.
The Buddha.

I have written this book with four purposes in mind.
1. *I believe the ego has corrupted the inner life of influential establish-ments with tragic consequences for humanity and the Earth. There is a spiritual vacuum running through our political, corporate, religious and social institutions.*
2. *I believe fundamental changes are essential in how we relate to each other and the Earth.*
3. *I believe thoughtful people world wide, including millions who are members of Green organizations, can benefit from the insights of the Buddha. The West largely ignores the teachings of the Buddha, thus neglecting a profound voice of sanity and moderation expressing unexcelled wisdom and compassion.*
4. *I believe Buddhists, and people with other spiritual values, can bene-fit from the insights of the international Green movement with its commitment to the welfare of the Earth.*

Significant change, if it comes, will emerge from the roots of so-ciety demand for change from the powerful and the privileged. We need a widespread nonviolent revolt against the ruthless self in-terest in our society and our indifference to the suffering of others around the world.

The Third World exports its food to the West for a perilously low price. OXFAM tells us that a cotton grower in Africa must spend a year's salary to buy a cotton sari. Why? Because she grows cotton bound for the Western paradise, receiving only a few cents a day for her labour. Low paid workers of the underdeveloped world support the weekly binge of the overdeveloped world.

Powerful figures, including political leaders, heads of state, roy-alty, religious leaders, scientists and heads of international institu-tions pay lip service to such ecological problems as global warming, damage to the ozone layer, destruction of tropical rain forests, over-population, famine and the rampant selfishness and violence of hu-man behaviour. Yet their policies of continuous economic growth

Introduction

destroy livelihoods, lives and the natural world. Our governments and corporations impede the urgent changes needed for environmental protection.

The Buddha said that desire, aggression, ignorance and fear support corruption and collective selfishness. The outer condition of the Earth is as much an effect of our inner life as our inner life is an effect of our outer life. Powerful political and business leaders are victims of social forces as much as they are responsible for creating them—their egos are part of the same loop.

This book explores the hard truths of human behaviour, our environmental impact and the significance of spiritual awareness and realization. It was not an easy book to write. Spiritual and ecological awakening includes inquiry into our own lives, into the lives of others and our political, business, social and religious institutions. Our entire manner of perceiving existence needs examining.

Unexamined assumptions curse religious and political life. The Green movement, too, has already formed dogmatic views and beliefs not dissimilar to the evangelical wings of religions. The Green movement is also at an impasse; it always has been, but now has the thankless task of having to acknowledge it. We appear not to know where to go, except to continue trying to force politicians and businesses gradually to introduce environmental initiatives, but this approach is a long, slow uphill journey.

The publishing world, which tries to keep its finger on the pulse of public opinion, hesitates to publish Green books because they can no longer get rid of those already on the shelves. Public attention to the environment is short-lived and fickle; it takes drama to create interest and that means suffering, destruction and further bad news. Only wars in places of strategic interest, the development of sophisticated weapons of mass destruction or massive earthquakes, floods and famines stir our attention.

The future of life on Earth appears uncertain. The Greens, professionals and volunteers alike, express an endearing innocence in trying to shift societies and governments away from promoting consumerism. It is one thing to stabilize our Western democratic institutions, introduce the welfare state and abolish the savagery of capital punishment (except in the USA) but the Greens campaign to end greed, corruption and destructiveness on Earth. Even at a local level the task is gargantuan.

In a two party state, the Green Party can only fantasize about power. Campaigning for the Green Party in Britain constitutes a nominal gesture of protest, not a realistic endeavour. I know from experience that standing (twice) for Parliament for the Green Party is a hopeless attempt to get elected. My local member of Parliament, who represents South Hams constituency, has a massive majority; the strength of local loyalty to the Conservative Party guarantees his re-election. Even if the impossible happened and the voters elected me to Parliament, I would hardly influence the nation's policies—not with 650 other Parliamentarians equally keen to have their voices heard. Not surprisingly many Green activists become disheartened and withdraw from working on global issues.

Nevertheless, I do not think *The Green Buddha* is a recipe for despair, but serves instead as an investigation into the very nature and experience of our world. For instance, I believe we take too much for granted in the ways we perceive and respond to situations. The world we perceive and our mental constructions depend upon each other, though we write and speak as if we were detached independent observers of global events with an exact knowledge of how things on Earth are. When we rely upon two forms of communication, namely painful information and personal responses to global issues, we become disillusioned, if not cynical, about the pervasive malaise of public indifference. Our attitudes then become similar to the attitude of those we wish to change. With rare exception, I have restrained from naming corporations and powerful political figures. To target specific organizations or individuals would detract from examining the overall greed, aggression and fear that haunt our world.

The Green Buddha makes no attempt to dish out further painful figures about the Earth and its future nor is it a "how to" guide. I explore the deeper issues and values concerning our relationship to the world. I believe we must question the whole model—and it is a model—of cause and effect. We think this model gives us access to the whole truth and have adopted it along with all its predictions. Also seeing the severe limitations of publicizing painful information and "50 Ways to Save the World," I propose an utter rethink about our beliefs. We assume there is only one world, that we are in agreement about what that world is, and that we are morally bound to preserve it at all costs. I believe that it is in our genuine interest to question all these assumptions. Throughout, the book I have drawn upon the wisdom of the Buddha's teachings.

There is a bewildering array of potential solutions to the problems. Some believe we are digging the grave for our species, others believe that life will carry on despite our lifestyle. Nobody, including Buddhists and Greens, can afford to claim they hold the right view of existence. For, if thoughtful people keep falling back on painful diagnosis and painful prescriptions, then the consciousness of caring people will not inquire deeper into the nature of things. We will stay in a groove, and remain imprisoned in an ideology of our own making. I refer to millions world wide who are members of various Green organizations as well as those whose lifestyles are genuinely sustainable. For sustainable living is an inadequate response to the need for *conscious* living. It is the bare minimum for a life of awareness and realization, though the international Green movement often makes sustainability an end in itself. Various campaigns to awaken the consciousness of people have failed in the face of widespread resistance or indifference to examining our way of life.

Many visionary movements have been tied to national aims, often with the hope of later exporting their vision to other parts of the world. But the Greens cannot do that. By virtue of the interdependence of the ecosystem, the Greens think globally, not nationally. Thus they have the unenviable and irrational task of changing consciousness, not of a nation, but of humankind. Vision, generally, means direction, and the appropriate strategy to take us from a specific Point A to Point B. What the Greens have to ask themselves is what is the nature of their vision and whether there is a genuine realism in this approach.

I have not completely avoided statistics nor have I ignored the "how to" strategy. I have however pushed for something deeper than endless preoccupation with the environment, our notions of what it is and our tactics for dealing with it. I have attempted a synthesis of his insights into the nature of existence with the insights of the Green movement and also investigated the impact of the Buddha's teachings on several influential figures in Western society. Without missionary zeal and religious dogmatism, Buddhism has become the fastest growing religion in Western society. There is a massive decline in church attendance, loss of faith in the Judeo-Christian culture and widespread defection from the church by priests, monks and nuns. Growing numbers of spiritual seekers turn their attention to the Buddhist traditions to see what they have to offer to those who recognize that the root problem in our aggressive and ambitious society is a spiritual one. The Buddha challenges the basic capitalist ethic of desire and personal gain as our raison d'etre, but he also demands that we look into our lives: we must say "no" to all that is harmful and insensitive. What the Buddha said and what capitalism says are incompatible. Awakening to life and truth is at the heart of the message of the Buddha and the Greens—the reason for calling this book *The Green Buddha*.

The interest in Buddhism in recent decades has caught the imagination of a wide range of people in the uphill struggle to bring a new paradigm to society. These include scientists, philosophers. environmentalists, psychotherapists, workers for peace and justice, community builders, and those of a meditative awareness from the world's religions and New Age movements. They acknowledge the debt they owe to the insights of the Buddha and the tradition that emerged after his death. People who turn their attention to Buddhism feel the spiritual support of a long-standing historical tradition—many Greens have taken a particular interest in the Buddha's teachings.

The Buddha's teachings of wisdom and compassion have an enormous practical application; ethics, meditation and realization are the essential foundations of the teachings. Both the Buddha and the Greens analyze cause and effect, action and results in order to end suffering. Yet the Buddha's teachings take a profound step further that is not found in the Green vision. The Green movement is missing the most vital realization—awakening to the Unconditioned, the end of cause and effect. With rare exceptions, the Green movement remains unaware of the significance of Ultimate Truth, unlocated in conventional understanding. As a result, the Green movement is prone to regarding spirituality as merely reverence for life.

The Greens tend to regard the essence of Buddhist teachings as ethical concerns about livelihood, respect for life and the spiritual discipline of meditation. Though these have a valuable place, the teachings stress complete spiritual enlightenment to Ultimate Truth. That is the best; anything less than the best is missing the purpose of the spiritual life. Conventional interpretations of time and becoming dissolve into the Ultimate Truth which reveals the Deathless. By attending to Awakening with our whole being, we realize the world in a different light. We recognize the difference between conventional understanding and Ultimate Wisdom.

The Buddhist tradition, the Green movement and the woes of the Earth fall into place. When spiritual enlightenment becomes the highest priority, we tread lightly upon the Earth. Full realization ends interpreting cause and effect, or action and results, as Ultimate. Realizing the Ultimate Truth ends suffering and anguish over global issues but not our action towards change. Penetrating into the Ultimate Truth provides a genuine service for peace and security in this world when we discover the demands of the ego are empty.

Christopher Titmuss
Totnes, Devon,
England.
1994

AN ENVIRON-MENTAL AWAKENING

Transmission of Teachings

I discovered that profound Truth, so difficult to perceive, difficult to understand, calming and sublime, which is not to be granted by mere reasoning, and is visible only to the wise.
The Buddha.

The Western upsurge of interest, exploration and practice of spiritual teachings from the East occurred in the last four decades of the 20th century when a sprinkling of Westerners were willing to learn something from Buddhism. Such spiritual seekers did not assume a role of superiority, nor did they travel to the East as sun-worshipping tourists; they went to learn. The regular flow of sympathetic Western minds into the Buddhist world has contributed in a small way to a new confidence among Asian Buddhists in the deep insights within their religion.

There is a growing number of people in indigenous Buddhist countries who are beginning to re-examine their own religious culture. Rapidly tiring of consumerism, they are probing beyond the outer appearance of the temples, tedious rituals and rigid forms. They recognize that they have overlooked some jewels in their religious rituals which surpass the desperate rush into the pleasure and pain of converting to wealth creating economies.

Western interest in Buddhism began during the 19th century. A handful of scholars, mostly British and German, took interest in Buddhist texts found in Eastern monasteries. They began to translate these texts from Chinese, Pali, Sanskrit and Tibetan. For several of these translators it was merely a work of scholarship, an intellectual challenge. But for a handful the teachings of the Buddha, the enlightened ones of subsequent generations and the wisdom and kindness of Buddhist monks, nuns and lay people influenced their lives dramatically.

In the early decades of the 20th century, small groups of people in the West began meeting together to discuss these teachings. By the 1920s, various Buddhist societies had formed in a handful of Western cities. They began to regard themselves as Buddhists, emphasizing observation of the five precepts, creating merit and conducting brief sessions of meditation, chanting and religious services. They wrote leaflets about Buddhism and invited monks from the East to give lecture tours in the West. University lecturers and Buddhist writers from the East also travelled to the West. Quietly and rather inconspicuously, the seeds of these teachings, known as the Dharma, were sown. Western Buddhists took particular interest in the paradoxical teachings of the Zen Masters. They explored the relatively new spiritual practice of meditation and the freedom to explore personal spiritual experiences with relatively little dogma. In the 1950s, Arnold Toynbee, the distinguished 20th century historian, wrote that the most significant event of the 20th century would be the bringing of Buddhism to the West; not the two World Wars, not breaking the atom, not nuclear fusion.

The late 1960s marked the arrival of the hippy era, flower power, an anti-authoritarian streak, mind-altering drugs and the overland trail to India. The philosophies of the East began to attract widespread attention among the young. The antiwar movement took notice of the nonviolent commitment and sacrifice of practising Buddhists, especially in Vietnam. The Buddhist monk and nun who immolated themselves in South Vietnam as a protest against the war of the US government upon the people of Vietnam became a searing image of the time. A tiny number of those who served as GIs in Vietnam stayed in Asia after completing their military service and took ordination as Buddhist monks. They readily admitted they owed a debt to southeast Asia for their part in the war against these gentle people.

The hippy trail began from Europe across Turkey, Iran, Afghanistan, Pakistan and India. Another trail ran from Australia through Indonesia, Malaysia, Thailand, Laos, Burma and into India. Thousands followed these routes in the late 1960s and early 1970s; some made contact with the Buddhist tradition. By the early 1970s there were 60 to 80 Westerners ordained as Buddhist monks in Thailand. Others were taking ordination in the Zen, Theravada and Mahayana traditions of the rest of Asia. Hippies, travellers, Peace Corps workers, ex-GIs and Buddhists who flew directly from the West made up the bulk of the ordinations.

During the 1970s and into the 1980s various teachers from the Mahayana, Vajrayana, Theravada and Zen traditions travelled to the West where there was a hunger for spiritual knowledge that did not divide the world into believers and unbelievers. Asian teachers, especially meditation masters, travelled to the West to give teachings and start spiritual centres. In the mid-1970s a handful of Westerners, who had engaged in sustained spiritual practices in Asia, were well enough established in the Dharma, that is the teachings of the Buddha, to return to the West to offer teachings. The main vehicle for giving teachings was a retreat ranging from a week to three months. Some Dharma teachers, including myself, dispensed with the religious forms while other Western teachers adapted the forms to our society. The seeds of a widespread international movement were sown and by the mid-1980s, the Western media described Buddhism as the fastest growing religion in the West.

Numerous Dharma networks were formed of spiritual practitioners from the retreats. Referred to traditionally as the Sangha, these groups consisted primarily of people in society dedicated to spiritual practises. Thus the three jewels of existence took root in the West—namely The Buddha, the Dharma and the Sangha—that is awakening, the teachings and spiritual networks. The handful of Westerners who took Buddhist teachings from East to West also took on the responsibility of ensuring that the body of teachings remained accessible and intelligible to a receptive but sometimes sceptical Western society.

Western teachers in the Buddhist practice of Vipassana, the insight meditation tradition, were generally only in their early 30s when they returned to the West—having gone to the East several years earlier. In time, Western teachers authorized other Westerners, who had never been to Asia, to teach Buddhist practices. "Practice" became a key word and by the late 1980s, more than 100,000 people in the West had participated in seven day or longer insight meditation retreats, which was only one of several Buddhist traditions available. Thus there was less need for Westerners to travel to the East as meditation centres and Buddhist based communities became established in the West.

The first wave of Western teachers in the mid-1970s had the task of transmitting teachings with the same authority accorded to a venerated master. It was a shock for some beginning spiritual students to find themselves listening to young Westerners both men and women, presenting an ancient Eastern tradition. To their credit Dharma students in the West of all ages and backgrounds expressed the same commitment and dedication as those who had travelled East. Thus Westerners inherited the 2500 year-old responsibility of Buddhism by continuing the tradition of offering the teachings of wisdom and compassion to sincere seekers of Truth.

Centres in Europe, North America and Australasia continue to mushroom. As one respected Theravada teacher who left the forest of northeast Thailand to teach for a period in London commented: "Teaching in the East is like keeping alive an old tree. But teaching in the West is like watering a young seed." Transmission of teachings to the West has taken place at a remarkable speed but not without pain. Human failings of certain teachers, both Western and Asian, became glaringly obvious as these ancient teachings made their way into a pleasure preoccupied western society. Issues around alcohol, drugs, money, power and sex continue to be examined in several Buddhist communities, particularly in the USA.

The transmission of Buddhism from East to West has not met with the approval of orthodox Christianity whose members will speak of Hinduism, Satanism, Buddhism and the New Age in the same breath. Buddhist values confront capitalism with its satisfaction of desires as the priority. But practising Buddhists are struggling to bring a spiritual awareness into our society whose problems are as gross as its successes. Many people say that the Buddha's teachings of awareness, nonviolence, tolerance, wisdom and compassion have profoundly influenced their lives though they do not use the label "Buddhist" to describe themselves. (Pollsters in Britain were unable to determine the number of Buddhists in the country owing to the common disregard of labels such as "Buddhist"—something which the Buddha, himself, endorsed. Labels can breed division and conflict).

Today, both popular and specialized bookshops contain a selection of books on Buddhism. These diverse teachings on wisdom and compassion offer skilful means for spiritual practice in daily life. The foundations of the teachings have their roots in down-to-Earth insights and interdependent action. Deep spiritual practices and an active ecological awareness capture the imagination of thoughtful people. Buddhism has aligned itself with the liberal wings of the Churches, such as liberation theology, and the peace, women's and environmental movements. It has joined the struggle against selfishness, violence, intolerance and the privatization of values. But the quest for Truth must remain the priority and these teachings from the East have a significant contribution to make towards enlightening consciousness.

In the East, Buddhist values of mindfulness, reverence for life and conservation must now compete with capitalist values of pursuit of self-interest, profit and privatization of the land. Political leaders in Asia promise their citizens a standard of living comparable to the European Union within 20 years. For this to occur it means dismissing 2500 years of Buddhist culture and values in exchange for the consumer culture with its destructive impact particularly on rural communities. But in this expanding web of interconnection, the seriousness and depth of Western Buddhism extends a positive influence in the East. Asian Buddhism and Western Buddhism have much to learn from each other.

Dharma teachings do not convert people to Buddhism and it is quite feasible that "Buddhism" and "Buddhists" may disappear during the next century. This is partly due to Buddhism's refusal to adopt a fundamentalist position, or use aggressive strategies to gain converts. Such behaviour reveals religious immaturity and a clinging to beliefs—anathema to the Buddha's teachings. The survival of Dharma practice depends on whether the realizations and insights of the teachings pierce the hearts and minds of those indoctrinated in Western culture. The central issue today is more than the survival of the Earth, or of the human species; it is what it actually means to be homo sapiens. The refusal to explore the nature and depths of our existence is abiding as homo ignoramus. Recent years have shown that the world's religions have become obsessed with their own survival and adopting fundamental beliefs is often their strategy for survival. Although there are perhaps some sects of Buddhism that might like to go this route, Buddhism generally is discovering a fresh direction that challenges the two central Western conceptions of the meaning of life: producing and consuming and belief in God.

Buddhism may need to adapt dramatically to become a revolutionary force in Western society. Consumerism challenges the deeper values of Buddhism while obsolete Buddhist rituals can suffocate the liberating spirit of the teachings of enlightenment. Thus practitioners of the Dharma have a duty to challenge selfishness and corrupted teachings to reveal a different vision through certain Buddhist practices, such as ethical guidelines; depths of meditative insight, wisdom and enlightened realizations, are of course indispensable to the spiritual life. So the transmission of Dharma teachings to the West has met with a favourable response since it works on the principle of providing a pragmatic range of spiritual practices suitable for any culture. For some, the absence of God in the spiritual life is a blessing.

Another attraction of the teachings is tolerance. While some religions demand total withdrawal from other beliefs, authentic Buddhist teachings never claim an exclusive way to the Truth but implore people to have faith in the wider spiritual life. Nobel Prize winner, the Dalai Lama, once told me that if a serious meditator was not benefiting considerably from the Buddha's teachings then the person ought to consider exploration of another faith rather than blindly adhering to Buddhism. The consistently tolerant attitude from this prominent ambassador of Buddhism reflects the acknowledgement and humility that no religion should claim all the answers to the questions of life and death that have troubled men and women for generations.

Buddhism endorses deep meditation and emerging insights that transform our perceptions and feelings towards self and other. Buddhist meditation teachers often specify sitting and walking meditation in silence and stillness with whole-hearted attention to the immediacy of the Here and Now. To sit and walk with depths of awareness and understanding is to realize the Buddha's mind, and this awakening of consciousness serves as a profound contribution to life on Earth.

The Shadows of
Consumer History

It is utterly impossible
To reach by walking the world's end;
But none escape from suffering
Unless the world's end has been reached.
It is a sage, a knower of the world,
Who gets to the world's end, and it is the sage
For whom the spiritual life has been lived out;
In knowing the world's end one is at peace
And hopes for neither this world nor the next.
The Buddha

When Christopher Columbus set forth on his voyage from Spain in 1492, he had the financial backing of the King and Queen of Spain, who promised him 10% of the profits. The Arawaks greeted him on his arrival in the Americas with food, water and gifts. Columbus responded by taking slaves. "With 50 men we could subjugate them all. Let us in the name of the Holy Trinity go on sending all the slaves that could be sold," he wrote. The conquistadors systematically slaughtered the peoples of the Caribbean. "Thirteen at a time they were hanged in honour of the 12 apostles and the Redeemer."

One historian asserted that 5 million died at the hands of the European conquistadors on the Caribbean Islands and 45 million died on the mainland. Then came the first imported labour force—slaves from Africa. They worked the slaves to death in mines, fields and the construction industry. For the next three centuries the slave trade continued. The colonialists destroyed entire civilizations. and more than 200 million died. Columbus was not the spark for the meeting of cultures, nor even for colonialism, but for genocide.

It is a world not far removed from today, from the sophisticated forms of trading in the latter part of the 20th century. Millions in the Third World die of poverty, preventable diseases, malnutrition, hypothermia, environmental degradation and industrial pollution. Every death is as horrible and as unnecessary as those by the sword of the conquistadors. Economic colonialism and environmental racism is still rampant. Economic development in the West has done nothing to alter the relationship between the North, the privileged at the top of the global ladder, and the South, those at the bottom. A case could be made that international trade agreements are so heavily weighted in our favour that the cost to the poor of the Third World is not so different from five centuries ago. Detached economic masters, directly and indirectly, work farm and factory workers to death on a pitiful income so that we can maintain and increase our standard of living. Those immigrants who have entered through the selective doors of Western immigration often hold the lowest paid jobs. The 1492–1992 quincentenary celebrations had a hollow ring.

The English launched the 18th century Industrial Revolution and the modern era of global colonialism, but only now, after 200 years of violating the Earth and its indigenous peoples are the Western masters noticing the human and environmental impact of this domination. The plundering of the poor nations by the wealthy ones takes at least seven forms:

1. *Importing goods from the poor nations at rock bottom prices.*
2. *Selling arms and weapons*
3. *Damming rivers*
4. *Mining*
5. *Deforestation*
6. *Construction of factories in the Third World (for cheap labour, absence of effective environmental legislation and maximization of profits)*
7. *Destruction of beautiful habitats to create tourist ghettos*

The dark shadow of Columbus continues. The decision to begin the process to protect the Western environment took root when we realized that the by-products of industrialism, such as the dumping of chemical and human waste, are destroying our own soil, forests, rivers, air and seas. The U.S. military alone generates annually half a million tons of toxic waste—more than the top five US chemical companies combined.

Global warming, the hole in the ozone layer and the destruction of the tropical rain forests also now worry Western scientists. Expansion of the seas through global warming would cause widespread flooding in low lying areas in the West. Insurance companies would have to pay out huge sums of money. The tourist industry would be affected. There would be more pressure on medical services with the thinning of the ozone layer and environmental damage leading to various cancers and other illness. Environmental pollution also affects the water supply, crops and marine life.

There is growing public acceptance of conceiving the Earth as a dynamic organism worth protection. This view also accepts that the organism is sick, that its natural immune system is getting weaker. In Africa, this sickness is a kind of gangrene gradually spreading over the region. Famines and regional conflict curse the African nations. The combined GNP of all central Africa is less than that of Holland. The corporate world reduces investment in Africa, preferring Asia or South America, thus leaving Africa to rely almost entirely on the dribble of aid as a source of foreign capital. USAID, the World Bank and IMF have cut their funding of projects in Africa; yet Africa pays back more money to IMF from debts than it receives from them. The West reduces aid to sub-Sahara Africa year by year. Quietly Western governments are agreeing to abandon Africa to its fate. The black continent will be left to die in the next century as a "matter of regret."

The World Bank and IMF exercise immense control over the fortunes of Africa. Originally a development fund, the World Bank effectively serves as the West's police for economic policy, particularly in Africa. The Fund and the Bank force struggling African nations to accept their fiscal demands. In order for poor nations to qualify for loans, they have to meet the targets of austerity set by IMF and the World Bank, otherwise these powerful organizations refuse to sign the cheques. The aid which is given does little to combat poverty in Africa. According to UNICEF less than 10% of IMF and World Bank aid goes to primary health care, education, family planning, farming or clean water. Instead, the World Bank funds large prestigious projects through the support of the corporate world. In Washington some of the loans from the World Bank to poor African nations simply travel around the corner to the IMF offices to pay off debts.

The prescription given by IMF has nearly killed the patient. IMF slashed rural development projects, education and health projects while prices rocketed and wages fell. Poverty reduction has not been high on the agenda of the World Bank, IMF or GATT (General Agreement on Trade and Tariffs) nor has protection of a fragile environment. The West exports about one million tons of dangerous wastes annually to Third World Countries because the wealthy nations believe the value of life in the poor countries of the world is lower. The World Bank, IMF and GATT continue to abide in the self deception that there is no alternative to their policies. They claim that improvement in the quality of life is on the way for Africa, though there is not a single statistic to support this view. Most Africans are becoming poorer with the passing of every decade.

UNICEF noted that during the last decade wars killed 1.5 million children and physically disabled four million others. War and regional conflicts forced five million children into refugee camps and 12 million lost their homes. Making war on children to such a degree is a 20th century phenomenon. Western governments, economic colonialism and the sale of military equipment must be held accountable for the current situation. The military and industry employ two out of three scientists so the daily war against children, adults and the environment can continue. Scientists deceive themselves by claiming they are patriotic and dedicated to protecting the citizens of their country; they belong to the export market. Governments say they continue to export arms to protect jobs at home.

Thoughtful people world wide experience compassion burnout as heart rending appeals to support worthy causes in the Third World fail to ignite action. Professional writers and layout artists design appeals so our hands reach for cheque books and credit cards, but the endless demands for money have numbed our hearts. For example, the famines in Africa get worse while the response of wealthy governments and the public gets less. We are resigning ourselves to allowing entire regions to starve to death due to our inability to summon energy to support relief agencies and make demands upon governments but no Western government will ever lose power because of its indifferent aid policy.

Consumer demand, corrupt governments, the international arms trade and the tight fiscal policies of Western governments and international businesses, as well as climactic factors, ensure famines will repeat themselves. Yet the West refuses to take any responsibility and instead offers a few miserable crumbs to salve our consciences. Since colonial times Western powers have spread the notion of the nation state though this was and remains a foreign concept for many cultures. As the world wide thirst for independence from colonialism grew the colonial powers sought to leave their final stamp on the places they had governed: national identity. They invited individuals from the colonies to the West, educated them in Western ways, values and ideology and sent them back to their respective homelands to form a nation state based on the Western model.

Trained in the West to use sophisticated military technology, the leaders returned, formed armies and waged war on dissident groups within the land marked as "nation state" or "neighbouring state." The obscene business of arms sales, particularly by Britain, USA, France, Russia and China provides a lucrative source of income despite the horrifying cost to the poor nations of the world.

Under the guise of independence, the Third World was economically and militarily recolonized. To import armaments and receive aid, Third World countries had to agree to our conditions. It is ironic that at a time when the Third world has conveniently and sometimes brutally agreed to identify with the nation state, the concept of the nation state is losing fashion in the European Union. "Don't do as we do, do as we say" is the barely hidden slogan of the European Union.

Privileged and powerful groups control rural masses, who provide cheap labour. The political-military-industrial class in the capital cities of Third World nations became colonizers in their own countries adopting the same arrogance towards rural peoples as Western colonists did previously. Within two or three generations, city planners, city dwellers and the politicians of the new nation states had forgotten their roots. The diversity of tribes, cultures and traditions became subservient to national aims. Any tribal protests against political or military rulers still leads to brutal forms of repression against people subjected to contemporary conquistadors.

To sustain control highly trained military personnel engage in undercover work for National Security. These undercover operations ensure that dissidents, poor people and intellectuals do not interfere with the strategic aims of central governments (who like to refer to dissidents using nonviolent means for social and environmental justice as agitators). Through the cooperation of the media, this marginalizes such opposition so that central governments can avoid examining their modus operandi.

Voices like Amnesty International have found themselves crying in the wilderness. For everyone released, through the cooperative pressure of Amnesty groups, countless numbers disappear into oblivion. For the rural poor and the shanty town dwellers in the city, human rights have no meaning. Authentic education familiarizes people with their rights but they are denied this opportunity. As nation states take hold over the world's populace the West sits quietly back and applauds its achievements of granting independence to these "nations" that the West itself helped create.

Western colonialism has left its indelible legacy through the formation of three groups of people—a political class, a military class and an industrial class—and developed the capital city as a power base. The farther people live from the capital the more deprived they became. Having little influence on the source of power, they form the underclass, systematically deprived of their traditions, cultures, values and often their land. Power and corruption entwine ensuring that the new classes maintain their wealth and privilege through exploitation of rural people.

Television documentaries report the problems along with the aid workers, environmentalists and economists dealing with large scale human and environmental tragedies. It slowly registers that we are ruining the Earth through our behaviour, making life intolerable for all. Yet though this message is unmistakable we manage to sidestep it; making a personal, social or national U-turn is not on our list of priorities. To those caught in the dominant social, political and economic viewpoint the necessary about-face in policy and practice is inconceivable.

Ecological organizations inform us that we have inflicted more damage on the Earth in the last two centuries than in the previous six million years of the Earth's history. Abuse of people and the rape of the Earth have become intrinsic to our lifestyle. When the environment suddenly became interesting there was the usual thirst for information, but knowledge became a compensation for making genuine change. By appearing to be well informed we present a deceptive mantle of progress.

In the space of five years, the UN has produced 2.2 billion documents on paper produced from forests. Overpaid staff write these countless scarcely read reports which are even more rarely acted upon. There is much doubt whether the immobile bureaucratic organizations that litter the Earth make any difference. But the politics of the environment have also become a convenient escape from dealing with local and regional problems of people and the environment.

Numerous conferences take place around the world focusing on world population, the holes in the ozone layers, deforestation, pollution, the greenhouse effect, expanding deserts and depletion of natural resources. Scientists, diplomats, senior civil servants, government officials and observers fly into these conferences, check in at five star hotels, deliver their papers, nod approvingly at the lectures of others, return home, file a report and then go on to the next international conference. Well-meaning, well-defined speeches serve to boost the egos of the individual, their employers and the nation state but do nothing for the welfare of the Earth. The outpouring of information is suffocating the spirit for change—the "environment" has become a metaphysic supported through language and endless analysis. Thus the "environment" that the experts refer to conceals exploitation and destruction, and it serves as a convenient escape from the real world.

Their "environment" is nothing more than a social relationship. The experts abide in a realm of self-other deception, a kind of mask. They appear to know what they are talking about but their environment is exclusively social relationships, conference halls and hotel bedrooms. They do not know the world environment they talk about because of their imprisonment in social forms. Experts do not reveal the Truth, rather their opinions can suppress it. Like people in power, they contribute little to real change through infatuation with their knowledge and conformity to their peer group.

Depths of experience rather than information changes people's lives. Outside in the genuine environment, the Gandhian tactics of strikes, fasts, nonviolent demonstrations, sit-ins, marches, boycotts and outdoor rallies have more local impact than endless UN documents, neglected resolutions and other international conferences. Thoughtful people working for wasteful governments and ruthless corporations find themselves marginalized. Staff are afraid to speak about their personal values. To do so hampers promotion prospects or places them under suspicion as to their commitment to their chosen career.

"Green" books focus on two themes: reporting global and environmental facts in detail, and "how to be more aware" in environmental matters. The first wave of books helped to spread information and probably increased the degree of public anxiety about the state of the ecosystem. The second wave of books encourages modification of our gratuitous lifestyle. Under the influence of news, documentaries and literature we use unleaded petrol, accept fewer plastic bags, buy recycled paper and place our used bottles in bottle banks. Governments pass laws ordering car companies to fit catalytic convertors to new cars. Having made nominal contributions to saving the planet, we carry on life in much the same way as before.

Production negates our efforts. For example, the massive increase in car production that the motor industry plans for the world in the next decade overshadows the value of catalytic convertors. There are 630 million cars on the world's road now; the car manufacturers have set their sights on 1000 million cars within 20 years. So, despite the barrage of information and the sincere efforts of dedicated and well informed people, change is minimal. Every manufacturing company has one strategic aim—to increase output and their existence is based on this principle. Though corporations engage in philanthropic gestures for the environment, they appear seduced by power and money. The cost to the Earth of their token

Green awareness is high.

Environmentalists have travelled countless miles by land, sea and air, exploiting resources, including acres of trees to publish propaganda. We exploit resources to send the message of reducing resources. Meanwhile the huge industrial machine, fuelled by production targets, charges on. There is little room for optimism, leaving thoughtful environmentalists in despair. Political parties of the left, right and centre have their own constituencies but the Greens work for radical change right across the political spectrum to implement a different value system.

If the growing number of pressure groups leaning on governments and the stream of "how to" books do not have the desired effect of significantly altering our behaviour, then we are still actively engaged in the abuse of resources. Apart from the words on the paper, there is no difference between the mountains of junk mail sent out to us by businesses and that sent by Green organizations. Nearly all of it ends up in the waste paper bin and at the local dump. We still focus our attention on getting a good salary, a good car with sophisticated ergonomics and a good holiday on a clean beach. Our junk mail, Green or otherwise now goes straight into the trash as we become bored, or despairing of the effort to recycle.

Well-meaning entrepreneurs forge ahead to address public concern by opening shops selling environmentally friendly goods. The notion of "capitalism with a human face" was born as Green businesses competed in the market economy. The value of these goods and shops became threefold:

1. *The goods remind the public to be user and environmentally friendly*
2. *They show that chemical and animal experiments are unnecessary for human safety*
3. *The public's demand for such goods forces the business world to take notice of the health of people and the environment*

However, Green goods cost the consumer a higher price. The business world makes the public pay more for having a conscience. Major companies see the direction of the market so they join the bandwagon; that is where future profits will be. If their share of the market declines in one area, they expand into another. Business people realize the public will pay more for "cruelty free" products, recycled paper and natural cosmetics. Such goods give the impression of bringing the consumer closer to nature. Green consumerism has come to have its influence in the market place; big business has moved successfully into "feel-good retailing." Shoppers feel good about products from shops whose windows are promoting a worthy cause. It also has become a successful marketing strategy to advertise Amnesty, Greenpeace or Save the Children Fund in shop windows. Customers purchase more goods so that a tiny percentage of the profit goes to worthwhile organizations, but it is all part of the "feel-good" policy that profit obsessed management initiates. Business acumen has persuaded the public to purchase more goods to save the Earth! Thus Green consumerism is part of the problem, not part of the cure.

We spend more time in shopping malls and High Street stores than in nature. Shopping is the norm whereas a trip into nature marks a special event. Our natural habitat has become display shelves of consumer goods; going to the mall expresses the last vestiges of the hunter-gatherer mentality. Economic growth depends upon this activity but deep inside, many women and men feel ashamed spending so much money, buying expensive goods for the home and keeping up appearances. It is not unusual that the greater the amount of disposable income the greater the guilt. User friendly shops make consumers feel good about themselves so there is some temporary relief from guilt.

Green consumerism is still consumerism regardless of content, no matter what promoters endorse or what new slogans ("cruelty free") are on the label. Buying cruelty-free cosmetics or returning bottles is a token gesture. It is vital that we do not deceive ourselves or each other by imagining that such actions are making a real difference to the problem of economic growth and the systematic destruction of the Earth.

This message (printed in clear child's handwriting) was to be found on every paper bag used by one High Street shop.

"New Earth Happy Packaging. You'll probably notice that our sandwiches now come served in paper wrapping instead of a box.

"That's because we figure the world probably could use 15,000 less tons of trash a year. And less trash means less trucks to carry it.

"Which means less gas and a lot less air pollution. Not to mention the reduction in packaging the packaging has to be shipped in.

"All in all, it's just one of the ways we're trying to make the world a nice place to eat."

Which high street business puts out this message on their paper bags? *Burger King.*

The international Green movement campaigned for years to force Burger King to stop destroying tropical rain forests for their cattle farms in Central and South America. Eventually Burger King agreed as more and more Green activists protested outside their restaurants. Recycled paper bags are welcome but, of course, Burger King continue to slaughter millions of cows on ranches elsewhere. The land used for cattle could provide far more food if used for grain, since it is no longer possible to recover the rainforests.

The other major meat chain, McDonalds, also promotes the consumption of cooked animal flesh wedged between a bread bun with french fries, as the central focus of its menu. Countless parents world wide experience doubt about such a diet for their children. McDonalds spends millions of dollars yearly in advertising to get young people to go to their fast food restaurants and actually ran advertisements telling children that hamburgers grow in hamburger patches. Children have a special love for animals so these advertisements obscured the painful truth of the process that brings animal flesh to throwaway plates. This deception takes children's attention away from the harsh fact that millions of cows annually get driven to the slaughterhouse. In Britain, the meat industry despatches 600 million animals a year to the abattoirs. (145 million tons of grain fed to livestock produces only 21 million tons of meat).

Meanwhile McDonalds cultivates the public image of their restaurants as a fun place to eat. McDonalds young staff engage in high speed work with strict hourly rates to maximize profit.

Coca-Cola, Pepsi-Cola, Budweiser beer, Levis, Marlboro cigarettes, Burger King, McDonalds, military hardware, satellite television, violent films, music, the armaments industry, the obsession with individual choice represent a dangerous trend to "Americanize" the rest of the world. The ruthless promotion of these products damages traditional cultures and decimates spiritual values. As a result, this trend contributes to nationalism in various countries and hatred of the capitalist West. Other Western leaders fear criticizing American corporations determined to engage in globalization of their questionable products.

Green consumerism bears little relationship to Green economics. A political analogy to this situation might be the era of strategic arms agreements signed between Russia and the USA during the 1970's. Despite the fanfare of international publicity and the heralding of a new relationship between the countries, it took the 1989–91 revolution in the former USSR to alter fundamentally the relationship between the superpowers. Like the international pacts of the 1970's, Green consumerism can only be regarded as a small step to profound change, not as any kind of end. Welcome as these minor changes are in consumer demand, they are on the fringe of Green economics. It is a pity that some lightweight Greens start proclaiming the new dawn in the middle of the night. It will take the drama of nonviolent revolution and widespread sacrifice to establish an authentic change of values.

Desire, Action
and Result

Look at those who struggle after their petty
ambitions, like fish in a stream that is fast drying up.
The Buddha

The meteoric rise of entrepreneurs in capitalism continues. High Street banks strike multimillion dollar deals permitting entrepreneurial gamblers to go into phenomenal debt. One noted Australian business tycoon was able to borrow as much as $700 for every man, woman and child in his country. With so much money in their hands, (largely from the deposits of small investors), banks dish out huge loans to these tycoons to stop corporations raising finance away from banks. Bankers and entrepreneurs form a mutual conspiracy as they strive to become to market leaders in their fields. Their aggressive drive and high risk finances have become the key to spectacular gains and equally spectacular collapses.

Governments admit they "could not buck the market" to force change but through promotion of the so-called enterprise culture governments are part of the problem. So much power accrues to the international money markets that elected governments find themselves helpless onlookers. Western governments do not govern. Gamblers rule nations.

Multinational businesses can ignore a nation's antimonopoly commission whose legal responsibility is to ensure some semblance of diversity for consumers. For example, numerous takeovers threw the newspaper and publishing world into complete upheaval. Employees who dedicated their careers to quality publishing found themselves axed. (New bosses lowered the common denominator of quality books to increase street popularity). Junk books, like junk food, sell more and thus make more profit. These entrepreneurs and their subordinates contribute to the decline of deeper values, culture, and literature. Friendships which existed for years collapsed as big businesses swallowed up family publishers. Control of the flow of insightful information and creative writing fell into fewer and fewer hands.

The financial pages of the press frequently oversimplify the degree of greed and corruption in business. They claim that these entrepreneurs who have failed "went one deal too far." They make the absurd assumption that if the predators in the marketplace had stopped before their last deal they would have been kings. The wheel of desire-action-result-desire-action-result traps ambitious individuals and institutions. Debts to banks have become so great that banks dare not foreclose on large companies in phenomenal debt to them. The heart of the corporate world remains far removed from managers and staff of small local banks working to provide a service to their customers. The foolish loans by directors of major banks result in directives to local banks to increase profit margins to recover losses. These directives generate pressure and anxiety at the local level. To recover their losses banks hike up charges on the small accounts of customers on modest incomes and the unemployed. Banks will provide a higher level of interest to those who deposit more money so that the rich can get richer.

Having vast sums of money to play with, empire builders in the business world purchase huge corporations, then sell off divisions retaining only what segments they want to keep. Nothing is sacred. The public heard of the tycoon who played around with millions of pounds from pension funds, once regarded as untouchable investments. Business tycoons resort to questionable forms of wheeling and dealing to maintain their empires. They shuttle large sums of money from one account to another. Accountants, auditors and bankers submit to this brutal game of Monopoly played with the savings of ordinary people. Employees, small savers and the environment world wide suffer at the hands of these merchants of money.

Big businesses team up to campaign to get their hands on as much of the Earth's resources as possible, or they form cartels to keep prices artificially high to increase their profits. Businesses work together the safeguard their interests. Rev Sun Myung Moon's Unification Church and oil, mineral and timber companies promote a grass-roots anti-environmental movement claiming "wise use" of the land. They equate environmental protection with the loss of jobs, coldly dismiss environmentalists as city-based intellectuals, and claim the Greens are nature worshippers and therefore anti-Christian. Their goals include:

1. *Opening up all national parks and wilderness areas to mineral and energy production*
2. *Ending the Endangered Species Act as such species have become "non-adaptive to their environment"*

3. *Making environmentalists who slow up corporate activities liable for civil damages*
4. *Logging all remaining old forests*
5. *Constructing national parks using the expertise of corporations such as Walt Disney.*

One major supporter of the "wise-use" policy is the American Freedom Coalition with 300,000 members. Organizations in the USA sympathetic to such proposals include the National Rifle Association, Du Pont Corporation, Exxon Corporation and some 200 outdoor clubs.

The motivation behind such proposals is maximising profits, keeping competitors and the international Green movement at bay and proclaiming market muscle. Power and control over the Earth and others give governments and company executives a sense of their self importance. Bankers can only see $$$£££ as they greedily calculate the interest that accrues to them in making more loans for mining, deforestation, building factories and roads. An international bank, BCCI, engaged in the biggest investment swindle of all time leaving thousands of investors broke. Greed and fear pervade the corporate world.

When gripped with this drive for more a board of directors resorts to any means to maintain control, and everything and everyone become subservient to this drive to achieve. There is a perverse pleasure when inwardly driven to get what one wants again and again. Aggression and fear underpin this drive. Rather than face these unresolved needs the ambitious and selfish act out on the world stage their compulsive needs for power and control and, consequently, others near and far suffer. Businessmen in the grip of arrogant desire and aggressive marketing have sold their minds and prostituted their existence.

Politicians, business people, sportsmen and women, entertainers, students and perfectionists are particularly prone to the pursuit of ends at almost any cost. They crave respect from their peers so press on to be admired through acquisition of power. However, the Buddhist texts view with disdain those who treat life as a chance to build up a personal reputation to impress others. The ancient texts of the East compare such people to a dung beetle who shows contempt for other dung beetles for having less dung. To put that into a modern idiom, we might say the life of those who pursue name and fame begins to stink—the bigger the name, the greater the love of fame, the bigger the stink.

Making a fortune on the stock exchange has become the dream

of investors perceiving that profits would provide them with power, property and privileges. Whether in a personal, business or political context, the thread of desire, action and result remains unexamined. Yet the welfare of the ecosystem hinges on developing the perception of the interconnection of desire-action-result. It is the task of responsible people to cast aside the obsessive drive for success and instead to question, without fear or favour, the whole process of self-interest, power and pursuits from beginning to end. Those developing a career in the corporate world may live in fear of disapproval. The business world demands employees appear corporately correct in attitudes, dress and lifestyle and conform to the methods and objectives of the company. Loyalty takes precedence over compassion. Employers treat with suspicion employees who meditate, participate in spiritual retreats, become vegetarian, refuse alcohol and do not show a cynical attitude towards others.

If governments do not set an example then what can be expected from the corporate world or the public? The free market extols a cutthroat attitude where the primary aim is to outsmart and upend the competitors. This approach causes economic censorship as the primary value becomes profit. Worthwhile ideas for the welfare of people and the environment get marginalized or trivialized thus stopping thoughtful business people from raising the capital to produce and promote worthwhile products. Despite the selfishness in society there are a wide range of people who selflessly engage in meaningful forms of livelihood. These selfless people are the salt of the Earth who apply their social and environmental awareness to peoples lives. Nonprofit organizations and charities offer alternative values to the corporate world where profit and high salaries rule supreme. In Britain there are more than 175,000 registered charities providing for the welfare of people, animals and the environment. All of these organizations have to run on a sound financial basis otherwise they go into liquidation.

There has not been a single serious and sustained appeal by any Western government or noted politician for the public to change their consumer values, to reduce their drive, or to reconsider their lifestyle. Governments hold up Japan as the example of a successful economy with low inflation, progressive management, a strong industrial base and dedicated workers. Even the Americans, who like to think they are the best at everything, view with envy the success of the Japanese. This view is full of projection. Envy of the Japanese leads to "Japan bashing," but it would be foolish to withhold criticism for fear of being judgmental.

The last thing the Earth can tolerate is an economy and set of values like those cherished in Japan. The Japanese government takes little interest in international campaigns for human rights or social and ecological justice, except as an international public relations exercise. Their fleet of fishing boats with nets 30 miles wide rape the seas. Their logging companies rape the forests of Asia and the Pacific Islands. In the space of a year they dispose of chopsticks equivalent to 10,000,000 planks of 8 feet by 2 inches by 4 inches. They tear up the Earth for its metals as the raw material for their world wide consumer market.

The Japanese people refuse to acknowledge the dishonour of abuse of the seas, forests and Earth. In wartime, Japanese soldiers refused to allow themselves to be taken prisoner as it was against their code of honour. Today consumerism has taken the people of Japan prisoner en masse and they express no interest in Buddhist economics despite centuries of Zen. All this is to their shame. A prayer of a 13th century samurai warrior reads:

"I make the heavens and earth my parents
I have no home.
I make awareness my home
I have no life and death.
I make the tides of breathing my life and death
I have no divine power.
I make honesty my divine power
I have no means.

I make adaptability to all circumstances my principles
I have no tactics.
I make my mind my friend
I have no enemy
I make carelessness my enemy
I have no armour
I make benevolence and righteousness my armour
I have no castle
I make immovable mind my castle
I have no sword
I make absence of self interest my sword."

Japan is winning the economic war at the expense of the spirit of the samurai.

Poor countries sell tropical forests at giveaway prices to foreign companies without replanting an equivalent area. Governments refuse to force companies to pay for the violence they inflict on the landscape and the ecosystem. Little can be expected from the UN since it reflects the total vested interests of the member nation states.

An inspired vision for peace and environmental justice touches a place of deep moral concern. A profound love of life and a liberated sense of something utterly unmechanistic about life will change our actions and our exclusive reliance upon the brain to manage the world. The human spirit has a capacity for action in the face of the most withering and destructive circumstances. But as the Buddha pointed out, we must awaken for clear action and policies to emerge. Our governments and the private sector are asleep on their feet.

If we wish to find Truth and justice we must stop the escape into consumerism and self gratification. We must examine our values, and realize an ecological wisdom rooted in comprehensive understanding of interconnection. We must change from addiction to desire-action-result to upholding ethics-awareness-wisdom. This means taking risks as values and awareness then matter more than our personal security.

The Truth must come first. Instead of being subservient to governmental and corporate interests, Truth will cease to be otherworldly and will be the force that dissolves fraud, cover-ups, social and environmental abuse. Fear of the results from speaking out will have no place for those who replace the drive of desire-action-result with ethics-depth of awareness-wisdom (which the Buddha described as the three disciplines of the spiritual life). Commitment to Truth radically alters consciousness, people and environment deserve respect.

International law, application of strict ethics in business, acts of Parliament and consumer awareness need to become a feature of thoughtful existence. This is no easy questioning as it is likely to bring us into conflict with those addicted to power and possession. Aggression, greed and the underlying psychological and social insecurities that make power and property so compulsively attractive must be pinpointed and guarded against.

Probing into companies' accounts reveals the sheer frequency of fraud that management embarks upon. One U.S. court ordered a firm of accountants to pay $200 million in fines for conducting faulty audits. Even accountants have now developed a reputation for cooking the books rather than for honesty and integrity. Not surprisingly, thousands of accountants in the USA face law suits from investors deprived of their savings.

Auditing company books accounts for most of the revenue of accountants. Auditors issue a letter to accompany a business's annual financial statement that declares that the statement is free from error. This letter, which investors once regarded as an assurance of truth, is reaching the point where it is no long worth the paper it is written on. Far too many auditors will rely on the information that the board of directors and management provide them with rather than investigate the truth for themselves. Yet auditors have a duty to shareholders and the public to uncover fraud wherever they can.

There are many occasions when auditors come across fraud. They have three option: to ignore the fraud as if they hadn't noticed it, to drop the account, or report their findings to the police. Few choose the latter. Since auditors are public servants, the law should demand that they report their findings to the authorities. That they are not required to do so is a further example of lack of ethics in the business world and government. Corruption has reached such a point in the USA that insurance companies have become reluctant to insure accountancy firms since investors may sue them for inadequate auditing.

Yet those who break the law and ignore regulations, must be held accountable for the damage that results. Obsessed with saving money, accountants and auditors impress their masters with their recommendations. They cannot avoid responsibility when they claim in their defence they were following orders. Wisdom is knowing the difference between social responsibility and the narrowness of a company's interests.

Greed and corruption operate at every level of business life from the board of directors, to management and through to the workers who comply with the unethical expectations made upon them. There is risk for workers, consumers and environment when a board of directors strives to maximize profits above all other considerations. The application of environmental law, skimpy as it is, requires the cooperation of workers who are willing to inform on decisions of the management that are socially or environmentally harmful. Loyalty must never overshadow Truth and justice.

To experience a user-friendly environment, there must be a sharp increase in health and safety factors and a willingness to hold environmental abusers accountable for the results of their actions. The corporate world and governments must change and take responsibility for the state of the world. This includes cutting out the obsession with profit and embarking on a sincere campaign to stop exploiting people and environmental destruction. The accountant or worker may have to risk his or her job for higher values, but providing information to the authorities can stop the actions of crooked companies. Every fraud risks investors money and every illegal toxic discharge risks cancer and kills land, water and air. Management and workers have a wider responsibility than fulfilling the demands of the board of directors.

The US courts fined one major US chemical company a record sum for the damage that its chemical waste had done to the soil. The company reported to the press they had ordered a "cleanup" of management and workers. The company fired workers including the worker who initially informed the police of the company's environmental abuse whilst the Board of Directors remained unchanged. It is worthwhile noting that during the time the company engaged in illegal dumping a popular "how to clean up your act" book reported the same company promised a 90% reduction in air emissions of hazardous chemicals. The company received glowing praise in the book for their pledge. Pollution of the mind often pervades the public relations exercises in the same way the activities of an industry can pollute the environment and people's lives.

If companies are to change, then they must reveal to shareholders and public a comprehensive view of their business affairs. We require legislation to force businesses, governments and the military to publish vital information including to:

1. *File (publicly) details of the impact of their business or activities on land, water and air*
2. *File details of toxic substances usage*
3. *Reveal information of annual reductions of air emissions and chemicals*
4. *Table pollution emissions from a company's various factories or plants*
5. *List accidental spills, complaints and fines*
6. *File details of procedures to prevent pollution*
7. *Publish charts to show use of resources against output of pollution*
8. *Publish financial estimates of company's annual impact on the environment*
9. *Answer shareholders and environmental organizations comprehensive questionnaires on their environmental record throughout the year*
10. *Appoint independent auditors and environmentalists to examine company's figures*
11. *Publish health and safety record of workers*
12. *Publish staff wages from floor sweeper to company chairman, no matter what part of the world the corporation employees staff.*

Sacrifice changes the formation of our desire, our activities and

hence the result. The worker who provided confidential information to the police about his company's methods of chemical waste
disposal had a priority different from his employers. "I know this
stuff is carcinogenic" he whispered into the mouthpiece of the telephone on his call to the police. "This company is killing our kids
every time they dump this waste in the bay." He sacrificed his job
for that phone call.

Green Knowledge, Green Action

It is not easy to see Truth
To know is to uncover desire;
To see is to have done with owning.
The Buddha

In the media, ways and means for radical change take second place to alarmist stories about the state of the environment. Through repetition, the language use about the global crisis tends to become tedious. Our common response is to turn off. In the face of this reaction Greens must not avoid the use of information altogether, nor resort to detailing the "how to survive" strategy to prevent future disaster. The Greens must try to discover realizations that run deeper than the endless preoccupation with the environment, our notions of what it is and our tactics for compelling change.

When we talk about the "environment," we talk about something at a distance from ourselves. In Buddhism there is no such word as "environment"—that is, an objective and independent world that surrounds us. In the West we attempt to understand the "environment" through knowledge. Reliance on knowledge inhibits us from understanding that life is an *environ-mental* relationship. We hyphenate *environ-mental* to emphasize the interdependence between mental attidudes and the envronment.Spiritual life and practices deeply explore this relationship without isolating the personal from the environment and vice versa.

Realization of Ultimate Truth is a vital factor for meaningful change. Spiritual depths, emotional contentment, an abundance of kindness and wisdom serve as the raw materials for those dedicated to a vision of a different world. We need to work towards a synthesis of the timeless liberating insights into the spiritual nature of existence with the insights of the Green movement. Human life and the environment share the same characteristic: their meaning is found through relationship. Independent self existence of the inner or the outer belongs to the mythology of objectivity. If we end inner selfishness that accompanies desire, we provide a noble form of human service for the Earth.

It is hardly surprising that our political leaders resist hearing about the state of the environment, its relationship to spiritual matters and the widespread corruption of the inner life. Political legislation for a sustainable lifestyle, modest and respectful to resources, holds no interest for politicians. Communism and the world's religions have failed miserably to dispel personal gain as the uniting force of our society. This burden has now fallen onto the Green movement. But the Green movement has failed to understand the significance of the inner-outer relationship, for there is no evidence to show that the average environmentalist consumes any less than anybody else. Support for the Greens is found in every sphere of society, yet it is a rare person who dramatically alters his or her lifestyle for the good of the Earth.

The teachings of the Buddha demand we say "no" to what is harmful and insensitive. But by saying "no" to our lifestyle we will have to renounce the consumer life, the use of travel other than by foot and virtually become like monks or nuns with only a handful of possessions. Countless millions world wide are already in this position, but for them it is involuntary. Dispossessed of opportunity, the poor struggle to secure the basic requisites of a nutritious diet, satisfactory clothing, a home and medicine. The Greens talk much about voluntary simplicity, but our lifestyles are not distinguishable from our neighbours. We simply *talk* about life in a different way.

We observe that tens of millions of people in Western society already lead a modest existence. Families work hard to avoid debt or to get out of debt. Though they may be bombarded with advertisements to consume more, to use more gas, fuel and electricity, their financial realities determine their restricted use of resources. The average consumer of necessity manages his or her home affairs rather better than governments manage the affairs of state. Governments are notoriously wasteful and indifferent to the growing national debt and show little regard to the global concerns of scientists and ecologists. Ordinary families cannot afford such indiscriminate behaviour.

Influential groups, such as banks, industrialists, the military and large donors to political parties, unite in an unholy marriage. Elected politicians and corporate leaders rarely witness impoverished environments because they can only relate to the world of employers, managers and employees. For this to change there has to be a force that shakes apart the conspiracy that exists between government and the powerful.

The brain has a remarkable capacity to absorb information on numerous issues. Knowledge of the "environment" is constantly competing for space with other fields of knowledge. Deep experiences of the interdependency of everything can have far more transformative power than information about the latest ecocrisis. We realize our love and commitment to the environment when we are mindful and responding to it in the Here and Now, not when abstractly analysing it, or during the occasional country walk. While walks in the countryside are a common form of leisure and exercise, few hikers realize the connection between environment and consumerism.

Many people love spending time in nature yet this does not change their lives. So profound inner questioning about what matters and what doesn't must accompany such activities. The combination of experiences, values, insights, creativity and action is the meeting ground of the best of any spiritual tradition and the authentic responses of all thoughtful people. Spiritual traditions, particularly Buddhism, have proclaimed again and again the importance of community for making changes. Information is a limited strategy to awaken people, and angry violent protests offend most people. We applaud creative expression when a new form of protest breaks out of old ruts.

The Green movement welcomes articulate people who can forge a new direction in public awareness and can convert the technical details of Green analysis and Green political policy into the language of street credibility. However, if we are impressionable, we might adopt leaders like religious prophets imagining they will lead us into the Promised Land. But there is no Promised Land— there is only the Here and Now. Articulate and well informed speakers have an elementary and useful role to play, but it is necessary to be aware of how inadequate the perpetual distribution of knowledge is as the answer to all Green prayers. Knowledge is part of the problem as much as it is part of the solution. We have become unquestioningly impressed with educational qualifications, informative books, speeches and debates on public platforms. It might be far more productive to regard the constant acquisition of knowledge as a burden on the brain, and indeed on life, itself.

As literature loses its force as a vehicle for change, poetry, prose, essays, novels and informative books have less clout. Books published last year make way for new books. Contemporary English literature lacks masterpieces of writing, either fiction or nonfiction that express global wisdom while deeply insightful literature is a rare phenomenon. Books primarily belong to the world of escapism; spy, detective and romance novels dominate the bookshelves as forms of escape from the harsh world of *environ-mental* and social decline. Being a clever writer has little to do with depth of insights into the human and global condition. Profound experience and realization of Truth needs to find its expression through the arts, otherwise we continue to be enchanted with cleverness. The number of performances of a play or the amount of money artists make diverts attention from the true potential of the arts to change and transform.

As public figures, we can go on talking until we become hoarse and as writers we can go on typing until the disk is full but first we must experience a depth of interconnection with life and understand the art of listening, learning and creating. The orchestra conductor who was crippled in a swimming accident said: "I have spent my life in the world of entertainment. I am now forced to live in the real world." Awareness and insights into the truths of existence reveal forms of insightful creativity. Attachment to a self promoting world inhibits an active exploration of silence, humility and depths of discovery.

The Green movement is currently far too dependent on the ideology of *environ-mental* management rather than challenging the underlying ideas that corrupt our world. We need to question this constant invasion of facts and the damage to the psyche of education from primary school to university. Experiences transform people's lives. Addiction to information, to the news and commentaries constructs endless conceptual realities. Knowledge often paralyses us from any effective action, and we either feel we don't know enough or that we really know—and neither provide the springboard for any liberating and participatory wisdom.

Knowledge intrudes into *environ-mental* awareness. One sign of alienation from the environment is observable in the commuter train. A reasonably high percentage of daily commuters become engrossed in their daily diet of newspapers and magazines. British publishers put out more than 2000 magazines every month. There are features on the environment in a wide range of magazines. Yet, there is a world of difference between reading about the issues and doing something about them

Whether they belong to Friends of the Earth or not, commuters stare idly out of the train, bus or car window. The cost of the daily grind shows as loss of intimacy with nature. Both newspapers and idle states of mind serve as barriers to an active realization. So we must ask: What will awaken the heart? Rather than concentrating on gaining knowledge, we must explore different routes to realizing the intimacy of human beings with each other and with the Earth. It is futile for the mind to shuffle between knowing a little and appearing to know a lot. Both are deceptions. It is not knowledge that we are short of but the inspiration to transform our life, to break out of the mould of mechanical existence, and live on the edge of simplicity with others in a communal respect for the ordinary.

We have become unfit for global understanding due to the weight of accumulated information. But refusing to live with self deception is the hallmark of innocence. We then face our own humility. We take risks to open up our life. If necessary, we abandon our career as it could mean a waste of our existence. We take risks. We learn to contribute to the renewal of community, actively sharing our lives with each other in as many ways as possible. We can allow ourselves to open up to silence, to take long, solitary walks into nature, to lie on the grass and feel the support of the Earth, to walk out willingly in the rain, to stay awake and alone in the middle of the night, to fast, to forget the television, and newspapers, and to rely increasingly on the poetry of life for insights into the environment. The megastars of the political and green world have fallen in love with their expertise and cleverness, they do not know how they burden us with their endless listing of problems and remedies. We delude ourselves when we assume that anyone knows what is going on in the world or that information is the answer.

Realizing this, we must be bold, and regard *environ-mental* analysis as only one approach to understanding our relationship to the Earth. We have the potential to respond to our awareness, innocence and the fragrance of silence. We probe together deeply into our experiences of existence to open up our inner life, to bare all. Accumulating knowledge about the state of the environment may lead someone to join a Green organization, but this is not necessarily a good sign. It is not an indication of any deep insight, merely a nominal gesture of support—often without interest to make genuine changes in the subscriber's life. Membership in worthwhile organizations is no substitute for deep experiences of the web of existence.

Membership and Action.
Constant growth of membership can be as much a harbinger of failure as of success. For with success there often begins the sacrifice

of the original deep values of an organization. Numerous well-meaning Green speakers moderate their views to gain support among influential peers on the other side of the ideological divide.

Increased membership of Green organizations does not facilitate more campaigning work, as organizers commonly believe. A large membership can hold the organization to ransom. Green organizations set their budget for the next financial year based on this year's receipts. They often fear to rock the boat by radicalizing their political remit in case subscribers rebel and membership declines. Green organizations are as growth obsessed as other organizations and they are becoming increasingly more conservative as maintaining the annual budget comes to matter more than fresh initiatives.

Motives for joining a Green organization, or any political party, vary. Some people who work in *environ-mental* organizations are avoiding their inner life and their reason for doing good is the chance to escape unresolved personal problems. Not surprisingly, there is often much stress and anxiety in the field of the "do-gooders." Office workers in Green organizations often find themselves saddled with routine desk work instead of campaigning out in the field. The usual personal addictions of television, alcohol, junk food and painful relationships affect the quality of commitment to the organization.

The organization, itself, keeps strictly to its remit and refuses to explore the relationship of the inner and the outer. Staff disregard such matters as "spirituality," "psychotherapy" as "states of mind." They treat such matters as belonging to staff's personal life. The focus on *environ-mental* management excludes attention to the interior environment of the organization. As a result, there is a significant turnover of staff; unresolved personal matters, conflict and poor working conditions lead to casualties.

Organizations working for people, animals and environment have failed to respond to the interaction of personality with issues. Praise and blame, admiration and envy, likes and dislikes sow the seeds for confusion and disappointment. Members of some staffs are afraid to discuss matters that worry them with their colleague. Green organizations refuse to campaign wholeheartedly about greed, hate, fear and delusion. These forces are dominant influences. "Successful" green organizations have adopted the silence of their opponents on such matters. Fear of ridicule, fear of taking a stand for deep inner values renders a certain impotency among Green organizations.

It is becoming increasingly more difficult for new Green organizations to get off the ground. Friends of the Earth, World Wildlife Fund and Greenpeace dominate the limelight. Their concern is growth and they largely control the Green market. Privately and occasionally publicly, they voice criticisms of each other. None of them see fit to finance groups independent of themselves, and to keep faith with the maxim that "small is beautiful." In this respect, these organizations are no different from the governments and businesses whose values they challenge. The unspoken belief is "big is beautiful."

The international Green movement gains much satisfaction through increased membership and publicity as the measure of success. To become a member of Green organizations is often a conscience alleviating activity. It helps assuage the guilt tied to our lifestyle. "I'm a member of Friends of the Earth" makes us feel better about ourselves but such membership has little to do with being a friend of the Earth. There is a preoccupation with membership, and the endless mailings of information, with pressure for money, catalogues of consumer goods and stories of St. George and the Dragon. Green organizations invite us to consume more through their catalogues so that in some unfathomable way we will consume less. More people are saying: "Please, no more information, no more goods, no more stimulation."

To their credit, Green organizations have adopted nonviolence as a basic principle because the public want organizations outside of government to be nonviolent before they join them. It is a pity that the public do not have the same attitude to the governments who employ the military to back up their territorial ambitions. On the one hand we support the Green movement and with the other hand we vote to ignore it.

It is useful to point out the extraordinary expansion of Greenpeace, an influential international organization. There is Greenpeace USA with its central office in Washington, D.C. and Greenpeace International, with its headquarters in Amsterdam, Holland. By the early 1990s in the United States alone membership of Greenpeace stood at more than 2.5 million with an annual budget of around $60,000,000—all achieved in 20 years. With more than 24 offices world wide, a full-time staff of 3000 people and a huge budget it has probably become the world's most powerful international Green organization, which no government can afford to ignore. One board member of Greenpeace International told me: "The money is pouring in at such a rate that I sometimes publicly tell people to put their money into other Green organizations."

Greenpeace has engaged in nonviolent action to bring an end to nuclear tests in the Pacific Ocean, to stop the dumping of radioactive waste and to save Antartica from exploitation. Greenpeace has enough power to make governments seek revenge. The French socialist government blew up the Greenpeace boat "Rainbow Warrior," and murdered a Greenpeace photographer in the process. It was inevitable that there would be such a backlash from a government furious with Greenpeace campaigners determined to stop nuclear tests, major polluters and whale hunting. (The French government agreed to award Greenpeace $8.2 million in compensation). Under the banner of Greenpeace, trained activists have risk their life and limb to shock the public into an awareness of the rape, pollution and decimation of the natural environment. To their immense credit, Greenpeace activists have not sought personal name and fame from their actions. In the Green movement they have became affectionately regarded as eco-cowboys.

Greenpeace has successfully exploited the politics of stopping but has contributed little to the politics of starting alternatives. Their activists have complained that the organization has become unwieldy thus stopping them engaging in widespread direct actions. Like other Green organizations their limited approach became glaringly apparent in the period up to, during and after the Gulf War. The Iraqi dictator, Saddam Hussein, set alight 500 oil wells in Kuwait as an act of revenge on the US and its allies. When the fires blackened the sky for hundreds of miles, turning day into night, one German documentary film maker commented: "Kuwait is Satan's National Park." In the immediate aftermath of the Iraqi military invasion of Kuwait, and for some months later, Greenpeace was thrown into confusion. Should Greenpeace USA and/ or Greenpeace International use its considerable influence and campaigning expertise to protect people and environment in the region from the ravages of an impending war? There were bitter arguments in the Greenpeace offices. Letters from members, including military personnel, warned them they would cancel their membership and financial support of Greenpeace if the organization opposed the USA-led military coalition.

Long standing members who had retained their radical roots, called for an international campaign to stop the war with its human and *environ-mental* destruction. Other influential members said such a campaign was against the purposes of the organization, that an antiwar campaign was "overtly political." There was fear of collapse of membership, which would damage their world wide operations. The same international board member of Greenpeace International told me: "I told board members peace is not simply an appendix to 'Green.' But other board members did not want to listen."

The USA-led war against Iraq got under way leading to the loss of 200,000 Iraqi military and civilians, 274 U.S. and allied soldiers and airmen, the firing of 500 oil wells and the pollution of the seas around Kuwait. The widespread bombing of Iraq's infrastructure—waterworks, sewerage, power stations, communications and industry—was the equivalent of launching a chemical warfare attack. As a result, thousands of Iraqis died of disease, sickness, malnutrition and hypothermia. Two Greenpeace offices in the USA closed down through a dip in financial support when some Greenpeace USA, campaigners began to organize protest against the war. Though Greenpeace International launched a modest criticism against the invasion of Iraq, they didn't want to risk further wrath from their conservative membership. Fear ruled the decision making process leaving some committed Greenpeace supporters with an unpleasant feeling.

It was much the same story with other Green organizations. The international Green movement preferred to hang on to its membership—to economic growth—rather than confront the second biggest ever avoidable human and *environ-mental* disaster in Asia since the dropping of atomic bombs on Japanese cities. The background to some of these difficulties in the international Green movement lies within the structure of the organizations, and the relationships between them. Greenpeace operates from a central and hierarchical standpoint. The organization claims that this enables them to act fast to meet a sudden crisis but experienced activists dispute this claim. Consensus certainly can be a slow and laborious way to make decisions but a conservative hierarchy of power can be equally frustrating.

Green cannot be separated from Peace. The days when activists dangled from bridges in front of nuclear battleships as a publicity stunt may or may not be over. What was effective in one decade can become ineffective in the next. The strength of organizations such as Greenpeace rests with its imaginative and courageous exploits which touch a receptive place in the hearts of the public. Greenpeace must endorse fresh ways of directing action, launch new initiatives and grant the membership greater responsibility. The centralist method of control in the Greenpeace organization is

European-North American-Australian now subject to internal debate and external criticism. There needs to be more accountability in Greenpeace in terms of financial matters and power politics. At the local level, Greenpeace members only raise money or collect signatures. This is hardly a sign of confidence in its membership.

The face and vision of Greenpeace and other First World *environmental* organizations may have to change. The strategy of the international Green movement seems stuck and unsure of its vision. Green action deserves thorough re-examination. The international Green movement must also acknowledge the significance of spiritual awareness and practices instead of fearing to introduce such a dimension. For years their activists campaigned together with strong moral conviction working under the auspices of a loosely knit organization. This spiritual component and passionate love for the Earth has become increasingly obscured through greater reliance on a cerebral and technocratic approach to global issues. Spiritual teachings and practices concerned with depths of being and daily reverence for life are often dismissed as a distraction to scientific analysis and boardroom meetings. Resources fall into two areas:

a) There is the destruction of the natural world and decimation of cultures

b) There is the depletion of resources within people.

Green organizations have concentrated on dealing with the first and neglected the significance of the second. The failure to inquire into the latter is an appalling error of judgement. Green luminaries have often left such matters to the dying Church, trapped in outworn and often irrelevant beliefs. The contemplative traditions, the teachings of the Buddha and those that experience a passionate and spiritual connection with existence have a lot to offer the Green movement. Access to deep inner resources is a vital key to the welfare of the Earth. Greens world wide have yet to wake up to the interdependent link of inner and outer. Without spiritual enlightenment, the international Green movement will remain stuck in its own patterns. The Green movement must take risks if it is to challenge the status quo of governments, industrialists and the military. Fear of falling membership is inhibiting new directions for the movement. The Green movement must risk the wrath of its conservative membership rather than risk stagnation.

The Green Credo

Let one fare unselfish in this life, while ceasing to
worry about various states of becoming.
The Buddha.

The Global View
The international Green movement has taken up environmental
standpoints that leave it short on insights into the dynamic relationship between inner and outer. Green beliefs need questioning
even if it means risking the passion to campaign for the Earth. The
world view of the international Green movement generally hinges
on a set of simple beliefs that have become obstacles in facing the
global crisis. It does more harm than good to assume beliefs are
worth clinging to. Dogma and ideology develop when we treat beliefs as absolute truths.

The unofficial Green Credo says:
1. *We are stewards of the Earth*
2. *Resources are worth saving for future generations*
3. *The Future matters*
4. *Time is running out.*

We treat these and other dogmas as truths carved in rock rather
than as ways of conceiving values. Challenging these beliefs provides a service to ourselves and the Earth.

1. We are stewards of the Earth.
Thoughtful Christians introduced the notion of stewardship to
counteract the questionable Biblical injunction "Man shall have
dominion over the Earth." In the West we assign ourselves a particular role that places us above the rest of nature, and imagine we
have a special part to play in the scheme of things. But there is nobody who can claim to be a steward of the Earth since we are all
actively engaged in forming its present condition. We are part of
the Earth. Hence the notion of stewardship, though more acceptable than ownership, falls into the realm of human mythology. If
we truly care for the environment, for the whole ecosystem, we
need to realize the emptiness of a separate identity and a special
role in the world.

We do not belong to a role, nor does a role belong to us, and it is arrogant to claim this. We belong to the nature of things. The idea of stewardship is a patronising view of life, a kindly form of global colonialism. So the dissolution of a special identity is vital. The Buddha suggested we realize "akincina"—be nobody, hold onto nothing, expect nothing and identify with nothing. Jesus put it succinctly when he said "Blessed are the humble, for they shall inherit the Earth." The world doesn't owe us anything; it was here first.

2. Resources are worth saving for future generations.

Information about the depletion of resources through the rapacious appetite of the mining industry, defence industry and agribusiness has not made an iota of real difference. The Green movement exhausts itself struggling to halt declining resources, but few can relate emotionally to such concerns. Reading that copper, nickel, zinc and lead will be exhausted within 50 years hardly spurs anybody into action. Industrialists refer to long term mining at board meetings, but their careers depend on output not conservation. Directors and geologists in the mining industry still possess the hunter-gatherer mentality continuing to tap into fresh deposits of raw metals, and strategic use of nonrenewable resources is only prolonging our current lifestyle. One possible solution to the depletion of resources is recycling consumer goods—the last link in the chain of exploiting resources. This end of the chain is worth tackling but the causes of our profligate lifestyles lie deep in the psyche of human behaviour. Thus to effect a real change equal priority must be given to digging deep into our inner resources.

3. The Future matters.

The international Green movement has adopted with unquestioning obedience, the conventional interpretation of time. It views the past, present and future as irrevocable and Ultimate Truth and consequently makes absolutist pronouncements bearing little relationship to the true nature of reality, which is Timeless. To radicalize our notions of time we must declare that ultimately the future does not exist. There is no Ultimate Truth in the notion of the future; it is a human invention. Since the future has no substance outside what we proclaim, we can declare that the future does not matter because it exists exclusively in the realms of imagination.

The Green movement has engaged in an exaggerated emphasis on viewing the Here and Now in terms of a cause with its effect coming at a later date. This puts out a message that global affairs will only get worse if we go on like this. Indirectly the message is also that the present situation is not yet bad enough, thus when we refer to the future in this way we provide a disservice to the Earth and the Here and Now.

4. Time is running out.
What does "Time is running out" mean? "Time is running out" is empty of Ultimate Truth since time is a human convention. So there is no point in stating this as people either disbelieve it or, by accepting such a statement as true, feel pressured and react aggressively or with anxiety. Or this rhetoric dulls our minds, yet we repeat it even when it ceases to touch our feelings or make sense. Numerous people in fields of work complain bitterly of their levels of stress through not having enough time. Stress belongs to the world of contemporary social myths, a concept used to obscure the interaction of fear, ambition, competitiveness and worry about tomorrow. The corporate world converted "stress" into a multi-million dollar industry of ways to treat or reduce it.

When we express optimism we live in a foolhardy world of our own making as any widespread analysis of global problems produces a serious prognosis. Famines, wars, dying species and widespread destruction of land, water and air are *already* the common currency of global life. Instead of taking past, present, future and the world for granted, it would be profoundly creative to examine these perceptions. We must inquire into the way we perceive situations and how we respond to them, as our present beliefs blind us to the nature of things. We imprison ourselves in our notions of time and cause and effect with endless conjecture about tomorrow or the next millennium. We imagine we are competing to save the Earth from those who compete to consume it. Spiritual teachings of awakening lead towards Ultimate Realization so that we do not become overwhelmed with concern for the fate of the Earth. The preservation of life, the so-called sanctity of existence, is rarely our primary concern, no matter how much we consider ourselves thoughtful human beings.

Nobody immerses themselves full time in the fate of the Earth; it is, at best, one of our many daily considerations. Everyday tasks take up most hours of our day and if some people devoted even more time to saving the Earth they would lose all peace of mind. The psyche of human beings and the world are inseparable but when we claim stewardship for the Earth we identify with our Green role. This identity can become an escape from realizing the inseparable cycle of humanity and Earth, and we become ecomissionaries bearing tidings of evolution or Doomsday. The endless struggle of so-called good against evil, right against wrong, for and against has bedevilled humanity since its conception. We naively dismiss spiritual awakening as irrelevant when we have decided what reality is.

We have a certain kind of self-assurance when we are busy trying to save the Earth, appearing convinced of the rightness of our position and the necessary remedies. We rely on painful diagnosis and prescriptions, which harm the enjoyment of life. When we do celebrate, we turn to gluttony followed by pangs of short-lived guilt. We need to explore self's behaviour and beliefs, both our own and the voices of influence in the corporate, political and military worlds. We must question their ego as much as our own so that we realize the emptiness of its formations. We must inquire into and expose egotistical claims wherever we witness them. Instead of preaching about the fate of the Earth we ought to concentrate on the presence of ego in the centres of power and its arrogant treatment of life. The ego of the powerful thrives on vanity and a vulgar sense of self importance. Let us find the wisdom to confront it.

Meditative awareness and profound spiritual teachings will enlighten us. The scientific theory, known as the Gaia Hypothesis, is making a distinguished contribution to a spiritual and global awareness. Since British scientist James Lovelock first proposed his hypothesis in 1979, Gaia has become a symbol for understanding our relationship to the Earth. Lovelock believes that the planet functions essentially as a self-regulating organism. Lovelock says that the Earth "constitutes a single system, made and managed to their own convenience by living organisms." Named after the Greek goddess of the Earth, Gaia has now come to represent a spiritual awareness, a holistic view of life on Earth, rather than the name of a deity. The meaning of Gaia has expanded far beyond the Lovelock definition.

It is unlikely that Dr. Lovelock intended such use of the word Gaia but its widespread contemporary use does accord with the Gaia of Greek mythology, which translates as the "living Earth.". The nearest equivalent in Buddhism to the Gaia hypothesis is the doctrine of dependent arising. The Buddha would not propose that the Earth and its atmosphere is a single unified system. Such a view does not take into account other influences near and far, seen and unseen, known and unknown that reveal the dependently arising nature of things. Yet the notion of the Earth and the biosphere as a single living organism makes an important contribution to our understanding of the inter-connection of everything. The doctrine of dependent arising belongs to a body of teachings connected to the nature of things. The Buddha regarded the concept of self-existence, whether of the individual or the Earth, as a limited perception owing to the tendency to isolate phenomena from the nature of things. Both Gaia and Gaya, the place of the Buddha's enlightenment, share the same pronunciation and both views share the same concern for all sentient beings. What Gaia and Gaya share in common matters more than the differences in understanding.

We need to explore, practice and apply the teachings from Gaya and the Gaia hypothesis to express a conscious life. We need to rediscover a respectful enjoyment of life that does not depend on exploiting the environment. We must care for one another and our local and global community. If concerned with famine let us all change our diet, reduce our weight, campaign to stop unhealthy food, drink and tobacco advertisements and ensure money, skills and resources go to those in desperate need. Let a percentage of our taxes go in practical forms of aid to the developing nations. If concerned with the excessive use of private cars and aeroplanes let us be aware of motives for travel, use energy resources wisely and publicly state the number of miles we travel each year by air and road. If truly concerned about consumerism, let's detail any investments, our earnings and what we spend our money on. Our individual and collective relationship to money lies at the heart of global issues. So "being open" has genuine significance for the Earth. The benefits are far-reaching. Otherwise we continue to live this double life, that is sustainable rhetoric with unsustainable lifestyle.

I believe we must:
1. *put to rest the myth of stewardship*
2. *end conflicts about conserving resources longer*
3. *stop obsessing about the future*
4. *dispense with the rhetoric that time is running out*

To end these beliefs, without falling back into the conditioned patterns of consumer culture, will require finding fresh realizations about ourselves, our world and the power of ego. By letting go of our attachment to basic Green beliefs, we stop declaring our claims on Truth. We can then acknowledge what is false and corrupt and let the Ultimate Truth present itself. By dedicating ourselves to realizing deep values, practising sensitive lifestyles and investigating privilege and social and environmental justice, we have the opportunity to access another dimension of understanding. The price for this is shedding our conventional credos and the dissolution of egotism, but for the sake of the Earth it is worth it.

As Greens, we campaign for a nonviolent revolution to change the wretched consumer value system that haunts the Earth and humanity. But an equal revolution must take place in our perceptions to reveal an authentic spiritual awakening. It is a feeble response for the Green movement to preoccupy itself with cleaning and tidying the Earth. Famine, wars and environmental destruction will continue to be features of life on Earth until the end of time. To imagine otherwise is foolish. There is the danger that such home truths may trigger despair—"What's the use?" But a critical inquiry into Green beliefs and socially conditioned attitudes liberates the heart and mind and awakens our existence so we act wisely amid the truths of life.

The Local View
Environmentalists find themselves on a treadmill when it comes to working for social and environmental justice. First, they become aware that either corporations or elected officials plan a major development that is unacceptable. This triggers a meeting of Greens to find ways to thwart the plans. The meetings produce press releases, leaflets, letters, more public meetings and occasionally initiate direct action. When protesters arouse enough public sympathy they may force the government or developers to stall their plans. But it is rare that environmentalists can halt a project, particularly when there are large sums of capital investment involved. Officials are frequently aware of potential public reaction and take this into account in their long term strategies.

Developers and governments bide their time. One or two years later they submit the same proposals to the planning authorities or, often, a mildly adjusted version of the first application. The Greens, and the rest of the public, are usually unable to muster up again the same degree of support for their efforts to halt the march of environmental abuse. The planning officials take this as a sign that the public has come round to their way of thinking. Developers proceed to tear up the land, usually for a self-serving purpose though they employ the rhetoric of public interest: that the local community needs another mall, or parking lot or office building.

Protesters often lack the resources to organize yet another campaign. Finally the local government agrees to the building application with token amendments. Up goes the concrete eyesore because people cannot mobilize themselves to halt the drive of developers. This situation repeats itself in democratic societies everywhere: there is public awareness of what is unacceptable, there is the campaign to change the situation with perhaps short term success and then there is the result. Is it any wonder that the mantra of environmentalists has become "What's the use?" The powerful vested interests succeed in getting their own way. They have the financial resources, the staff and sharp public relations expertise to defeat the amateur efforts of part-time protesters. They dash to pieces worthwhile public campaigns.

The only solution to this state of affairs is dramatic change. As the Green Party proposed, there must be an active participatory democracy at the local level instead of centralized control from national government and only weak local government. For this to occur, it means:

1. *Local referenda on decisions affecting local communities*
2. *Setting and collecting of taxes by local government*
3. *Proportional representation to express a broad view of concern*
4. *Freedom of information so that the public has access to information affecting their lives*
5. *A Bill of Rights to protect all citizens*
6. *Worker and tenant participation on boards and governing bodies*
7. *Local government and industries to make available to the public detailed reports of the environmental impact of their activities.*

LETS

At the local level there are small groups and individuals struggling to find alternatives to the current economy with its obsessions around making money. In 1986 Totnes, the main centre in Britain for "alternative" values, launched the first LETS (Local Exchange Trading System), a community information system through which local people and businesses can receive and supply services and goods—without necessarily having to involve money. After a rocky start, it finally got under way in the early 1990's quickly involving hundreds of people in the local community.

LETS, a non-profit organization run by its members, provides the opportunity for the local community to develop its needs. LETS offers a sophisticated barter system where those with needs and providers find each other through the network of members. LETS offers the full range of skills of blue and white collar workers and the unemployed. The view that everybody has a talent which they can offer lies at the heart of the LETS system. The network recognizes that people can offer to bake bread, to provide child care, car pool, use equipment too costly to buy, give therapeutic treatment, write business documents and so on.

Reflecting the belief in a community focused economy, LETS rejects the present economic system tied up with greed, profit, debts, fluctuating interest rates and customer exploitation. Payment for goods and services can be in both a unit of currency called "acorns" and cash. Each member has a LETS cheque book from which he or she can issue credits to others from their own account. The LETS computer stores account information—with no interest on either credits or debits. Any member may know another's balance and turnover.

Obviously LETS does not have the power to be regarded as an alternative economy, but from such small seeds may come (decades ahead) the potential to challenge the narrow economy of money for goods or services. Today it provides a potential lifeline to the unemployed who can use their otherwise unmarketable skills through LETS. After a person receives a service, she or he writes out a cheque crediting the person for the amount agreed. The LETS administrator enters it into the person's account and debits the purchaser's.

LETS offer a way of rebuilding local communities, generates a cooperative neighbourhood atmosphere and the opportunity to learn, share and offer skills to others. At the time of writing, LETS in Totnes makes available around 1000 different skills. Local government ought to coordinate such systems as LETS for an entire local community as part of its public service. Just as every local community has a library of books, so community libraries of household and gardening appliances, tools, workshops, offices, bicycles, computers, tapes and informative videos ought to be made available to the general public through exchange of skills or at a modest cost. Such initiatives would reduce the demand for personal ownership, cultivate community relationships and reduce the pressure to make money to acquire goods. Such community cooperation would place less demand on the scientific and industrial base of society thus contributing to safeguarding the environment.

The corporate world has already noticed the successful introduction of bartering in the local community. So a growing number of companies are beginning to place their goods and services in a flexible pool from which members can "buy" and "sell" without using cash. For example, one company offers goods to a certain value in exchange for other goods in the pool or for credits to buy at a later date from the pool. This principle works well for those with little cash but with a surplus of inventory of goods and services. The pool can also help in terms of bad debt relief as payment can be made through entering excess stock into the pool. Barter companies can help members find the goods and services which they need. As with LETS, bartering relies on trust particularly when offering credits to members of the pool. At the local level, goods and services within LETS supports ethical values and community. Companies using barter pools see it as a convenient alternative; they cooperate with other companies to expand their "sales" of goods and services. To its credit, the method of barter, locally and internationally, makes a shift off the money obsessed economy.

It is a plain and hard truth of community and environmental activism that overcoming powerful vested money interests is a Herculean struggle. The powerful dismiss those engaged in ways to find alternatives to the money market using ethical principles and investments. Intransigence in government dashes to pieces many campaigns to change values from craving for profit to caring for principles. Current tactics to stop abuse of our world at the local and global level still remain largely ineffective since politicians remain out of touch with the cutting edge of meaningful change.

At the present time, any spin-off in terms of increase in membership of Green organizations is largely irrelevant. Councils water down objections of dedicated groups until the final agreement is hardly worth the paper it is written on. Locally, thousands of Green candidates may stand in local elections with hardly a handful in Britain managing to get elected. Elected Greens form a tiny minority on their councils; they have the unenviable task of keeping to their principles or making pacts. At best, Green minded councillors may slow down development plans or speed up the introduction of recycling projects. But they experience frustration in the struggle to challenge the obsession with economic growth that fuels the desire to exploit natural capital resources for profit.

It is as if environmentalists are trying to knock down a prison with a hammer. Hopes to achieve worthwhile goals often end in disappointment. But despair relates to results, not to action. I believe it is vital that we radicalize our thinking so that our participation in efforts to change this crude and violent world is not tied to the hope, optimism and romantic idealism that readily become despair. Environmentalists consistently confront the hard truths of having little effect locally or globally. We imagine that because we work hard for the Earth we deserve a major response. Despair is born from the failure of cherished hopes—not through joining uphill struggles.

It is largely futile asking the rich and famous to jump on the environmental bandwagon. Their lifestyles are incompatible with Green economic analysis. The super rich and the rich use their wealth and influence to ensure they locate their homes in the most beautiful of environments. They then support strict building regulations so their personal environment remains protected from further development. Not surprisingly, the rich and the famous like to support environmental politics while turning a blind eye to the environmental degradation of the poor sometimes living a few kilometres away from exclusive homes. The NIMBY (not in my backyard) ethos pervades the rich in their views on environmental politics.

The Green movement has aimed some of its criticisms at consumers rather than specifically targeting those mindlessly wasteful of energy and resources. The super rich, the nouveau riche and the ambitious middle classes certainly have to be held accountable for the current decline in the quality of life. When the wealthy and the famous expound Green values the hypocrisy becomes slightly nauseating. "Don't live as I live, live as I say" is their dictum.

The Green movement has failed to protest about the gap between words and actions. Prominent Greens associate with the wealthy, the pillars of the Establishment, to secure their financial support and signatures. They make no personal nor any public criticism of unacceptable lifestyles, but in a Green revolution the lavish lifestyles of the rich and the famous would vanish overnight. The Earth and its people cannot tolerate the excesses of those who wallow in high living. The rich withdraw from the real world retreating into large private estates isolated from human and environmental suffering. They will pay huge sums of money sucked from the underprivileged classes for their exclusivity. When the rich speak of Green values from their isolated towers of luxury, they hasten the end to their days of living in a privileged existence with their excessive consumption of precious resources.

There are wealthy and famous people who are extraordinarily generous. They give money and time to the Green movement and various charitable causes. Unattached to money and property, they share their privileges wisely with those far worse off. But there is a suspicion already among grass roots activists that for many in the wealthy sector, their primary concern is the "feel-good" factor, not the environment, nor suffering humanity. The bottom line shows that the rich resist any changes whatsoever to their personal lifestyle. The publicists for the privileged like to cultivate a public image of environmental responsibility for their clients while ignoring their clients' scale of disregard of environmental values. But we often ignore this form of personal hypocrisy since name and fame impress many people. Thus we put aside our critical faculties when it comes to the egotistical and ostentatious lifestyle of famous individuals who proclaim their concern for Green issues. We are more comfortable criticizing the impersonal government or multinational corporation.

Green values are attractive to a tiny minority of the rich and famous, who can promote a "good cause" without personal sacrifice and remain popular among all political views of the public. Green politics transcend the vested interests of any major political party, so individuals can promote environmental issues without identifying with the left, right or centre. For some, this smacks of mediocrity and convenience and the refusal to take a stance while others happily add their name to a worthwhile Green endeavour knowing that it is politically safe. The tiger has no teeth. A signature on a Green petition represents a very poor substitute for a transformed life, an unpretentious lifestyle and a sustained campaign for inner and outer change.

Consequently environmentalists have developed a cap-in-hand mentality; they feel flattered when the rich and famous offer their names to the latest Green cause. Green organizations politely write letters to the rich and famous asking for support instead of voicing criticism at their selfish use of resources and huge incomes. Strength must be found within Green values and commitments rather than through pursuit of acceptability. Passion for issues makes the difference, not cultivating the support of megastars belonging to a destructive way of life.

In recent years there have been numerous bizarre manifestations of the use of wealth. An American billionaire publisher flew 600 guests to his 70th birthday party in Morocco. The cost? $2 million. One corrupt politician's wife said: "A million dollars here, a million dollars there, it's so petty." The super rich share her view. Heads of nations, corporate leaders, entertainers and royalty pay a fortune to satisfy their countless whims. They call it "living with style." Companies pay an after dinner speaker thousands of dollars to be entertained. Amidst the cigar smoke hangs arrogance and vanity.

Green organizations compromise their beliefs for the endorsement from those living in wealthy ghettoes behind barbed wire, bodyguards and sophisticated alarm systems to protect their possessions, their personal hold over their environment and their person. As environmentalists, we lose our way through adoration of name and fame, forlorn hopes and unexamined beliefs. There is something offensive about entertainers who jump on the environmental bandwagon, then fly home each night from public concerts in a private plane having squeezed their fans out of as much money as possible to watch them perform. We belittle ourselves and our Earth when we compromise our vision: when the mega-elite deserve criticism rather than adulation, we should give it. It is a betrayal of values to play the superficial social games that characterize our society.

But, also, questioning the "sacred cows" of the Green movement is imperative. The size and scale of global or local problems may have a dispiriting impact on the heart thus contributing to compassion burnout. Spiritual wisdom and practices, the capacity to be steadfast in the Here and Now, and to be free from inner investment safeguard the heart and mind from burnout. Few people become so dispirited as those who take the moral high ground—unless wisdom supports the moral basis for political awareness.

Spiritual awakening, the realization of Ultimate Truth, is an indispensable feature for action. Ultimate Truth reveals the timeless nature of things, sees through conventional realities and embraces all perceptions, views of life and the Earth. Such realization transforms perception, decimating constructed beliefs and bypassing hopes and fears. We pay the greatest respect to the Earth and its people through ruthless inquiry and committed awareness. What happens to the Earth will dishearten those living in the realm of hopes and fears. There are other ways of being in this world. The international Green movement with its noble values must challenge its contemporary credo so the light of awareness permeates perceptions. This awakening will reveal immediate and compassionate action rendering irrelevant worry over the future and the results of actions.

As If Nothing Mattered

When ideas are unprofitable, liable to censure,
condemned by the wise, being adopted and put into
effect, they lead to harm and suffering,
then you should abandon them.
The Buddha

Sensitive people experience sadness over the degeneration of our values, our way of life and the intransigence of the Western mentality. Many influential people have deeply rooted psychological problems around power, profit and efficiency that they resist addressing. Trapped in fixated mental states, the same hardened views get repeated as reality. Having cooperated in this peculiar blindness, we pursue an excessive share of resources for ourselves as though this was a healthy response to living on this Earth. We hook into the ideology of individual choice. Neither our religious, scientific, philosophical nor psychotherapeutic traditions offer an adequate interdisciplinary questioning, nor insight into our addictive selfishness. While those in uniform emphasize discipline, the armies of religious and spiritual believers are often unwilling to develop a disciplined way of living: the rhetoric of "go for it" infects consciousness. Economists have declared that the consumer is king. Ego ravages the Earth.

To maintain our lifestyle we exercise control over other economies, particularly those of the Third World. Inequitable trade agreements, selling arms, bank loans, Western education, the secret services and occasional military invasions ensure our domination. Leaders of poor nations approach us cap in hand, travelling the Western world looking for investors. Western businesses and governments disregard the human and environmental costs of their investments in the Third World; the bribing of government officials, civil servants and company bosses ensure contracts. Aid appears to be linked to trade agreements, massive projects such as damns and even major arms deals.

The West has sought to divide the world between the developed nations and the developing nations. The mythology of progress embraces this view. It would be more accurate to speak of the over-developed peoples and the out-of-development peoples of the world. The world's poorest billion inhabitants receive 1.4% of all global income while the world's richest billion receive 83%. The exploited poor on the land and in factories create national wealth without benefiting from it. Exploitation of environment and people serve as the raw resources for maximization of profit. Even the World Bank admits that the poor get the raw end of environmental abuse. Large nation states, such as the USA, Russia, China, Brazil and India, as well as small ones, marginalize millions of people below the poverty line.

Third World countries owe Western governments, High Street banks and other businesses billions of dollars. They attempt to pay back these loans through exploitation of natural resources, but the debts continue to increase owing to interest rates and further loans. Impoverished countries export precious resources to the affluent and greedy economies of the West. To pay off their debts, some African countries continue to export food in the midst of famine. Paying off of debts and exploitation of resources cancels out any beneficial effects of overseas aid.

With rising interest rates and falling prices poor countries have to export more of their agricultural produce, their wood and their minerals to the West so the debt does not grow. The high street banks lent money to poor countries because they saw the opportunity to establish a global banking empire. The Third World policy of the banks proved calamitous as they endorsed mountains of debts. This suited Western governments for the debts gave Western nations leverage over the economies of the poor nations, but the desire of the West to maintain its pole position as creditor means that the poor of the world do not even get to the starting line.

Third World countries are unable to generate enough cash crops and manufactured goods to pay off their debts. They are in desperate need of capital to produce essential requirements for their equally desperate peoples. Yet the Western merchants, particularly multinationals, mercilessly pursue their vested interests. The industrial sector, including clothing and household good factories, exploit cheap labour free from union pressure. A worker in Indonesia receives on average about 29 cents from a pair of running shoes that cost $79 in the West.

The unholy alliance of governments, banks and businesses investing in Third World countries ensures Western capitalism's domination of the world's economies. Overdeveloped countries keep a grip on the underdeveloped countries through this economic disparity and control over their money supply; Third World Countries have little hope as they are on a downward economic spiral. We have plundered the Third World and built a wall of self protection around ourselves through tight immigration control. Self-serving trade and compassion are incompatible, and, sadly, in the West today the latter is expendable.

GATT (General Agreement on Tariffs and Trade) makes a concerted effort to ensure that all agreements work in our favour no matter how much suffering these policies generate to the poor of the world. GATT aims to liberalize free trade despite the cost to poor countries dominated by foreign competitors. By removing remaining trade restrictions, multi nationals will increase their profits dramatically since Third World countries will have no power to stop imports. In the name of aid, the European Union dumps surplus food on Africa, sometimes at the expense of local African farmers unable to compete.

Transnational companies control 70% of world trade. The over-developed nations try to force other governments to stop subsidies of worthwhile projects (such as forest replanting) or end safety regulations (such as the dangerous use of hormones in meat). There is constant fear of another nation having an unfair advantage, and again and again, fear and greed determine decisions. GATT indirectly supports the transport industry—more and more trucks on the road, ships at sea and cargo aircraft—further damaging land, water and air. GATT works against the community-based principle of local consumption of local products and places free trade before environmental protection.

According to the Agriculture Council of America, the USA uses only 10% of its disposable income to buy food compared to 16% for France, 29% for Thailand and 53% for India. We complain when food prices go up, not generally because we cannot afford to pay more, but because of the desire to spend our money on other "things," such as vacations in the sun. Tropical gardens of the Third World become tourist ghettos to satisfy the exotic desires of our society. Hoteliers even seek out Himalayan caves used by Buddhist and Hindu monks for centuries, to entice newlyweds to spend a honeymoon in a cave—yet another attempt to satisfy the Western fetish for novelty.

The USA has consumed more natural resources in the past 40 years than the whole of humanity in the past 4000 years. This is truly different from a simple recycling project 2500 years ago. Ananda, a close companion of the Buddha, told a ruler that the Buddha's spiritual community made their worn-out clothes into bedspreads. Then the sangha cut up the worn-out bedspreads into dusters and finally the used-up dusters were used to repair cracks in the walls.

Reducing economics to market values reveals our deranged thinking. For example, consider obsession in sports. We invest hopes, fear and rage in the name of a team or individual with whom we have no personal contact. We believe it really matters whether our team wins or loses. With hardly a mumble of protest, we read reports that a club has sold a single footballer to another club for £5 million. This is more than double the amount the British government offered in aid to two million environmental refugees in Bangladesh, who lost everything in the face of freak weather conditions. These cases are not anomalies in the economic life of the nation, they are symptoms of neurosis. Our obsession with wheeling and dealing reflects the gross disparity between economic and human values. People who blatantly prosper from exploitive investments live with little compassion for others. We take the view that those who are not even as high as the bottom rung of the ladder only have themselves to blame. "That's their choice" we say; this view is regarded as rational.

An ugliness of perception and thought reveals itself in certain foreign policy. There was the unpardonable horror of the Indonesian massacre of one third of the population of East Timor. The death toll was similar as a percentage of the Timorese population to the holocaust of Buddhists by the Khmer Rouge in Kampuchea during the 1970's. A former British Defence Minister commented on television: "What is it that is so dreadfully special about East Timor to the British people?" Yet the West had provided the Indonesian government with sophisticated weapons, including fighter-bombers and tanks, to attack a defenceless people.

Another elected member of the British parliament made a vicious public comment illustrating obscene political arrogance. Ten days after 120,000 Bangladeshis had drowned in floods and hurricanes, he commented that meanwhile even more babies had been born in that country. This absence of compassion and savagery of opinion is not an isolated instance. I believe politicians who make such comments are in serious need of psychotherapy. The loss of 120,000 people is the equivalent of every voter in nearly two British constituencies dying from a storm in a matter of a day or two. Does he have any possible notion of the grief such tragedies generate to loved ones, relatives and friends? Regrettably the voice of that Parliamentarian is not alone but found in every tier of an indifferent society unable to think beyond its own self interests.

Socialists have contributed somewhat to understanding the nature of selfish economics, but they have tied themselves to state planning and job creation no matter how soul destroying the work. Some socialists envy the rich whom they like to blame for the problems of humanity. If only this was the truth, it would at least simplify the problem, its cause and its solution. But economic matters embrace a complex web of circumstances which neither the economist, political analyst nor this author can possibly hope to identify adequately. We are all in this economic mess together. In "Animal Farm," the classic novel analysing a socialist society, George Orwell coined the slogan: "Everybody is equal but some are more equal than others." With the fate of the Earth, we might say with some accuracy: "Everybody is responsible but some are more responsible than others."

At home and abroad, desire and pressure around money generate problems between business firms and within individual businesses. Desire and ambition can cause the collapse of a business or widespread redundancies as much as changes in the market place or public demand. Outside forces cannot be divorced from the profit obsessed psychology of management, hungry for bonuses. The Buddha's teachings on right livelihood are about work and the fruits of work, usefulness of the product and the atmosphere in the workplace. This gives us the opportunity to live with wisdom and contentment while simultaneously giving compassion and protection to others and the Earth. If companies cooperate we can find collective ways to alter current values. Contemporary and classical economics, whether of the left, right or centre, act as if nothing mattered but profit, efficiency and production. The responsibility for the energy and environmental crisis rests largely with the over-developed world.

If governments, banks and corporations switched to zero growth and explains the reasons, the public would adapt to the fresh situation. Shareholders must examine their desire for constant annual increase in real value of their shares. Economics must address the issue of a safe, just world which employs clean technology. If guided by insights into the malaise of the Earth, the way of defining economics will change. The current priority given to economic efficiency means producing more output for every unit of input. The focus on efficiency ignores the rapid absorption of energy resources and the limits to growth.

Inspired by E.F. Schumacher's chapter on Buddhist Economics in "Small is Beautiful," the international Green movement points to a value system that includes an interdependent awareness and a steady state economy that is linked to essential needs rather than desires supporting personal vanity, extravagance and excess. Current economic policy with its proliferation of harmful products damages the health and wellbeing of people. It is ideology of *Economics as if nothing mattered* rather than the power of *Economics as if life mattered*. Buddhist economics—including right livelihood—embrace values, cooperation, sustainable work and the production of goods shaped by ethical considerations.

As an act of compassion, all Third World debt must be cancelled to give these countries an opportunity to start afresh. Once released from the vice-like grip of Western business practices and trade agreements, they have the opportunity to engage in a sustainable and worthwhile existence supporting the specific needs of all the people and environment. But simultaneously Third World leaders must end their practices of corruption and obscene abuse of their peoples and environment.

The US government brandishes the sword of the free market world wide so that working life becomes synonymous with personal gain. This value system ensure that the less well off lose out. In the USA a million smaller farms have disappeared in each decade since 1950. Sixty per cent of the budget of the European Community goes in farm subsidies. The large agricultural estates milk and farm the system rather than act as caretakers of the land. When small farms are no longer subsidized it affects the health and social fabric of local rural communities. When profit reigns supreme it leaves an ethical void in local community life.

The intention of the agribusiness is to flood domestic and overseas markets with cheap produce to make small farm financially inoperable. The agribusiness then takes over the small farms. It is a similar story in supermarkets. They can purchase from the agribusiness in such large quantities that they can sell their items at a cheaper price than small shops can buy the same goods at wholesale prices. Governments and businesses conspire together to take full control over land, production and consumption and to relegate entire local communities to becoming servants of powerful market forces. Big business generates the deception that the benefits of the agribusiness, supermarkets and large retail outlets benefits the consumer—despite the danger to the livelihoods of millions of people struggling to keep afloat a small business. Soulless transnational corporations cash in on consumers desire for cheaper products. On average products in the local supermarket travel around 1000 miles. Market values degrade community values. The free market is not giving people what they want but telling people what they want and then selling it to them.

Economists are questioning the basis of their claims on objectivity. Prominent economists, including Nobel Prize Winners, have acknowledged the significance of altruism in economics. Their breakthrough articles have appeared in the influential journal, American Economic Review. One Nobel Prize winner, Paul A. Samuelson, wrote: "Mesmerized by Homo Economicus who acts solely on egoism, economists shy away from altruism almost comically." Under the title *Altruism and Economics* another Nobel Prize winner, Herbert A. Simon, wrote: "Economic theory has treated economic gain as the primary human motive. An empirically grounded theory would assign comparable weight to the other motives, including altruism and the organizational identifications associated with it. This theory would recognize that human motives change over-time." Under the title *How can Altruism prevail in Evolutionary Environment*, prominent economists Theodore C. Bergstrom and Oded Stark remarked: "If natural selection favours those who receive high pay-offs, and if altruists get lower pay-offs than selfish individuals, then evolution will tend to eliminate altruists."

To bring altruism into economics does not go deep enough. What is needed is compassion to serve as the basis for economic policy. Economists and their employers often accuse their critics of not living in the real world. They claim that the world of figures and forecasts is the real world. From a Buddhist standpoint, those who live in the real world express compassionate awareness as the founding principle of their work. Such an awareness must replace conceited claims to scientific objectivity.

Insightful economists can see clearly that desire and fear are the shadows of economic analysis which must be taken into consideration in neoclassical economics. Awareness of interdependent arising affects motives. Fear of unemployment, fear of whether raising taxes will alienate voters, fear of pollution laws controlling business expansion all affect political decisions around the economy. The corporate world strives to use labour saving technology to maximize profits since labour costs eat into profits. Labour is treated like machines or raw materials. Workers become expendable when labour costs rise more than consumers' desire for the product. The private sector then passes over the problem of support for unwanted workers to the government and the public sector.

Desire and fear dominate perceptions in insidious ways as the brain of the worker, businessman or politician avoids addressing such underlying influences. Unsafe weapons, unsafe nuclear plants and unsound market forces arise from minds distorted through desire. The underlying psychological forces then continue to exert immense pressure on the public and private sector to produce and consume more. Surplus production, unhealthy produce and trivia saturate the market economy. This also leads to the West exporting more and more goods to the middle classes of the poor nations. Free trade becomes the means to maximize profits in dealing with the Third World. The big operators dominate the global market, and this desire to make money now runs deep into the global psychology. Wise economics of the middle way includes insight into the interdependent nature of things.

The rich get richer and the poor become poorer. One in five in the Third World are starving; one in five in the West are grossly overweight. Countless millions of people world wide are 50 to 100 pounds or more overweight. People dig an early grave with their knife and fork. Of course, obesity is not linked only to greed. Insecurity, stress and the bottomless pit of unfulfilled emotional and spiritual needs contribute to the eat, eat, eat syndrome. There is the forlorn hope that consuming more will relieve the ache of the sullen emptiness of a despairing life. Others get overweight through living off the fat of the land. With their contemptuous disdain for others, they prefer to gaze up at the stock exchange figures rather than look down at the gluttony protruding beneath. Far too much of the profits goes into the hands of the shareholders instead of investment for a sustainable world.

Despite the countless psychotherapy books that line the bookshelves of shops, we rarely find books that deal directly with the addictive desire for more in the form of success, money and personal identity. The opposite is more likely to be encouraged: "Know what you want. You deserve it. You should give it to yourself." Therapists' clients also respond with the classic line: "I have to look after myself. I have to listen to my needs." Self interest takes priority over economic and environmental costs; protests against such addictions are treated as irrelevant or interferingly moralistic.

The vast numbers of therapists, priests and counsellors do not discuss environmental problems with their clients. Those trained in the helping professions generally fail to realize the relationship between the addictions of the client and the impact on the environment, both natural and social. Personal finances and the environment require as much attention as religious people give to God and psychoanalysis gives to childhood influences. It is narrow minded to adopt the Freudian view that our parents hold substantial responsibility for any suffering that has come our way. Poor diet, pollution, pressure in education, advertising, television, money—the human environment—deserve attention and understanding, too. We cannot lay all the blame for our problems on sin or our parents.

Therapists feel comfortable working with clients' anxieties, jealousy, child abuse, depression or food issues generated through emotional needs that have not been satisfied. But they rarely ask why their clients are wining and dining so frequently. They may never ask why their clients are purchasing an expensive car, a bigger house, antique furniture, pursuing a bigger salary or playing the stock market. There is no behaviour as insidious and dangerous as those left unexamined and unchallenged. Owing to democratic selfishness, we have become beggars at the sense doors—determined to satisfy every whim for what we want to see, hear, smell, taste and touch.

In the Buddha's talk on the "Exposition of Non-Conflict" he said that we have the responsibility to examine the two extremes of selfishness and self-hate. One must let go of those desires that are "low, vulgar, coarse, ignoble and connected with harm, and one must let go of self-hate that is painful, ignoble and connected with harm." He also said that those caught up in selfishness overrate themselves and those caught up in self-hate underrate themselves. Both overrated and underrated ideas lead to extreme views and contribute to conflict. Obsessing over money, career and the future is dwelling in these extremes of self love and self-hate. For example, women, and to a lesser extent men, have become constructed around their feelings about their body. The fashion industry largely caters for a narrow range of sizes and shapes. It is no wonder that so many women experience feelings of lack of self worth. The same industry now targets children knowing that children will demand from their parents the latest style of clothes. Parents have to cope with enough daily pressures already.

Ask teenagers what they want from life and the chances are they will say they want to make a lot of money. Many state this with embarrassment, but there are many young people who are serious about the pursuit of money above all else. We condition children from early years to think this way. Parents worry more about their children's financial circumstances than about their values and commitments. Some young people experience a brief period of idealism and service in the world. After a few years they say they have to live in the real world—making money—so they spend the rest of their lives reacting to the demands of their conditioned ego and a competitive society. The aims of the ego ignore the cost to the under privileged and environment. So called success generates workaholics while others languish in despair in unemployment. The concept of sharing skills and employment is alien. The evolutionary economics of greater selfishness govern our lives.

Restraint and Responsibility

It is hard to know a man by his appearance,
Nor can you judge him on a passing glance
The unrestrained can go about this world
Wearing the guise of men that are restrained;
For there are some who, hidden by a mask,
Glitter without and are corrupt within,
Like jewels counterfeited out of clay.
The Buddha

The attempt to define clearly what is a human need and what is greed has never seriously entered the political debate. The personal and political willingness to examine the differences and to put the results of that inquiry into practice is vital to the health of people and the environment. Right now as I sit here in an airport lounge, I can see on the table a phone order fashion magazine selling clothing such as double breasted evening suits and silk sarongs. The title of the magazine is "Complete Essentials." I propose that the publication ought to be renamed "Complete Inessentials." It is an excellent example of the confusion between needs and desires.

The mantra of the West is "that's their choice"—as a vague response to questionable behaviour awnd lifestyle. We have become indoctrinated into believing in choice, but there is little genuine acknowledgement of how the mind is conditioned. Our notion of choice contains the illusory idea of freedom—that a person or family could really choose something else at any moment, if they so wished. Capitalist propaganda conditions the lives of people as much as Communist propaganda. Violence and rage in family life often revolves around choice or the lack of it. When we imagine that every action of an individual is a matter of choice, we can never understand them. But conditioned forces, both past and present, determine behaviour, and we employ the mantra of choice to escape inquiring into these forces.

Mesmerized by advertising, we are not able to perceive the difference nor the consequences of this inability to change our priorities. Our mind and the environment become tortured through choice. We are losing our power of inner authority to say "No." By grasping the rhetoric of marketing goods we lose our right to say "No" to what we get offered. That capacity to say "No" shows restraint and is an act of responsibility.

Economists and manufacturers do not concern themselves with the differences between needs and desires. Since World War II governments and corporations have marginalized the debate about wise use of resources. Today we wage war on the Earth and, like Pontius Pilate, wash our hands of responsibility. Since economics concerns itself with the maximization of production, it focuses on the use of resources, human, animal and environmental, to fulfil the range of both needs and desires. Since the line cannot be clearly drawn then the present economic system is likely to continue. Economists will prefer to focus on their figures and graphs and are unlikely to enter into an obscure debate about the differences between needs and desires.

The conventional economist does not take into account that:
1. *Certain resources used for production are nonrenewable*
2. *The renewable resources are being depleted faster than we replace them*
3. *The cost of environmental destruction goes unmeasured*
4. *The widespread cost of different forms of chemical and waste disposal born from manufactured goods is ignored. Economics do not take into account the impact of pollution upon people and the environment*
5. *Profit and loss balance sheets take priority*

It is the task of Green economists to bring these and other environmental welfare ideas and their underlying ethical considerations into the arena of local, national and international economic debate. But Green economics also can begin at home. As householders we could examine the items in each room in our home— assuming we are fortunate enough to have more than one room— and probably identify countless things which are superfluous to genuine needs. We can reflect on needs and desires. We can make approximate estimates of the value, time and work involved in what we have surrounded ourselves with.

We only have to watch an old movie to notice how sparsely furnished the rooms were. New economics, then, is making space in our lives for space. It is the willingness to ask ourselves and each other about the necessity of pursuit of property and possessions. It is to poke ridicule at the persuasive voices of the market place and to regard that which we make last for a long time as being of greater value than that which is technologically modern or treated as an antique.

Green economics is based on compassion, and the simple edict that both environmental and resource management matter in economic analysis. Conventional economics ignores the human and environmental cost of production and distribution of goods. Under the present system, if there is less production there is less employment and fewer consumers so the choice is full-time work or unemployment. Conventional economics generates unemployment through even mild fluctuations in the market place.

One spate of fear running through the stock exchange can set off a financial crisis in governments and corporations. Governments often curb public spending to reduce inflation and set limits on wage increases in the public sector. The reduction of public spending means purchasing fewer goods. With less goods to produce, it means companies lay off staff. Fewer goods means less demand on natural resources but greater pressure on people—creating anxiety over making ends meet in the face of high interest rates and fixed incomes. Inflation makes people's lives miserable. Economic growth eats up natural resources damages people's health and their environment. The poor continue in their poverty.

When there is unemployment crime, family conflict and social unrest there is increased demand on the health service—a cost which is not taken into account. The unemployed millions whether short or long term become victims due to the availability of capital. This is not only apparent at a global level, but also at a national level as there is now a degree of poverty in the West, particularly in the USA, which brings reminders of life in the Third World. The acquisition of wealth blinds the heart to poverty.

The spend, spend, spend mentality does not provoke the same public outrage directed to unemployed teenagers who steal a flashy car to go joy riding. Yet there is a relationship between the two—the wealth of one works to the disadvantage of the other. It is not enough for bishops with liberal views and left-wingers to say that unemployment is responsible, the issue runs deeper than that. Social unrest has its roots in the wretched values of a society which is rampantly superficial, where the ego gives itself licence to be on the make again and again. We actually envy the behaviour of tycoons. There is much to celebrate in life, much to enjoy and take delight in, to laugh and be playful about. But when it comes to spending substantial sums of money on whims it is a sure signal of the size of how egocentric behaviour is haunting the Earth.

Worried about future employment, students dare not challenge the ideology of the state that demands their submission. Traditionally, idealism and youth merge to generate an alternative range of concerns to those the state imposes. The current educational climate has successfully exercised sufficient pressure on students so they are concerned with their personal careers. Unemployment and social hardship generate a rebelliousness among the young on the streets, which is expressed as crime. But unemployment also hits hard-working students, who have slaved for countless hours to qualify for nonexistent jobs.

It is unlikely that radical change will work its way down from the top through legislation and national and international agreements. The goal of governments is to put more money into the pockets of everybody regardless of their present economic realities. Since this is their prime aim they will, by necessity, drag their heels about implementing any changes, which inhibit overall economic growth. Green economics will be kept at bay while governments pay lip service to the condition of the environment but take no serious action.

Western governments ignore thoughtful Green economists, environmental scientists and the Green Party of various nations who appeal for change. Implementation of ecological critiques of existing economic theories never gets under way. Politicians use the available money of their nation, either earned or borrowed, for carrying out their respective policies, not for introducing radical alternatives. I believe the responsibility of governments and the public extends to several areas.

1. Governments and the corporate world must implement fresh legislation, both national and international, to protect human and natural environments. Currently, governments are content to pursue their vested interests or leave the corporate world to introduce, often very reluctantly, any restraints on the use of resources. Strict environmental legislation of resources is an urgent necessity.

2. Reports from the government and corporate world of the environmental impact of their activities must be made public instead of being suppressed. Successful production of consumables that are environmentally friendly must come largely from local materials and for local use. There is a pernicious slowness of governments and the corporate world to interfere in the activities of a profit motivated economy.

3. As long as we view natural resources as capital, we shall continue to destroy life. When there is, for example, a severe tax on use of resources and products that harm the environment, it will motivate companies to explore clean technology. Thus prices must be

regulated to discourage the production of goods that harm people and environment. Three methods exist for change—law, taxation and voluntary efforts. Since the latter is not working, laws and taxation must be adapted to the needs of the environment.

4. Motorized transport pollutes the environment when office workers pour into the city in their cars. Neighbourhood offices need to be introduced to support a "walk to work" policy that reduces dependency on cars and oil. Reduction of cars would end road building and all the environmental abuse entailed. There is a need for workplaces to support their local community and reduce the negative environmental impact of travelling to and from work.

The Ministry for the Environment receives a tiny slice of the national budget compared to the Ministry for Transport. This current policy would be appropriate if the purpose of the Transport Ministry was to reduce the number of cars and road building. The duty of the transport minister should be to offer an environmentally friendly way of life, not to scar and pollute the countryside.

5. The days of huge central offices, symbols of power and oppression, must end. Interdisciplinary teams of hybrid communities based in small, neighbourhood offices should have the important function of contributing to a renewal of community life. Fax machines, modems and computers have the capacity to revolutionize the 9–5 work syndrome. Computer networks can end imprisonment in skyscraper offices. Employees must demand neighbourhood offices and a shorter working week, not bigger salaries and overtime. Employers must cut their own salaries and find self respect and fulfilment through other means.

6. Governments and the corporate world must listen to the voices of people working on small farms, in small businesses, and the few self supporting societies. International cooperation can ensure that impoverished people are protected. Hundreds of years of Western colonialism precluded the opportunity for the West to learn from other cultures because we grossly overrated our own importance, but this can change.

7. Science must view itself in relationship to people and the Earth. The scientific and business community could introduce an environmental work ethic and reconstruct the conceptual frameworks in which science operates. Scientists and economists must first realize that the agent, the action and the world are not three separate entities; that is simply a notion of language, a reductionist belief. Then research could relate to the needs of people, animals and environment rather than be born of the notion of supremacy

of the agent over the world with profit as the supreme good.

8. We need to understand the psychology of desire and the consequences of the wanting mind. We need to look at the spiritual vacuum, and the psychological and social attitudes that drive people to desire more. Our universities are breeding grounds for selfish desire, ruthless ambition and arrogant lifestyles. Creative and imaginative challenges, spiritual and psychological disciplines encourage alternative values and a genuine sense of self worth that money can't buy. When maximizing wisdom, compassion and a fearless integrity becomes the strongest motivation for existence it will replace the crude addiction to selfish pleasure and profit.

9. We need to examine and address our widespread addictions. For example, 46 million Americans smoke daily causing the greatest burden on health care services. Even more get addicted to maximizing their income. Thoughtful organizations can challenge the corporate empires that thrive by cultivating artificial desires. The social support system for inner change is pathetically weak, as we continue to indulge our addictions in the forlorn hope that we will stop the habit in the future. Our society has little genuine concern for the addictive personality, though such behaviour drains personal, family, social and environmental life. Addictions include the abuse of smoking, alcohol, junk food, drugs, gambling, money, profit, sex, power and the desire to impress.

For more than 2000 years Buddhists have been taking the vow "to save all sentient beings." With more species under threat, with countless numbers already extinct, this vow has come to have a fresh significance for the Earth, as an active reminder to value sentient life. As a species ourselves, we have to concentrate our minds with purposeful awareness on participation in the Here and Now. Otherwise every human endeavour since cave dwellers first scratched drawings on their walls will have been in vain.

Beliefs which have guided Western destiny destroy life. It would be naive to dismiss the selfish advantages of the current economic strategies for our society, but from a global standpoint we operate from a small mind and a painfully narrow political and philosophical basis. Green economics will take more money from our pockets, but current economic ideologies will cost us the Earth.

Choice.
What Choice?

There are six bodies of choice (or volition):
choice among visible forms, sounds, odours,
flavours, tangibles and mental objects.
The Buddha

As a society which worships choice, we have perhaps distracted ourselves from the essential choice of life. The proliferation of objects generates a poor semblance of choice between one item and another. But choosing whether to commit ourselves to personal gain or to realization of wisdom decides the present and future. If we do not consider embracing the latter, we will continue dithering about what career is going to further our personal ambitions or what brand of cigarettes or toothpaste to buy. When we examine such areas of our daily life, we observe that conditioning, indoctrination, addictions and financial status significantly determine our activities, thus making a mockery of the notion of real choice. Realization and insights break the spell of conditioning and destructive patterns.

Education

Education does not serve the genuine needs of all children, of the community or of the Earth, but remains subservient to the demands of the State and the corporate world. Thus education requires a radical overhaul to turn emphasis away from the obsession with knowledge and competition and the pressure of passing examinations. For example, a pupil may be a wizard at repairing things but education offers no real opportunity for him or her to show these skills. This child can be considered a dunce in the classroom when it is the failure of education to address his or her particular gifts. The current curriculum focuses primarily on the ability to articulate ideas and solve problems on paper. Education fails to address equally the whole person, including the intellectual, creative, emotional, physical, social and spiritual being. Thus education is narrowed minded, to the extreme.

For radical change in schools and universities, education must:

AN ENVIRON-MENTAL AWAKENING

1. *Shift away from becoming clever to embrace an holistic view of activities, skills and responsibilities.*
2. *Include development of practical skills in terms of diet, exercise, creativity and maintenance. Right livelihood, the environment and community life must serve as a "back to basics" foundation in education.*
3. *Question the measurements that proclaim some children as being more clever or bright than others. We must recognize the failure of the education system which neglects to recognize and cultivate the various potentials of all children.*
4. *Increase considerably outdoor activities, connections with the local community and teach skills to deal with issues of life. Experience must take priority over theory.*
5. *Invite a wide range of people with particular knowledge and experience from the local community into the classroom to speak on issues of importance and give children first-hand experience of local institutions such as local government, hospitals, homes for the elderly, prisons, courts and factories.*
6. *Change to widespread cooperation in the classroom to appreciate that many people work more effectively as part of a team rather than alone. Friendly competition has its place on the sports field.*
7. *Expand accessibility to educational establishments rather than retain a system based solely on public examinations as the criteria for entry.*
8. *Include teaching and understanding of the interior environment, including the spiritual, physical, sexual, emotional and mental spheres of life.*
9. *Change the law that demands that all children attend school throughout each school day or face retribution. Pressures, bullying, unhappiness, fear of failure and alienation contribute to children avoiding lessons. Teachers, parents and pupils must cooperate to find a satisfactory arrangement for school attendance.*
10. *Form decision making bodies for teachers, parents, workers, students and local community to draw up the school curriculum rather than conforming to the State imposed system.*

Authentic education enables conduct and wisdom to shine. The current trend is moving away from such a vision. The business world is now turning its attention to winning over the minds of young people. Private corporations are moving into private education in the USA as a money making venture, and one high street chain has opened private high schools. Sales of news, documentaries and advertising have gone to 10,000 schools in the USA with around eight million student viewers. Schools sign a contract that 90% of students must watch a 12 minute programme of education and advertising in its entirety daily. In return, schools get a satellite dish and a television for each classroom. Through use of computerized instruction, classroom assistants and advertising instead of fully qualified teachers, these corporations who invest in schools believe they can make education into a profitable venture. The long term aim is to reduce money spent on state education, cut taxes used for education so that the corporate world can make money while directing children's minds to corporate objectives.

Medicine

Medical science treats the body as a machine divided up into various parts. The industry devotes massive sums of money to research to deal with physical pain and ill health but neglects various causes for sickness. The medical establishment generates the view that the health of the nation will improve through devoting even more public money to a technological solution to ill health. It has been estimated that 80% of the national health budget of Canada is devoted to prolonging the lives of those who will die within ten months. Medical science largely fails to take into account the sickness of people due to:

1. *addictions, habits*
2. *diet, weight*
3. *emotional life, stress*
4. *environment,*
5. *pollution, pesticides, radiation, food additives*
6. *lifestyle*
7. *posture, exercise*
8. *social life*

Health care ranks low in the scientific model which concentrates its attention on symptoms showing sickness and pain. Health depends upon the willingness and ability of people to live in an integrated and sound relationship with themselves, with each other and their environment. To support the old adage that prevention is better than cure, it requires widespread cooperation of government, science and society. Massive sums of money promote high technology and sophisticated surgery which benefits a very tiny minority. If such money was allocated to improve the quality of life, then countless more people would live healthier and happier lives. Independent research needs to be directed to evaluate alternative medicine and to monitor the toxicity and side effects of conventional medicine. Potential hazards for health are found in the food and water supply, the air we breathe and in addictive behaviour.

The commercial, industrial, military, scientific and pharmaceutical industries affect the health and wellbeing of people. There is insufficient data of the impact of those industries on people and their environment.

There is a growing and widespread disillusionment with conventional drugs and scalpel-based treatment of sickness as the cure for all ills. There is still a schism between the medical establishment and alternative medicine. Orthodox medicine has marginalized alternative medicine enabling the pharmaceutical industry to control the health of people world wide. The range of alternative medicine, including acupuncture, Bates Method, herbalism, homeopathy, natural childbirth, naturopathy, osteopathy, shiatsu, spiritual healing, meditation and so on, have the expertise to restore to health those whose lives are blighted with all manner of sicknesses. The West must let go of its arrogance and include in any government health service methods of healing used in other cultures.

Orthodox medicine took prominence during the past 120 years as drugs became more powerful and diagnosis more precise. The essential premise is that these drugs attack the invader with the scalpel to follow up, if necessary. While this basic strategy works, and with some speed, the method fails to treat the whole person—mind, body and spirit. The quick cure may not be the lasting cure. The drugs the doctor prescribes may trigger other consequences including a gradual weakening of the natural defence system.

Numerous medical scientists world wide are dedicated to finding cures to the wide range of sicknesses. However, influential figures in the medical and scientific establishment believe there is no alternative to improving health care other than further specialized scientific research. Many medical scientists are well-intentioned but they dare not make public protests against their employers since they rely upon grants from the government and pharmaceutical industry, who define their fields of research. The economics obscures the way to change. The drive for a particular cure often goes unexamined, for example AIDS.

The medical establishment have told us without doubt that the HIV virus causes AIDS, therefore all research money must go to find a cure for the virus. There is fierce competition between the drug companies to find and market a cure; they claim HIV-AIDS is a simple cause-effect syndrome about which there can be no argument. When AIDS was diagnosed there was immense pressure to produce quickly a drug to treat it. The US Food and Drug Administration usually takes 10 years to test drugs before permission is granted for use by patients, but AZT became available within 20 months. AIDS sufferers accused Wellcome, the manufacturer of AZT, of profiting from their suffering after the drug company priced the drug at $188 for 100 capsules. This cost the AIDS sufferer about $10,000 a year to take the drug, the benefit of which has been questioned.

The argument against HIV as the cause of AIDS deserves greater debate among medical scientists. This uncertainty between certain members of the medical profession and the drug companies generates confusion and immense personal suffering for a growing number of AIDS sufferers. Wellcome claims AZT slows down the progress of AIDS. The side effects of AZT include chronic headaches, nausea and muscle fatigue. It is not unusual for some AIDS sufferers to be told by their personal physician to take this drug to slow down AIDS and for another doctor to warn their patients off the drug altogether. Medical experts who dispute the HIV-AIDS theory claim:

1. *The prolonged use of various drugs causes AIDS (acquired immunodeficiency syndrome).*
2. *There are people with severe immune deficiency who are not HIV positive.*
3. *One third of AIDS cases are intravenous drug users.*
4. *Drugs, such as poppers, are mutagens. Psychoactive drugs, including nitrite inhalants, generate AIDS.*
5. *HIV is a virus that the body can carry without necessarily causing AIDS.*
6. *Infecting chimpanzees in laboratories (the animal equivalent of concentration camps) with HIV show they have not come down with AIDS.*
7. *On average haemophiliacs who are HIV positive do not have a shorter life span than those who are HIV negative.*
8. *AZT, a heavy antiviral drug taken every few hours for the treatment of AIDS, is toxic. The side effects can damage the patient's health.*
9. *AZT has little or no effect in delaying the onset of the disease.*
10. *Government funding to find a cure for AIDS rests on the belief that HIV is the sole cause—through blood transfusion, sexual activity and use of needles.*

If the medical scientists and the pharmaceutical industry are correct then they are saving countless lives. Their grave warnings about unprotected sex, care with blood transfusions and use of needles deserve widespread public respect and acknowledgement. If the basic conclusion of the same scientists and the industry is wrong then countless lives and billions of dollars have been wasted. If major abuse of drugs, toxic medicine, chemicals, malnourishment and intense stress matter as much as the HIV virus in causing AIDS then medical scientists, doctors and the pharmaceutical industry will have made the greatest error of judgement in the history of medical science.

In the final analysis, life embraces birth, ageing, pain and death. Neither conventional or alternative medicine will overcome these events in the experience of existence. For that to occur there must be awakening and liberation.

Tobacco

"I get born, consume, die," said a piece of graffiti on the leather coat of a youth. Corporations export the view: "I consume therefore I am" to every corner of the world. The tobacco industry is not an atypical example. Tobacco barons, based in New York and London, see the decline in the number of smokers in Western society so they turn their attention to producing slim cigarettes for women, promotion of sports that attract the attention of those with disposable income, target teenagers and engage in modern art advertising to hold our attention on their ads for a longer time. The companies also target the ranks of the growing middle classes in the Third World. Smoking cigarettes supports industries that are:

1. *successful at destroying the health of their customers*
2. *abusing valuable land for tobacco crops*
3. *annually persuading millions world wide to become addicts*
4. *increasing nicotine content of cigarettes sold in the Third World to speed up addiction*
5. *employing every deceit imaginable in advertising to encourage smoking including playing on the emotions of danger, tension and fear.*

Based in New York, the Council for Tobacco and Research, a propaganda arm of the tobacco industry, attempts to fudge the widely accepted medical view of the direct relationship of smoking to lung cancer. Money takes priority over morality. For the Council, their lawyers decide what results of their approved experiments are made available to the public. The Council cheats the public through holding back vital information about the health hazards of smoking. Every year it is as though everyone in several cities in any country experience a slow and painful premature death due to the effects of inhaling cigarette smoke. More and more Western courts acknowledge the "right to health" of the nonsmoking public who have had to endure an environment polluted by cigarette smoke.

Cigarettes are one of the most deadly forms of addiction available to people. Scientists say that nicotine is comparable to cocaine as an addictive substance. Nicotine, a dangerous but legal drug, consists of an acrid poisonous alkaloid found in tobacco. The US tobacco industry has admitted adding 599 chemicals to cigarettes, including ammonia, an insecticide that causes liver damage. The industry manipulates nicotine levels to keep smokers hooked. They also add 100 more chemicals to cigarettes exported overseas.

Science magazine says that the success rate for quitting for two years is one in five serious attempts. This destructive drug is difficult to quit because cigarettes are cheap, easily available, compact and portable. It only takes the loss of will power for five minutes to get hold of and light up a cigarette. Cigarettes require no equipment, are socially and politically acceptable and widely advertised. There is no immediate sense of harm to the smoker's life, despite being more than 4000 chemicals in cigarettes. The suffering of cancer, lung and heart disease usually arrive after around 30 years of regular smoking. Although nicotine is the main addictive substance in cigarettes, smoking also becomes habitual as a way to occupy the mind, affect the mood and suppress agitation. Those who hate themselves or have a low sense of self worth indulge in habitual smoking to block out such feelings; smoking is then used to withdraw from the immediate environment.

Heavy smokers are five times more likely to have lung cancer, heart disease and strokes than nonsmokers. One third of women suffering from the embarrassing problem of urinary incontinence can often trace their problem to smoking. Smoking causes conditions such as wrinkles, yellowing of teeth, bad breath and pollutes the environment. Tobacco companies use their brand names to advertise nontobacco products in order to associate cigarettes with pleasure, entertainment, progress and success. The industry targets young people in their world wide advertising campaigns to ensure early addiction. The poor find it harder to give up smoking as they report that it is their only pleasure.

Alcohol

Alcohol, another duty free good, often goes hand in hand with smoking. Unhappiness, despair, broken homes, accidents, heart, liver and stomach disease, violence and death reveal the true cost of alcohol. Alcoholics with a family will spend as much as 50% of disposable income on their addiction, as much as 80% if they are single. One in seven employees have alcohol problems in Germany.

(Glossy alcohol advertisements will often feature a sketch of despair in the background).

"Vodka rules Russia and whisky rules the West" carries some element of accuracy. Governments and corporations entertain guests by providing them with an endless supply of alcohol and cigarettes. Years of drinking and smoking result in cutting (surgery), burning (radiation) and poisoning (toxic drugs) to destroy parts of the body damaged through such substance abuse. There is nothing much that can be done to relieve the terror, anxiety and suffering on hearing that one has a few months to live. Health care cost due to alcohol abuse and tobacco use needs to be included in the price of a glass of whisky or packet of cigarettes. Alcohol and tobacco companies ought to be forced to build hospital facilities for all their customers who are diagnosed as ill due to tobacco and alcohol. The Law should demand that doctors warn all patients off cigarettes, and abuse of alcohol, as part of the treatment in any visit to a clinic.

The tobacco and alcohol industries provide the highest form of revenue for the government from the taxation of products. Fear of loss of revenue through taxation means that governments only take very modest gestures to curb alcohol and tobacco use. Any government seriously concerned for the health of the nation would immediately ban all forms of advertising of cigarettes and alcohol and halt all exports. The public and private sector would have to take responsibility to provide all workers in both of these industries with alternative employment on the land and in other factories. Businesses act on the notion that they are providing a function for the public. They will deceive themselves and the public, lie and suppress information in order to hang onto their share of the market regardless of the suffering they bring upon people.

Television

Television viewing is an addictive activity for the mind, via eyes and ears, often alienating people from each other and their environment. Statistics show that people in Britain and the USA watch on average around four hours of television per day. The average viewer will spend 10 years of their life, if they live until the age of 70, staring at the screen. Even with the remote control, many feel powerless to use the "off" switch. The choice of viewing of only very specific programmes is rarely an option; it seems that television generates a magnetic field that is hard for viewers to break out of, except to go to bed. The real choice is whether to have the set switched on or off. But the addictive factor denies that choice leaving the majority of people of entire nations stuck in a mental vacuum absorbing soaps, commercials, violence and ball games. Television makes no effort to encourage viewers to switch off to break the addiction.

Nearly every single home has a television and some have three or more - for the living room, kitchen and bedrooms. Television keeps people largely inactive, glued to the screen and thus non-communicative. Television thus suppresses emotional, creative, intellectual and physical life. It significantly undermines community life and generally produces apathy towards social action. Yet few programmes stir people to skilful action. Powerful images impregnate the brain affecting behaviour and values. Spotting a face that appears regularly on television generates public interest, even huge crowds. (Politicians chances of election increase significantly if the broadcasters regard them as telegenic). Successful megastars of television and the big screen have a grip on the public mind. They serve as the willing, or sometimes unwilling, pawns of management peforming to the demands of their contracts to fulfill the vested interests of corporations determined to dominate the national or global market.

For many families, television has become a substitute for a baby-sitter. even though figures in Britain show that most adults agree that TV violence encourages criminal behaviour in children. In a survey, 22% said they have witnessed youngsters copying violent or disturbing behaviour they have seen on TV. However, television mostly runs at the behest of the corporate world. In the USA, television viewers, both adults and children, watch on average more than 20,000 commmercials per year. Every commercial is designed to spellbind viewers again and again so that they associate and identify themselves with the product.

The corporate world now targets the world's five billion people making satellite television an indispensable feature in its future plans. Accelerating world wide interest in various forms of family entertainment, international sports and instant news ensures producers can sell consumers their products in millions upon millions of homes. Around two billion people will watch at home a major sporting event, such as the final of the World Cup in football while another billion people on the Earth cannot even afford to buy a pair of shoelaces, let alone shoes. Two out of five people in Britain will watch regularly the same weekly soap opera.

Sales of products increase after appearing on television ensuring again that the primary duality of the world is producers and consumers. The production of choices hides the truth of the problems inherent in viewing day after day the technology of coloured dots emanating as fast altering pictures, and its impact on global life. Change will come through people realising what is happening Here and Now. We have become programmed to say "yes" instead of finding together the capacity to say "NO" to daily addictions. That realization of the necesssity for change only shows itself in acting for change not in complaining. Addictions and obsessions have to be abandoned so that we start afresh, so our activities respond for the genuine welfare of life. We must not be afraid to dispense with what we have formerly identified with.

Governments

Governments tend to operate on the naive belief that information cures social problems. When any problem gains enough public attention, such as AIDS, alcohol, crime, drugs, tobacco, unemployment or environmental abuse, governments generate carefully orchestrated short-term advertisements in the attempt to increase public awareness. But consumerism is an addiction itself, a widespread social problem that generates immense suffering in individual and family lives as people go into debt in the "buy, buy" syndrome.

Government advertisements do not cure addiction nor influence significantly the cycle of desire-action-result. When there is no change then governments imagine they are not putting out a clear enough message so their advertising agencies compete with the agencies that corporations employ. Advertising has become a form of social engineering, a tool to manipulate consciousness, to feed or stop the obsessive drive. The initial responsibility of governments is to ban advertising of substances and goods that damage the health and happiness of its citizens.

The causes and conditions that generate suffering and pain for people and the environment require penetrative understanding and subsequent action. The current view rests on modification of symptoms instead of looking deeper into the nature of our social relationships. To change direction we have to take risks. We must not be afraid to question the institutions that act on our lives.

The relationship between information, conclusions and action deserves widespread attention. Governments and corporations continue to neglect the suffering of people, animals and the environment. The size of the gap between available information and action is horrifying. For example, information on climatic swings is available, space cameras reveal the size of the hole in the ozone layer and the loss of forests. We have precise information on the way we poison land, water and air. Yet governments and scientists take little action as a result of this information. Chemical companies claim they work in the public interest, yet continue to ignore their contribution to damaging the environment.

With global problems the public has to rely upon governments, yet they are as complacent and as secure in their respective ideologies as ever. What our governments demand from the public through their orchestrated advertising is something that they are not able to do themselves, namely change. They want the public to change certain addictive activities, such as crime, excessive debt or avoidance of financial responsibility—all burdens to the state—but refuse to change themselves.

Change comes through people realising what is happening Here and Now. That realization only shows itself in acting for change not in complaining. We are living in rare times since we have no previous model in our society that works, and no set of stereotyped beliefs to cling to. The old ideologies have to be abandoned so that we start afresh, every action must be a response towards the genuine welfare of life. We must not be afraid to dispense with what we have formerly identified with. Our democracy with its competitive basis is not serving the urgency of the times. Loyalty to a particular political party is often a primary motive for giving it our vote.

This change of consciousness invites a different order of participation in the world. It has nothing at all to do with the humourless, selfish and mechanistic mental constructions that tie the public's mind to the past. The old ideologies share a common perception; a general indifference to people and the Earth and a worship of unenlightened self interest in the name of the people. These ill conceived notions of what matters are redundant. We must seek fresh and appropriate political forms respectful to the life of our Earth and the experience of living Here and Now.

The Wheel

One who has crossed beyond the rough and
dangerous road of cyclic existence and self deception,
and gone beyond, free from doubt, I call a noble being.
The Buddha

Bihar, the second most populated state of India, languishes in cultural and social deprivation where poverty, corruption and apathy rule. The rest of India looks upon Bihar with disdain. Bihari citizens are often unwelcome in other states. Biharis lack credibility in the eyes of millions of other Indians. Much of Bihar exists in a semi-feudal condition where exploitation, violence and a degenerate culture are the norm.

Statistics show that Bihar has the highest murder rate (around 4500 per year), more terrorism, kidnapping and violent crime than anywhere else in India. The literacy rate of 23% is the lowest in the country. Biharis are paid the lowest wages, have the fewest cultural activities and cinemas, and the biggest gap between rich and poor. Today Bihari labourers on public sites are paid about the same as their forefathers received in silver at the time of the Buddha, 2500 years ago. Bihar has the lowest per capita income and the largest percentage of people below the poverty line; millions of the poor are known by their caste name of Musahar—"rat eaters." More than half of the Bihari population live in "excruciating poverty."

Honest Bihari politicians constantly struggle to stop the widespread corruption in the state, including among their colleagues. In Patna, the capital of Bihar, politicians must show an extraordinary degree of integrity to avoid temptations in the form of bribes, slush funds and financial gifts for favours. Bihari politics regularly feature assassinations, threats and accusations. At times, polling booths and votes are bought and sold. Caste and patronage dominate education; spurious doctors and quasi medics abound amidst a virulent and repressive caste system. Power, privilege and caste determine even one's place on the bus. Local dignitaries evict passengers seated immediately behind the driver to take the seat for themselves and they often refuse to purchase tickets. The poor sit further back or on the roof.

Feudalism, political corruption and intimidation of the poor reach their zenith in the Bodh Gaya region, where the Buddha was enlightened. For example, the eight-mile country road from Gaya railway station to Bodh Gaya is highly dangerous, neither pilgrims nor locals dare travel on the road at night due to bandits, known as dacoits. If there is an accident on the road, drivers will flee for their lives. In Bodh Gaya, the local feudal landlord, the Mahanth, amassed 13,000 acres at the expense of the local villagers. Though Indian legislation calls upon large holdings of land to be returned to the poor, the Mahanth remained unflinching; it took years of court cases for the poor to recover their land. Landlords in Bihar use guns, wealth and power, as well as the arm of the State, including at times the police, to terrorize the poor into submission. Armed guards, day and night, accompany the current respected local district magistrate in Bodh Gaya.

Ten minutes walk from the Bodhi Tree, next to the Thai Monastery, stands the village hamlet of Mastipur where, in 1993, the Sri Lankan government built brick homes for the villagers on the condition they took a vow to stop brewing illicit liquor. After agreeing to take the vow, the villagers said they could not eat the bricks of their new homes. They resumed brewing the liquor, catching rats and sending their children out to beg.

Massacres, social unrest and bonded serfs are common in the State of Bihar. Coupled with a harsh environment, these pressures on the poor become overwhelming. Famine, floods, disease, waves of deaths from hypothermia add to the hardship. In the peak of summer, parts of Bihar become the hottest inhabited places in the world. Decades if not centuries of wholesale destruction of the natural environment have contributed to destructive change in weather patterns.

Every year during the winter months thousands of Buddhist pilgrims from all over the world make their way to Bodh Gaya—in central Bihar—as an act of devotion and faith in the Buddha and his teachings. Tibetans travelling down from the Himalayan kingdoms and other parts of India make up the majority. Most Tibetans travel as sincere pilgrims generating loving kindness and compassion world wide through their prayers, devotional practices and rituals. But over the years there has been ongoing resentment of some of the Tibetan pilgrims in Bodh Gaya. They have earned themselves a reputation for being extremely tightfisted, arguing over the smallest transactions in the village. Some Tibetans bring with them the carcases of animals to cook, which are regarded as offensive by the local Hindu population, who are mostly vegetarian. The Dalai Lama, himself, rarely visits Bodh Gaya fearing that he could be used as a target for anti-Tibetan feeling.

Tibetan merchants are buying boys, aged 6–12 years, from desperately poor families in Bodh Gaya, for between 150 (£3.30p) to 500 rupees (£11) to use as child labour in their settlements in other parts of India. The boys are taken as serfs to work in Tibetan refugee settlements in Karnataka, Mysore and Himachal Pradesh. Bodh Gaya parents who sell their children rarely see them again, nor receive news from them, nor do the parents receive any money by mail, as promised. People in the village are afraid to approach the authorities for fear that the Tibetan merchants will kill their children. The author has in his possession photocopies of certificates of sale of children. These children are deprived of all human rights, including their home, friends, family, education and income. One eye witness in Mysore told me the children's Tibetan masters force the boys to work long hours doing the most menial tasks.

Until the last three centuries, Bihar, where the Buddha gave most of his teachings, had a long history of spiritual, philosophical and cultural development. The colonization of the region by the Moghuls and then the British ended this period. Today, despite everything, the people of Bodh Gaya and surrounding hamlets accept and accommodate the tens of thousands of Buddhist and Hindu pilgrims who visit the area during the winter months. The presence of pilgrims gives much needed support to the local economy. What is remarkable is not that the poor in Bihar ask for anything, but that they ask for so little. Asian and Western Buddhists have raised funds to provide schools, clinics, a leprosy project, a home for the dying, as well as teachings on wisdom and compassion. The author has been giving spiritual teachings annually in the Thai Monastery in Bodh Gaya since 1975.

Siddhartha Gautama was born on the full moon of May between two trees in the Garden of Lumbini in northern Bihar near the foothills of the Himalayas. His mother, Queen Mahamaya, was travelling in the royal carriage to Devadaha, her family home, to have the baby after leaving Kapilavatthu, the capital of the Sakya Kingdom. Halfway between the two cities she went into labour and gave birth to her son beneath the shade of the Sal tree in full blossom. Siddhartha's mother died a week later leaving her sister, Pajapati, to raise the baby.

His father, King Bimbisara, ruled over the Sakya kingdom from his palace in the capital. The prince married the beautiful Yasodara but by the time Siddhartha had reached his late 20's he was beginning to have profound doubts about his future. For the first time he experienced the reality of witnessing an ageing person, a very sick person and a corpse. The thought arose in him:

"Youth, the prime of life, ends in old age and death; our senses fail us when they are most needed. We lose our vigour and health when disease creeps in. Finally death comes suddenly perhaps, and unexpectedly puts an end to this brief span of life. Surely there must be an escape from this unsatisfactoriness, ageing and death."

So at 29, insecure and unenlightened, he left his wife and young son, Rahula, to engage in the quest for the "supreme security." After six years, Siddhartha arrived at Urevela, modern day Bodh Gaya. The river, Neranjara, ran near the village where there were trees which gave him shade. In one of his talks in his old age the Buddha recalled the location saying that it was "a pleasant spot soothing to the senses and stimulating to the mind. I saw a delightful stretch of land and a lovely woodland grove and a clear flowing river with a delightful ford and village for support nearby." Seeing a large tree, the asathatha, a sacred fig tree (ficus religiosa), he sat and meditated. He said: "I attained enlightenment under the tree."

He spent another seven weeks at the riverside in the woodland grove before setting off to make the long walk to Sarnath on the outskirts of Varanasi. It took him about two weeks to reach there where he gave his first talk on the profound significance of the middle way in the spiritual life. The title of this talk is "Turning the Wheel of Dharma." It was the turning of this wheel that became his life-long mission from age 35 to 80. Day after day he spoke of the necessity to turn to the Truth, and the way the Truth of things affects our lives. In that talk he urged his friends to discard everything that was not essential for the spiritual life. The news of a man declaring he was turning the Wheel of Dharma spread rapidly.

The Steering Wheel

In comparison to the Wheel of the Dharma, the wheel of the bullock cart or of the motorcar is of minor significance in the development of humanity. During the Buddha's lifetime and until the 19th century travel was by foot, horse, cart or carriage. The world was relatively quiet, road accidents were rare, maintenance of transportation was simple and inexpensive. Life was focused around the local community. There needed to be strong motivation to make a long journey; wandering mendicants, salesmen and government officials regularly passed through the towns and villages, but otherwise it was quiet. It was a far cry from today's society where the building of roads and car parks and the manufacturing of cars and trucks take priority over community life.

We claim we have come a long way from the days of the bullock cart. But we have paid a price for our motorway madness. Naively we have confined the language of development and progress to the mechanical world; giving priority to adapting the environment to meet our demands has contributed to the neglect of our inner environment. Scratch the surface of many people in our society and beneath the confident mask of success there is an alarming depth of dissatisfaction. Life in the fast lane breeds aggression and despair, yet our society and leaders are unable or unwilling to shift the focus of existence off industrialization onto environmental awareness.

An example is the internationally notorious M25 Motorway that encircles London, one of the largest cities in the world. To a fanfare of self-congratulation, the British government spent billions of pounds building this motorway. At its opening, Prime Minister Thatcher described it as "perhaps the most important piece of transport history for London...a major step towards making the capital a pleasant place." The government, transport officials and roadbuilders propagated the myth that the M25 would greatly reduce traffic into the city when completed. When the motorway opened the average speed of traffic in London was still slower than when the Buddha lived in Kapilavatthu, the Sakyan capital.

The car is a powerful symbol of our plight. One television advertisement shows spectacular film of a horse and rider galloping at full speed through a variety of environments. At the end of the advertisement appears a luxury car braking quickly at the edge of the ocean. The advertisement claims that the car "drives like it's alive." It is of course a total fabrication, but it's no wonder so many motorists converse about their car in terms of "she" or "he." When an object of the mechanical world is regarded as a feeling, perceiving being it shows an alarming alienation from the natural world.

In the skies above London, planes circle around the two major airports in a queue waiting for permission to land. By the turn of the century the London airport authorities anticipate handling one million passengers per month at London's airports. This is equivalent to moving the entire population of London in nine months. A 767 passenger aeroplane carries 24,000 gallons of fuel—enough to take the average family car one million miles.

The constant struggle for space in the skies is repeated on the ground. The orbital M-25 proved a disaster. The motorway encouraged more and more motorists to drive into the city centre. Within two years, it became the busiest stretch of motorway in the world and contributed to making the capital an even more unpleasant, polluted, and noisy place. The average speed of traffic in London was reduced further, to the point where motorists in the city rush hour envy the speed of traffic 2500 years ago. Some sections of the motorway built to take 80,000 cars a day have to accommodate more than 200,000 cars a day. Obsessed with misplaced notions of development, the government's solution is to increase the number of lanes.

Massive roadbuilding plans are announced weekly in various countries around the world. There is little or no consultation with local communities. New roads and more motorway lanes invite more traffic onto the streets and into the cities. Friends of the Earth and the Green Party want to see the use of derelict railway lines, extensive rail links, cheap and easily available bus rides and more use of cycles. The place of work and home need to be in close proximity, but since the sacred cow of the West is the car, progressive solutions are dismissed. Current transport policy is guaranteed to make matters more desperate than they already are. Harsh experience and sensible alternatives take second place to worship of the car.

A motorist, who had lost his way, was driving along a country lane when he spotted a farmer cultivating his field. The motorist stopped and shouted across to the farmer: "What was the name of the last town a few miles down the road?"

The farmer said: "I don't rightly know."

The motorist grimaced and said: "What's the name of the next town down this road?"

The farmer said: "I don't rightly know."

The irritated motorist said: "You mean to say you don't know the name of the last town nor the next town?"

The farmer smiled and said: "That's right. But I'm not lost."

In our obsession with the car and going places we have lost our way. Road maps will not help. We refuse to consider the personal cost through worship of the car, we override the interests of millions who hardly drive or do not own a car. Thousands upon thousands of hours of our lives are devoted to the car; the cost of a used car often works out at much more than a year's disposable income. Every spare penny may go into paying for the purchase, maintenance and repairs of the car, and the garage can be one of the biggest rooms in a home. Most people use their private car to get to the shops and cannot imagine shopping without it, so huge supermarkets are built on precious green land to cater to motorists.

Motorways have become long, narrow scars of concrete and tarmac across the Earth; the constant production of cars means the constant growth of unmanageable problems. Road planners and architects deceive themselves and others when they claim more roads, bridges and tunnels will cure traffic snarls and lengthening traffic jams. Multistorey car parks deface the skyline. Cars generate 700 tons of pollution annually, particularly carbon dioxide; they are responsible for 13 per cent of the total carbon dioxide emitted. More and more cities are shrouded in polluting fumes from cars mixing with ozone. Satellite pictures taken of the hole on the other side of the ozone layer show that it is nearly twice the size of the USA with an alarming thinness in various patches.

Cars, whether unleaded petrol is used or not, are a significant health hazard affecting particularly the young, elderly and sick. Traffic conditions significantly contribute to stress, anxiety, aggression and a foul temper. Death from traffic accidents amounts to some 100,000 people in the West every year and more than a million are seriously injured. Another hidden cost of the car is car crimes; more than a quarter of police time is spent dealing with car related crime, accidents and traffic problems. The continued acceleration in car production has meant reorganizing the lifestyle of communities world wide. The car has become an expression of advanced technology, a symbol of personal success. It has become such a desirable product that cities, towns and villages are built according to the needs of motorists rather than to the needs of the community.

Car manufacturers determined the average "life" span of a car as seven or eight years. Endless novelties in design and performance ensures a faster turnover with millions of new cars being added each year to our congested roads. Two out of three cars on European roads are less than five years old. Green activists in Europe seriously discussed taking worn-out cars back to the factory of origin and dumping them outside the gates as a protest against the car industry's unwillingness to produce a car that lasts, and for its refusal to take back what it produces. Instead countless car dumps deface the city and countryside.

Cars have become a symbol of freedom, an expression of individualism and a comment on our values, therefore an extension of our mind. No government is willing to engage in an utter rethink of its transport policy when millions are employed in the motor industry and life has been geared around the worship of individualism. We have become dependent upon the car, but the challenge is to find the political commitment to end this dependency through adequate communal transport systems with accessible integrated networks. We also need psychological insights into the power of the car as a symbol, our desire to impress and our infatuation with the new.

Today there are many who refuse to go to work by bus, train or underground because they think they are above such forms of transport. Such perceptions speak of the success of the car industry. Governments and businesses are afraid to promote public transport for fear of losing massive revenue from the car industry. If they did, we would have the opportunity to rethink our way of life, and to liberate ourselves from the burdens and anxieties of car dependency, car debt and endless hours of expensive motoring for unnecessary goods in unnecessary shopping malls.

If we own a car, then we must examine our relationship to it. What are the purposes for its use? What are our responses when it breaks down, or is in a collision, or stolen? What are common states of mind when driving? What does the make, size and year of car say about our values? There is something distasteful at the sight of well-groomed left-wing politicians driving around in their luxury personal cars. The Buddha invited those concerned with turning the Wheel of Dharma to discover "moderation, calm, insight and transcendence."

The Wheel of Dharma

The Buddha's teachings on mindfulness and insight are extremely subtle; for example, everything we do, even the most familiar act such as stretching out an arm, is worth being mindful of. This power of mindfulness can arrest the movement of the arm before the hand opens a car door, signs a letter, or authorizes questionable legislation affecting the lives of people and the environment. Sublime discoveries await us when we are willing to be mindful of all the circumstances unfolding in our life in the Here and Now. The Buddha said that sustained mindfulness is the direct way to overcome sorrow and regret, and realize the deepest insights.

The Buddha explained that he turned the Wheel of Dharma to end those actions which contribute to painful results. He concerned himself with the science of living, to be applied during any era of the development of humanity. He constantly pointed the way to a life of wisdom and delight rather than adherence to possessions.

Dharma teachings are not concerned with returning to a pre-industrial way of life, nor evolution into a utopian existence, but wisdom withstands the test of time, and the changing circumstances of the human environment. The unsatisfactoriness, pollution and harm caused by current transport policies requires much greater purposeful attention than either governments or manufacturers are willing to show.

From highlighting the importance of our relationship to the Earth and spiritual teachings, the Buddha also turned his attention to the experience of joy through contact with nature. Clearly the outdoor life meant a great deal to him. He loved walking, sleeping out under the stars and contact with the countryside and clean air. Being mindful of our feet touching the ground from moment to moment communicates intimacy with nature. Trees played a significant role in the Buddha's life. His birth, enlightenment and death took place under a tree. On many occasions, he turned the Dharma wheel while sitting beneath a tree, giving talks in city parks and in the rural environment.

The Buddha was compared to an elephant as a symbol of endurance and strength. He told people that they had to learn to endure harsh words with the same fortitude as the elephant who is shot by arrows in battle. We have also to pull ourselves out of unacceptable situations like the elephant which pulls itself out of the mud. The Buddha frequently referred to flowers, particularly the lotus, which can grow even in a dirty pool on the side of the road. He compared human beings to the lotus: "There are people like the beginning of the lotus stuck in the mud, there are others who are like the stem of the lotus growing through the water and others who are just beneath the surface. A fourth kind of person has fully blossomed like the lotus on the water." He used the beautiful lotus on the water as a symbol of those who have transcended the murky waters of life.

The Buddha distinguished between the beautiful fragrance of flowers and the beautiful actions of people. He said neither the fragrance of jasmine, nor the sweet smell of sandalwood can travel against the wind, whereas the thoughtful actions of people can pervade everywhere. Of all the perfumes, including lotus, jasmine and sandalwood, the perfume of an ethical way of life, free from harming others or oneself, is the best of all. The Buddha compared the spiritual life to birds. He said there are birds which follow the path of the sun by means of their "miraculous power." In the same way, the wise free themselves from selfish demands and temptation, and go beyond this unsatisfactory world. Like the flight of birds through the sky, the path of those who are liberated is difficult to follow.

Time and again the Buddha referred to environmental life to illustrate a wise way of living. As we undergo transformation ourselves so does the world in the way that we perceive and respond to it. The very nature of things embraces *environmental* being, a vast field of endless mystery that remains hidden in any mechanistic bias. At the age of 80, after giving teachings for 45 years, the Buddha died between two sal trees during the night of the full moon outside the village of Kushinigara. It is recorded that on his last night he "plunged his weary body" into the River Kauttha, dried himself, put his clothes back on and went to the sal trees in the mango grove. As the Buddha lay there on his death bed with his head facing north, petals from the sal tree began to fall gently onto him. As the Buddha was dying a wanderer called Subhadda pressed to ask a question. Ananda, the Buddha's attendant, was reluctant to allow a question to his dying teacher but the Buddha permitted the man to come forward.

Subhudda said that there were many famous religious teachers who claimed enlightenment and to have realized the Truth. Subhudda wanted to know how he could tell whether their claims were true. The Buddha told him not to concern himself whether others were enlightened or not. The Buddha's last words were: "All conditioned things are of the nature of decay. Work out your liberation with diligence." Until his last breath, the Buddha concerned himself with turning the Wheel of Dharma for human beings to arrive at enlightenment.

The Buddha's teachings concentrated on the immediate experience of the Here and Now. He had no appetite for engaging in speculative theories and assiduously avoided concepts which could be interpreted in various ways. He would explain with painstaking care the way events unfold and the influence of the constructions of the demanding self. He often told wondrous mythological but simple stories to get across a point. A constant thread in his teachings was the interconnection of people with each other and the environment. His stories revealed the way one event led to something else and what happened as a result, occasionally with a dry sense of humour. "It is more important to increase our understanding than to increase our circle of relatives," he once remarked.

The Buddha adamantly refused to speculate about the beginning and end of the Earth. He would not participate in the acrimonious debate between religion, science and philosophy about how the Earth, or human beings began; he said claims to know about the origination and cessation of the world were merely views and opinions. Such standpoints had no bearing on the spiritual life. He once remarked that he did not dispute with the world but others disputed with him. Dharma stories point the way to the original blessing of existence, which is pure, bright and unstained.

The Buddha did not behave like a proselytizing religious missionary, preferring dialogue and meditation as vehicles for understanding. Neither sophisticated technology nor intellectual brilliance were his criteria for a cultivated and developed human being. On one occasion a religious cult was arguing among themselves at a lodging at Udumbarika. While this row was going on the Buddha's name was mentioned and they compared him to a buffalo who circles around but would never enter into debate with such a sect. As it happened the Buddha was nearby and the cult asked him to comment on their spiritual practices. The Buddha listed some of the dangers of those who live in extreme ways. He said they became intoxicated with conceit, desirous of attention, judgemental, deceitful and attached to their views. He told cult members that they could attain liberating realizations within a week. The leader of the cult appeared anxious; it seemed to him that the Buddha was trying to attract some of the cult members to follow him. Sensing this, the Buddha told him that he was not looking for followers:

"You should not regard it like that. Let him who is your teacher remain your teacher. Or you may think, he wants us to abandon our way of life. But you should not regard it like that. Let your way of life remain as it was. Or you may think, he wants to draw us away from things that according to our teachings are good, but you should not regard it like that."

It becomes clear that the Buddha constantly pointed out the features of an enlightened life which set humanity free from conflict and suffering. He did not use his wisdom to form a sect but gave teachings to enable people to see through any problems they encounter with existence. From the very outset, he adopted an attitude of trust and confidence in people's potential to realize for themselves the deepest truths of life. Through realization, people do not have to rely upon the beliefs and claims of others. Even the insightful words of the Buddha are not to be treated with absolute conviction. His duty is to point to That beyond conceptions, and it is in this spirit that he turned the Wheel of the Dharma.

THE HEARTFUL BUDDHA

The Four Divine
Abidings
(Four Brahma Viharas)

1. *LOVE, DEEP FRIENDSHIP, LOVING KINDNESS 0(Metta)*
2. *COMPASSION (Karuna)*
3. *SPIRITUAL JOY (Mudita)*
4. *EQUANIMITY, (Upekkha)*

The Buddha declared that insight and understanding into the nature of life are the supreme value of human existence. He exhorted all those who listened to him to devote their lives to realizing Nirvana, the end of suffering. Wherever there is nonviolent ethics, awareness and wisdom, there is an expression of the Buddha's teachings. The Buddha never let anyone forget the priorities of a wise existence, a mindful and conscious life in which wisdom penetrates the appearance of dissatisfaction and suffering, subtle or intense.

He proclaimed these four heartfelt ways of living to be a blessed state, accessible to those concerned with the depths of the spiritual life. Such divine states of consciousness are available when we know that connection with others, animals and the environment matter as much as self interest.

Love

Not a mother, not a father, nor any other
relative will do so much;
a well-directed mind will do us a greater service.
The Buddha

For the first immeasurable quality of heart, the Buddha used the Pali concept "metta," a love free from sensual desire. Metta means love, deep friendship and loving kindness. Metta is the active communication of the heart, mind, speech and body for the happiness and security of all life, near and far. It is born out of insight and understanding of the nature of sentient and nonsentient life. Like compassion, metta expresses a love and respect for life which knows no boundaries.

Punna, who had practised the Buddha's teachings for years, decided to go and live in an area notorious for violence. The Buddha's conversation with Punna illustrates his uncompromising conviction about the power of metta. Punna told the Buddha he was going to live in Sunaparanta:

The Buddha said to Punna: "The people of Sunaparanta are violent. What will you do if they insult you?"

Punna replied: "I will say: How good these people are. They don't throw clods of Earth at me."

"What if they hit you with clods of Earth?"

"I will say: How good they are since they don't beat me with sticks."

"What if they beat you with sticks?"

"I will say: How good they are since they don't stab me with a knife."

"What if they stab you with a knife?"

"I will say: How good they are since they don't kill me."

"What if they kill you?"

"I will say that, due to Dharma practice, I do not have illusions about the nature of the body." The Buddha said: "Good, good, Punna. You will be able to live in this violent district."

Realizing the significance of love comes through absorption into an abiding deep friendship towards all existence. The Buddha said: "One relates to all beings in one direction with a heart endowed with metta; then likewise in the second, third and fourth direction and in the same way upwards, downwards and across. One continually relates everywhere with a heart endowed with metta—untroubled, free from enmity, vast, enlarged and measureless." The force of metta becomes the ground of being of our heart, the predominant feeling experience whenever we are in contact with people, animals and the earth.

The capacity for love and friendship knows no measurement. There are exquisite forms of communication that warm the cells of our being like a radiant sun bursting through a cloudy day. This generous and kind spirit can reach down into our deepest recesses running beyond the pains of life. Beneficial environmental conditions provide the space and atmosphere for love and healing to flower. We forget that metta often requires initially a kind and supportive environment for the fullness of its momentum to be sustained in a difficult environment later. The Buddha was aware of this and endeavoured to provide a loving and supportive places for the realization of spiritual depths.

Metta can pervade the very depths of others. Love heals. It takes away, or at least accommodates, the pain, the fears, and the intensity of vicissitudes that can beset even the most well-intentioned life. This presence of metta reveals an emotionally healthy human being, who has the power to ignite happiness in others. The walls of the ego, the forces of negative resistance wither and crumble.It is this marvel of global design, this exemplary personification of goodness, which enlivens the listless mind and uplifts the human spirit. When those whose impoverished lives experience authentic metta, their personal, social and environmental conditions can undergo dramatic change. The Buddha perceived it as a sacred duty to bring metta into the world. The conditions for its manifestation include awareness, accessibility to the heart, activities that consider others as much as ourselves and not obsessing over our personal existence.

Wisdom expresses the four divine abidings—love, compassion, spiritual joy and equanimity.These four profound states of consciousness flower from ultimate realization, but when they manifest without knowing Ultimate Truth, they may become blemished in subtle ways through the ego. When self identifies with any of these four sublime abidings it obscures the Ultimate Truth where ego has no hold.So the Buddha added a note of caution to those who misunderstand the role of metta. We acknowledge and venerate those who generate kindness at every opportunity, without fear or favour, but living with a heart filled with loving kindness, like an instrument of the God of Love, has limitations. The Buddha explained that spiritual life expands further than the fullness of loving kindness and devotion. Love of God, for example, can fulfil certain human needs and the noble concern for others, but the Buddha did not regard this as the ultimate goal of the spiritual life.

He said: "One then reflects in this way: Even this liberation of the heart, which is love, is produced and intended. Whatever is produced and intended is impermanent...One understands this. One becomes established in this (wisdom)." From the standpoint of pure experience, no one can sustain the loving mind from moment to moment, not even saints. Love or deep friendship is born from conditions, which are subject to change.

Love, deep friendship and loving kindness towards all beings has earned world wide respect for Buddhism. But sometimes the insider's view of Buddhism's relationship to metta is not entirely favourable. As the Buddha commented: "When you see what is for your genuine welfare you must apply effort. When you see what is for the genuine welfare of another, you must apply effort. When you see what is for the genuine welfare of both you must apply effort." Traditional Buddhism deserves some criticism for not making enough effort for people, animals and the environment, instead spending too much time in navel gazing, worship of the Buddha and an introverted monastic life. Metta is active, not passive feelings.

The Buddha said one who sustains deep friendship even for the duration of the snap of the fingers is leading the spiritual life in that moment.A life of metta is qualitatively different from a life of ego-centric desire—one lives expansively and the other narrowly. The Buddha used the example of food to illustrate the differences. "Endurance of fire is preferable to addiction to food," he said.When we are obsessing over food, we are wasting it. Genuine enjoyment for what we eat comes from appreciation of those who provide food as much as from the taste. Through kindness, we understand we eat to create energy to serve others. Awareness of the extensive food chain nourishes the heart, food is not wasted when we eat with such an attitude. The Buddha concluded that "such a person can breathe easily."

Unless there is wisdom, love can communicate signals of personal need and a desire to gain the approval of others. It becomes a means to increase feelings of self worth by securing attention through acts of kindness. Metta is free from these kinds of motives, whether hidden or conscious. It is a force born of a stable heart, equanimity and a mind abiding with clear comprehension.In the

Parable of the Saw, the Buddha said metta is strong, durable and able to cope with all forms of abuse. It is a love which is impervious to sullen reactivity, unshakeable and born from the realization of Non-Duality.

During one of his talks, the Buddha said we should make our hearts deep and immeasurable like the Earth. He said we must abide like space which cannot be painted and like a great river which cannot be set on fire. The Buddha recited a poem which spontaneously came to him while speaking to monks, and he requested his listeners to meditate upon it. The Buddha herein revealed his love of the Earth and all sentient creatures, whether living on the Earth, in the soil, in the air or in the water. It is a beautiful statement of love for every form of life.

"One should be capable, honest, straightforward,
Receptive, flexible, humble,
Content, easily supported,
With activities, with few possessions,
With steady senses, wise.
Considered in his actions and not mimicking others.
He should not engage in low conduct at all,
That would arouse the criticism of the wise.
May all beings be at ease, secure;
May they all be happy in heart.
Whatever is a breathing being,
Stable or unstable without exception,
Long, or those who are large,
Medium, short, subtle, gross.
Visible or invisible,
Distant or near,
Beings or those yet to be born,
May they all be happy in heart.
One should not cheat another,
One should not be proud with respect to anyone anywhere.
One should not wish others harm
Through anger or aversion.
One should cultivate an unlimited loving heart
Without obstruction, anger or opposition,
To the whole world
Above, below and across.
Standing, walking, sitting or reclining,
He should be resolute in this mindfulness,
As long as he is free from fatigue,

Here this is called an immeasurable way of living.
Free from harmful views,
With correct conduct and vision,
Having removed desire and attachment to objects,
One is certain to come to deathlessness.

The Buddha stated that there are 11 benefits for those committed to living with deep friendship towards all life forms:

1. *One sleeps well*
2. *One wakes with contentment*
3. *One does not experience nightmares*
4. *One is respected by others*
5. *One is loved by nonhuman beings*
6. *One is protected*
7. *One will not be harmed by fire, poison or weapons*
8. *The mind easily becomes calm*
9. *One dwells with clarity*
10. *The complexion is bright*
11. *One dies without confusion*

The Buddha did not speak in an absolute way with regard to these benefits. He himself frequently was abused, and his cousin, Devadatta, attempted to kill him. An elephant nearly trampled him to death, and the Buddha probably died from a meal accidentally containing poisonous mushrooms. Nevertheless, those who abide with love and deep friendship feel safe and secure in this world. They know it is their home and they have nothing to be afraid of.

Such comments can sound like mere fine sentiments or a series of platitudes. What is vital is the expression of love and deep friendship and that we find the wisdom to transcend egotism. Religious teachers have told us that love is supreme. They have converted love into a universal ideal often far removed from the day to day truths of our lives. Religious love also can communicate a wimpish sentimentality—a passive, softhearted response to surrounding problems—but this certainly was not what the Buddha intended. In such interpretations, the *concept* of love can become a hindrance to the spiritual life, it then has a dulling effect on consciousness rather than an awakening one. For example, we often react negatively to such platitudes as "love thy neighbour," The Buddha does not order us to apply metta to life, he saw it as a powerful and healing force emerging from understanding life. Authentic metta shows a state of fearlessness with the capacity to bring people together, to make others feel a sense of their worth and value as human beings.

Without wisdom, we tend to form our views of others according to the way others treat us. In the ancient commentaries, written about 1000 years after the death of the Buddha, Buddhist scholars said we have a relationship with three types of people: those we love, those who are strangers and those we dislike or hate. One visualizes and reflects on the first kind of person to generate feelings of love and deep friendship for their happiness and welfare. Then one proceeds to the second and third kind of person until there is a deep heartfelt love for all others. In this absorption no distinction arises between oneself and others. The function of this meditation is to enable us to treat others as we wish to be treated ourselves.

But spiritual practice never guarantees a transition from this meditation on love to active love. Its impact on consciousness may only generate pleasant feelings of kindness to all sentient beings. Whether these meditations alone without action do any significant good in the world is debatable; in certain circumstances they could even do harm. Warm pleasant feelings in meditation towards the wretched and unacceptable features of sentient existence are an inappropriate response to painful realities. Those who engage in loving kindness meditations may inadvertently use these feelings to obscure the awareness of the conditions for suffering going on all around them. The meditator has then confused metta with passive feelings of acceptance and the heart becomes entangled in spiritual delusion.

Unable to cope with the suffering world, an individual could withdraw into these meditations to feel comfortable. Loving kindness meditation does have a place, but those who practice this meditation must understand that loving kindness is the action not the "feel-good" sensation. Otherwise metta is reduced to cherishing a pleasant inner feeling, a deepening passivity, and harbouring a handful of kindly thoughts. Adopting a passive response allows the barbaric and cruel ways of human beings to continue; just sitting on our backsides sending out loving thoughts is not the solution.

The fire of communication and action test whether authentic loving kindness meditations have carried into daily life situations. To imagine that directing loving thoughts is as worthwhile as facing issues undermines meditation as a springboard for action, and meditation then becomes alienated from life. Metta is direct service, unburdened by religious beliefs or notions of doing good and involves no desire to convert others.

The Buddha frequently reminded spiritual seekers that others matter. "May all beings be happy," is one of his frequent refrains. But, again, we need to be mindful that our universal statements do not sound glib. Such statements have a useful purpose to remind us of the larger vision of life, but their repeated use loses impact and becomes rhetoric. We then philosophize about the world rather than responding to its immediate needs. The infrequency of the Buddha's remarks about metta indicates that realizing the Truth of things took priority over loving kindness.

The insights of the Buddha encourage us to examine every feature of daily existence. Out of trust in the capacity for people's transformation through insight, the Buddha encouraged us to view and respond to daily events with a heart free from selfishness. He acknowledged the place of metta as a vehicle for social, political and environmental change. His teachings of loving kindness, compassion, spiritual joy and equanimity refute the position of the detached observer, who remains aloof from harsh realities, for the detached observer can only function at the expense of love and deep friendship, no matter how gregarious the personality. The detached observer, whether politician, philosopher, journalist or meditator, must examine his or her motives with an insightful awareness.

Love with wise action is the antidote for the diseased mind filled with violence, hate and negativity towards others. When latent and unresolved attack and defence patterns surface, they form a justification for violence. We become embroiled in the desire to pursue revenge or destroy others with whom we are in dispute, and uphold the view that there is no other choice but to respond to the aggression of others in a like-minded way. When there is detachment and lack of inner peace and equanimity, we become prisoners of our dualistic mode of "us and them"—the basis for violence. Our rows and conflicts with each other then perpetuate violence in the world rather than solving it.

The Buddha said: "Hatred does not cease with hatred but with nonhatred. This is an eternal teaching."

Those who work for peace and justice must find peace within themselves and with each other as a direct contribution to peace on Earth. Otherwise we find ourselves caught up in anger and resentment, overprotecting those we cherish through blindness rather than wisdom. In a talk by the Buddha, the Parable of the Saw, he points out to Molliyaphagguna that he is becoming more and more angry because of his defensive and protective attitude towards women in spiritual practice. The Buddha and others observed that whenever fault was found with any of the women's activities, Molliyaphagguna would leap to their defence, becoming angry with the critic. The Buddha told him to uphold an attitude free from negative speech, to continue to show concern for women and to develop a loving mind. The Buddha added that these same attitudes are to be adopted even when a woman is struck.

Although the Buddha declined to offer any technique to generate love and deep friendship, he encouraged people of spiritual practice to act to make all beings happy and to allow them to live in safety. Words of the Buddha such as "sabbe satta sukhita hontu" (may all beings be happy) and "sabbe satta avera hontu" (may all beings be free from danger) are expressed with the frequency of a mantra in some Buddhist traditions as a constant reminder to act for the welfare of others. But it must be pointed out again that well-meaning slogans are no substitute for direct action.

Compassion

If you do not look after each other,
who will look after you? Let him who
would look after me look after one who is sick.
The Buddha

"The soldiers who crucified her husband and raped her 12-year-old sister to death will do it again. And again. And again. And again. And there's nothing we can do to stop them."

This was the headline of a full page advertisement placed by Amnesty International, the human rights organization, in a Sunday newspaper. Wrapped around this headline was the gruesome account of soldiers entering a village in Arakan Province in the Buddhist country of Burma, forcing a shopkeeper to be a porter for the army. When he collapsed, said the report, the soldiers nailed him to a tree, cut off his penis and put it into his mouth, severed his nose and ripped off his eyebrows, and eventually thrust a bayonet into his chest. The soldiers then gang-raped his sobbing wife and repeatedly raped her 12-year-old sister, who died from a heartbroken convulsion five days later.

The advertisement also said that it is certainly not the only atrocity taking place in Burma. Readers are told that nothing can be done because the military junta in Burma "doesn't give a damn." By taking out this full page advertisement and by graphically describing this atrocity, Amnesty International obviously hoped to shake the typical Sunday morning breakfast table reader out of his or her apathy into an active compassion. They were trying to force the reader at least to write a cheque and become a member of Amnesty.

World wide there are Amnesty groups who engage in constant letter writing to governments which abuse human rights. These organizations expose alarming stories of injustice in their advertisements. The power of the written word and the impact of photographs on the imagination and sensitivities of readers sends a shock wave through our nervous system. No doubt this is the intent of Amnesty International and similar organizations when they advertise in such a way. They, at least, have the courage to spell out the brutal facts of human rights abuse. But it leaves a certain unease: this strategy to arouse compassion may instead trigger a backlash of indifference from readers. Though these tragedies need to be spelt out loud and clear, they lose their potency through repetition.

In the same newspaper another advertisement appeared. The headline says: "Please don't look away." Charity advertisers are already acutely aware of the public's tendency to glance quickly over and away from their appeals. Readers prefer to spend time in the fashion or sport pages—compassion takes second place to consumption and entertainment. The text of the second advertisement concerned a little girl in the neighbouring Buddhist country of Thailand, who lives in an orphanage. A Catholic priest, Fr. Raymond Brennan, takes care of her. He looks after children without a home, without sight and without hearing. It costs £15.12 to support a child for a month. Both advertisements appealed to the compassionate heart reminding us of life outside our tiny circle of associates.

But such advertising is a high risk strategy, although vivid accounts of suffering can have a significant impact on our emotions. These advertisements may persuade some people to become involved with the work of Amnesty, or with charities working to end the suffering of people and animals, or environmental destruction. Other readers are unable to absorb such nauseating accounts of suffering and will avoid reading such reports in the future. Some others will read with an air of apathy while they butter their toast. The repetition of these advertisements eventually has a numbing effect and charities will find themselves sorely pressed for fresh ways to engage the public's compassion and generosity. There is no easy solution. Becoming peripheral, compassion then competes with consumption; we concern ourselves with the welfare of others only in our spare time.

Compassion is awakening the heart at the expense of entertainment for the self, we cannot rely upon full page charity advertisements for this to occur. Again, we have to ask ourselves serious questions about our values, the way we live and if we really care about anyone or anything. The duty of spiritual teachers is to wake us up, to be honest with us, not to convert us to a religion.

The heart's attitude to a situation reveals the difference between compassion ("karuna" in Pali) and love. Love expresses a heartfelt friendship with all forms of life. As an expression of love, compassion reduces or ends suffering. Love and compassion are distinctive features of a happy person. Inspired by the life and words of the Buddha, the Buddhist traditions acknowledge and emphasize the significance of compassion in a meaningful life. Every activity of body, speech and mind, including meditation, is to be regarded as an offering for the welfare of others.

The Tibetan Mahayana tradition talks about a mother's compassion for her child. The mother does not have to think about her love for the child, but responds naturally and directly to its needs. There is no necessity to develop compassion for the crying baby—the response is immediate and heartfelt. Tibetan lamas frequently use this analogy while giving Lam Rim teachings (Graded Path to Enlightenment) to Westerners only to be rebuffed. Some Western Buddhists tell their Tibetan teachers that they were frequently neglected by their parents who placed career, pleasure and personal needs before the needs of their children. They urged the lamas to stop using this analogy because it implied that their mothers and fathers were models of compassion. They told the lamas they were not loved as children, or were even abused. Lamas found this incomprehensible, they believed that the love and compassion of a mother for her child went together like wood and trees. But conflict, suffering and abuse, whether sexual or violent or both is common in our society among rich and poor alike. "Spare the rod, spoil the child" was a dictum familiar to every parent for generations in Britain.

To know ourselves, to understand our past and our present without regret, supports compassionate action. The caring human being is not born lucky but has been willing to accommodate the past and take risks in the present. We not only learn to trust in ourselves but also to extend trust to others. Together we can vitalize compassion rather than naively imagining that we have to rely entirely upon our own efforts. Awareness, interconnection and the applying of spiritual teachings can permeate the vast space of our hearts and release conviction in the value of our actions.

Everyday life provides the opportunity to contribute to the welfare of others. We do not have to become spiritual teachers, or missionaries. By doing so, we might miss the essential point of the Buddha's statement about the emptiness of self existence. Being a "Buddhist" might also obscure this realization. A compassionate contribution towards healing religious divisiveness reveals the emptiness of all religious labels and identities. At best, labels are a convenience; we must examine our beliefs so we access the Profound that stands beyond labels.

Leading Buddhist teachers from the traditions of the East have flown to the West to serve the Dharma. The Buddha encouraged travel for people's welfare. "Go and travel for the welfare of everybody, for the happiness of everybody, out of compassion for the world, for the benefit, welfare and happiness of all beings. Teach the Dharma that is beneficial in the beginning, beneficial in the middle and beneficial in the end." One British Airways pilot announced to passengers as the plane touched down in the USA: "Welcome to Boston, America. You have now completed the safest part of your journey." It was a cutting commentary on a violent society where people are at such risk on the streets that they are much safer flying in the air. The average life span of a Black man in Harlem is 46 years—less than in Africa.

In some respects Dharma teachings are distinct from religious beliefs which càn isolate groups of people from each other and from the Earth. Dharma teachings cannot convert people to an "ism," but point the way to the realization of wisdom and compassion. The Dharma of wisdom and compassion, the active realization of interconnection, contributes to keeping the ecosystem in accord with wisdom. Human beings, creatures, land, water and air dwell in co-existence. According to the Dharma, wisdom and compassion reveal that people, creatures and the environment share a profound and deep sense of intimacy, of contentment and pain with all their surroundings. The wisdom of interconnection reveals itself through our personal, social and political realizations and actions.

The Buddha said that those who follow the way of the Dharma should think of themselves as warriors who wage war on greed, hate and fear. Compassion serves as an antidote to these corruptions of the mind challenging current political, psychological, social and economic analyses by pinpointing and responding to the causes and conditions for suffering. However, we can become filled with self righteous anger; then we justify our aggression and despise others. We imagine that we have the right view and thus can easily project our unresolved hatred onto the Burmese soldiers who raped and murdered the village people.

Such negative emotional reactions, though understandable, support a world already overburdened with reactivity. Our minds become as polluted as the world. Our righteous anger does not end the suffering of numerous victims in Burma, the rise of neo-Nazism, licensed brutality or injustice but adds to the amount of hate in the world. There is enough rage in this world already.

Certain people are quite vulnerable to these obscene tragedies: to relieve their guilt and identification with the situation, they try to do something good. It is not uncommon for those engaged in compassionate work to experience doubts about the validity of their actions: failure to bring about change can damage feelings of self worth. We sometimes become thoroughly confused about our underlying motives for trying to do good in the world. Some may question whether their real motive is to serve the interests of others or merely their self interest. However, any personal satisfaction that comes from activities to relieve or end suffering is a minor consideration. Yet doing good fails to overcome guilt or the need for self worth, so compassion must be supported with ultimate wisdom and self-understanding. Otherwise compassion is not sustainable, and the preoccupations of self overwhelm it.

No doubt numerous individuals at their Sunday breakfast tables thought to themselves, or said to the person opposite them when they read the Amnesty story: "Oh, it makes me so angry. How could such a thing be allowed to happen?" I doubt whether this is the response that interests Amnesty. I suspect the question they want the reader to ask themselves is "What am I going to do about it?" Compassion transcends outrage, pity and despair. There is no point in pleading and struggling to sustain life on Earth if this includes continuing barbaric treatment of people towards each other and the Earth. The Green politics of a sustainable world must be accompanied with a campaign against consumption, aggression, fear, and the growing cynicism in our society. Enlightenment must take priority.

There is a further dimension to the tragedies taking place in Burma and elsewhere. Many of those who inflict harm on others also believe in the rightness of their action. They see what they are doing as a necessary and viable course. In the most perverse way imaginable, the Burmese army, and the military junta who turn a blind eye to such savagery, may think they are teaching the villagers a lesson. By making an example of one family, they may think they are protecting the others from rebellion and subsequent massacre. They may not for a moment imagine they are doing wrong, evil or engaging in an orgy of violence.

Our outrage at violence against an innocent shopkeeper and his family could be similar. "Those soldiers ought to be hung, drawn and quartered," we might say. The violators of life, the victims and the newspaper reader may all end up sharing the same violent view. "The eye for an eye" mentality runs deep, born of self-righteousness. We have a duty to dig deeper into ourselves rather than identifying with our initial outburst, then we can confront situations with a different heart and mind. The transformation of consciousness reveals an active compassion. We can either work to end suffering or feed the global licence for revenge.

Theologians, philosophers and political leaders like to present sophisticated arguments to rationalize the "just war." They sanction the use of the military and the damage it causes, bringing much suffering through rape, murder and carnage. Destroying a community's infrastructure results in disease and long-term environmental damage. There is little difference for the victims whether aggressors justify their actions or not. People who live in the shadow of their leaders suffer because of the unresolved psychological issues of these people. Civilians and conscripts alike are condemned to unimaginable pain by events for which they are not responsible and which they have no power to influence. The notion of the "just war" belongs to the pathology of religion: for example, historically, the views of Christianity have frequently taken precedence over the ultimate wisdom of their founder.

There are, of course, countless stories of compassion in war. Compassion can reveal itself as a heroic deed to save a life or in simple expressions of a sensitive awareness. During the Gulf war soldiers carried a badly wounded Iraqi soldier into the US forces field services hospital. An officer, the surgeon, turned to a young nurse aiding the wounded man and said: "What's this? One of the enemy?" The volunteer nurse replied: "No sir. It's a human being." Our attitude towards what we are doing can actualize compassion. While the surgeon could eliminate suffering and still not realize compassion, the nurse could hear the cry of pain from the Iraqi conscript.

In his wisdom the Buddha frequently highlighted the immense value of love, compassion, joy and equanimity, but made it clear that we should not identify with their expression. "If one with a clear mind teaches another, he (or she) is not bound to it by his (or her) compassion." Investment in results, a sign of attachment, obscures the wisdom which safeguards us from unrest and despair.

Meditations on compassion, similar to those on love, can lead temporarily to a withdrawal from the world to expand and ground the heart in wisdom and presence. We have to consider seriously our relationship to spiritual teachings and global concerns. Do we drop out from social activity to find solitude? Do we move away from our culture, work or study to realize the nature of things—before becoming involved in the problems of the world? The Buddha was aware of these genuine concerns. Such choices can produce concern, particularly for those who strongly feel the plight of others. For them, time to look into their own existence first may be vital.

If we feel unprepared to engage in active compassion, then we must look deep within to realize what it means to live an enlightened life.

The Buddha said that he had lived in the forest out of compassion for people in the future. He withdrew into the forest with the intention of expanding his insights and understanding for the future welfare of others, thus the intention to go deeply into ourselves can express compassion. One senior member of the sangha, Maha Kassapa, well known for his austere way of life, only wore rags, lived in the forest and dwelt alone. He told the Buddha he did this out of compassion, but Maha Kassapa, unlike the Buddha, did not have the intention to return to the conventional world. Maha Kassapa's intention was that his lifestyle would serve as an example to others. It would encourage people in society to question how they were living and inspire them to follow a way of life of renunciation of demands upon the world and its resources.

Even a cursory examination of his talks reveals the immense concern the Buddha had towards society. By today's standards, he chose a somewhat extreme voluntary simplicity as part of his teachings. Such an approach was a challenge to the level of consumption in society. Today there are a growing number of women and men devoted to the spiritual life, whose primary possessions they keep in their back pack. They dedicate their lives to spiritual practices, homelessness, travels to the East and time in various communities. With their handful of possessions, Buddhist monks and nuns, who are serious meditators, also touch society's conscience, getting people to question their addiction to consumerism. Contemplatives from the various religious traditions have an indispensable role to play in pointing the way to freedom from ostentatious living and personal vanity.

It is not accurate, as some scholars have written, to describe the Buddha's teachings as encouraging withdrawal from the spiritual needs of society into a self isolating monasticism. Certainly there are numerous historical examples in the Buddhist tradition of abstention from concern for social peace and justice, but it goes too far to imagine that this is what the Buddha taught. Today the 227 rules (known as the Discipline or Vinaya) for Buddhist monks, need adaptation for the contemporary world. Some of these rules have become irrelevant and impractical due to social and climatic factors. The rules serve as the yardstick for discipline and act as practical guidelines for a pure and simple way of being. Monks and nuns need to add fresh rules to the Vinaya as acts of renunciation such as to:

1. *abstain from eating animals, birds and fish*
2. *abstain from watching television*
3. *abstain from wearing silk robes*
4. *abstain from travelling first class*
5. *abstain from using first class hotels*
6. *abstain from smoking*
7. *allow a maximum of two hours per day for rituals,*
8. *give strict priority to spiritual practice and service over study*
9. *make the same Vinaya available to women and men*
10. *enter into periods of meditative solitude, under guidance of a spiritual teacher*
11. *monks and nuns to share together experiences and challenges of the Vinaya and monasticism*
12. *engage in daily exercise*

Religious traditions can move away from the original spirit of their founders, thus it is vital that we discern the difference between the original spirit and some of the unsatisfactory features that have emerged in the tradition. The Buddha's efforts were to ensure that the personal conduct of the sangha was commensurate with the message of wisdom and compassion. It was his refusal to ask of others what he would not ask of himself that gave such authority to his teachings. This dissolution of the gap between words and action is a hallmark of enlightenment. Spiritual teachings of liberation then flow easily between the voice of the teacher and the heart of the listener.

There are some orthodox Buddhists who voice the rather strange view that the preservation of the teachings comes first. One has to give up "doing good" for others, such as working to end poverty and injustice or attempting to apply environmental ethics. These voices dismiss such issues as nothing more than temporal matters. "Why concern oneself with such passing issues?" they argue. "By being involved in the problems of the world we get lost in the world." For them, doing good is like a band aid which blocks the opportunity for realization of the Ultimate Truth and enlightenment, which is beyond good and evil.

We certainly have to look at any attachment to doing good which becomes an escape from the realization of enlightenment. But the great danger with such conservative voices is that they encourage spiritual seekers to lose interest in the fate of people and the Earth through clinging to limited standpoints. They treat life on Earth with a certain disdain. Such voices—and they are not unusual inside and outside of Buddhism—can inhibit a spontaneous predilection to end suffering, as a natural expression of empathy with others, as natural as the responses of an emotionally healthy mother to her child.

There is a compassionate story in the Buddhist texts which bears some resemblance to the story of the Good Samaritan in the New Testament. The Buddha said: "Friends, it is like this. An ill, suffering, very sick person is on a long road. There are villages far off in front and behind him. He has no suitable food, suitable medicine, suitable companion, nor a guide to the village. Another person on the long road sees this situation and establishes compassion and care for the sick person with the thought that this person may be free from all misfortune and misery."

There is no discrimination with compassion. It is this realization that makes compassion a profound way of living and an expression of an enlightened life. For Truth is deep, profound and beyond measurement.

Spiritual Joy

Victory breeds aggression. The defeated live in pain.
Happily the peaceful live, giving up victory and defeat.
The Buddha.

Spiritual joy ("mudita" in Pali), the third of the immeasurable ways of living, is the capacity to experience joy, not only within ourselves as a spontaneous state of being but also to experience joy for others. Joy is the outcome of a healthy emotional and spiritual life. The sublime sweetness of joy graces consciousness in expected and unexpected situations. Among the ways spiritual joy arises are in:

1. *treasuring the five ethical guidelines*
2. *the depths of meditative absorption*
3. *the manifestation of considerate creativity*
4. *the love of aloneness*
5. *serving people, animals and the environment*
6. *the capacity to let go of fear and addiction*
7. *living an integrated and grounded life*
8. *receptivity to momentary occurrences*
9. *insights into the nature of things*
10. *stepping into the unknown*
11. *the deep touch of immensity, where the formations of mind have no hold.*

Spiritual joy is different from securing material or emotional pleasure. These result from the deliberate pursuit of a particular sensation or object with the aim of gaining it. We have to do something to get pleasure. Though the same objects may give spiritual joy and pleasure—such as a walk in nature—there is a difference of attitude between the two. Pleasure is a response often born from self-interested activity while spiritual joy comes from the depths of our being and suffuses consciousness. This joy deepens receptivity for fresh insights into our relationship with the nature of things.

The substitution of pleasure for joy damages our green world to an alarming degree. In the pursuit of pleasure and personal satisfaction, we develop multibillion dollar entertainment and tourist industries. We regard natural wilderness in all regions of the world as opportunities for exploitation and blatantly interfere with every natural environment. In wreaking damage on our world we simultaneously damage our health and the health of future generations.

Ironically, we demand that our children take care of their presents, but we have a different yardstick for the gifts that life offers us. We chastise our spoilt children, discipline and reprimand them, but at the global level we behave far worse than they do. Becoming the last word in spoilt behaviour, we selfishly and ignominiously do what we want, where we want and when we want. Who is there to set boundaries around our behaviour? Who is there to say "NO." There seems to be no guiding hand to limit our behaviour. No wonder life deprives us of daily joys.

We observe that profit and prestige have become paramount, a collective neurosis; we wish to take advantage of every situation available despite the consequences. When we experience an undiluted intimacy with the environment, such as being in natural forests, we can recognize these places as a sanctuary, a cathedral to life. Spiritual joy interconnects with the autumn leaves spread like a carpet, or the poetic thoughts emerging from seeing the dawn mists hanging in a valley, or the bursting through of a rose bud after a lifeless winter. Our home is this ecosystem and the Earth our garden with its diversity of organic and sentient life. Home is not where the heart is but where our feet are.

Yet the outpouring of painful information about the fate of the Earth is beginning to take its toll on the emotional life of those committed to a sustainable world. Ideological debate within Green organizations have become common currency. Some environmentalists and lovers of nature experience the intrusion of painful knowledge into their perceptions and feelings of beauty. Beautiful landscapes, forests and the open sea become less exhilarating as images of death and destruction loom in our mind. The natural world then fails to provide spiritual renewal.

When a lover of the forests, who also campaigns to protect them, goes into a forest he or she becomes aware that the agribusiness and mining companies destroy an acre of forest every second to satisfy the consumer market. Such facts intrude into his or her experience of beauty and awe. Painful information thus abuses the deeper intimacies of our emotional connection with nature. The wounds and scars on the Earth have a similar impact on caring and conscious people. Not surprisingly, the natural world is having to compete with painful information about it for a place in people's hearts. Sensitive people report experiences of despair in beautiful locations. People and Earth have a mutual impact on each other in the moment to moment unfolding of interdependency.

The Buddha's love for the Earth, an aspect of his spiritual joy, expresses ecological wisdom. The beauty and wonder of particular environments touched him. He loved to take people deep into the heart of the forest where they would meditate for many hours together in the sitting, walking, standing and reclining postures. He encouraged men and women to spend time alone in a cave, far from the crowd. He and his spiritual companions went on long hikes across the country of the Sakyan people and neighbouring kingdoms. They spent many nights sleeping under the stars on the edge of villages. As much as possible they lived an outdoor life. All this had an immense appeal. Application of the Buddha's teachings and deep penetration into the natural world mutually supported an enlightened life. The Buddha knew that we cannot get what we already have; the true gifts of life come from profound receptivity and a dedicated awareness rather than from desire and striving for achievements. Joy is the fruit of that realization.

Having little appreciation of the value of forests, we find ourselves today forced to adopt a materialistic view to try to save them. The International Tropical Conservation Foundation in France encourages consumers to "adopt a hectare of land" in a tropical rainforest by paying so much per hectare. Consumers then feel they have made their contribution to forest protection when they write out a cheque. Of course, there is some merit in these gestures, but it requires changes in international law brought about through a sustained concerted public campaign to stop the destruction.

The Buddha did not allow his spiritual community (the sangha) of voluntarily homeless ones (bhikkhus and bhikkhunis) to cut down trees. He made it one of the disciplinary rules which ensured sustained respect for the human and natural world. Such disciplines also heightened the consciousness of householders who needed trees to build their homes, carts and carriages, and for fire wood. In those days the people replanted trees as acts of compassion. The spade followed the axe. Today a Buddhist monk in Thailand ordains trees to deter the Buddhist government and logging companies from further desecrating the forest.

In spite of the systematic destruction of natural habitats, we have the capacity to live very happy lives. Spiritual awakening reveals our interdependence with the Earth, the capacity to respond to the beauty of life. Joy is available when neither goods, money nor future are the primary focus of interest. We can know a depth of contentment and appreciation which is hard to comprehend in the light of global information. There are genuinely joyful people in the world who are not naive, not unaware of the nature of circumstances. But they have reached deeply into themselves, and know that intimate exposure with life exudes an indescribable sweetness. Such people bring much needed joy into the world. The purchase of furniture made from tropical hardwoods is no substitute for spiritual joy, a joy which is not for sale.

Spiritual joy also arises as a response to outer situations. The Buddha stated that love, compassion, joy and equanimity know no limits and are therefore immeasurable in scope. Thus we are able to rejoice at the happiness and welfare of others. Such joy arises when a loved one recovers from illness, when we witness a depth of love and happiness between two people, when a father welcomes his new baby into the world, and the countless ways we observe the peace, happiness and wisdom of other people. These are occasions for the arising of spiritual joy.

When we are in competition with others, consciously or unconsciously, we are prone to experiencing envy. Others have what we want. The mind then obsesses in the "if only I had" syndrome. Through the media, we stare enviously at the so-called super stars with their meaningless extravagances. Our government harps on about the success of other countries, telling us that we have to work harder, expect lower wage settlements and compete if we are going to enjoy the fruits of prosperity. When we compare our economy with other Western nations, our politicians encourage us to be envious of them. They have a higher standard of living than we do, that is, more disposable income. We believe we should strive to equal or surpass them—no matter what the personal, family and environmental cost. If we compared ourselves with the poor nations of the world we would find little to complain about, and access to contentment and compassion would then be possible.

When we unfavourably compare ourselves with others we become resentful and cannot wish them well. The success of others throws us back on ourselves, our inadequacies and neuroses so that we never feel happy at seeing others happy. We become jealous of others who are receiving the love that we desperately want. This experience, one of the most painful and cutting of all emotions, reveals the antithesis of spiritual joy, the loss of love from another can provoke a destructive fury.

The inability to cope with change—insecurity—supports jealousy. Time and the growing fungus of dependency on a relationship makes us acutely vulnerable to the intensity of that heart wrenching sensation. The ones we love can never guarantee us the continuity of their love. The suffering that comes with jealousy becomes a warped proof of love, a measure of deep commitment and loyalty. But jealousy is not a product of love, it is the outpouring of pain due to blindness and the perpetuation of unexamined assumptions. Spiritual joy, along with deep love and friendship, is liberation from the proclivity towards jealousy, not the excuse for it.

Others have what we would like. They seem to have acquired, with or without effort, experiences, possessions and positions which we want. But spiritual joy is the antidote to envy, referred to in the Buddhist tradition as the "opponent force." We have the wondrous capacity to rejoice and celebrate the wonders and miracles of daily life; we forsake the opportunity for this when we indulge in secret or overt envy of others. As with numerous other aspects of the Buddha's teachings, spiritual joy is an ongoing challenge to consumer values, and the emotional and social consequences of a competitive society.

But then comes, as it inevitably does, the question that begins with "How...?" "How can I be free from jealousy?" "How can I stop being envious of other people?" "How can I find this spiritual joy?" Caught within a particularly unpleasant psychological pain, such as jealousy or envy, we want to find a method that enables us to resolve it. Joy becomes immeasurably attractive when depressed, particularly when others get on better with their lives. However, personal suffering indicates that we have to look deeply into more of our life than this one instance of depression or envy. "What fundamental changes am I prepared to make in my life?" might be a useful place to start. "Am I willing to make contact with thoughtful people" is another major consideration. Painful emotions are the fruits of unsatisfactory ways of living.

The Buddha offered comprehensive teachings. He did not oversimplify life offering only a couple of commandments for our guidance, but examined daily life and exposed an enlightened awareness. If we have been living an unexamined life, it is necessary for us to make a fresh start, to examine the various facets of our life, and our attitudes, and inquire deeply into our mental and emotional processes. The Buddha pointed out the need to meditate and reflect upon change, the nature of suffering and the impersonal nature of mind-body experiences. Making significant changes in our life entails risks—risks that may affect those close to us and ourselves. But are we going to go on living in envy and jealousy, or are we going to free ourselves from such nightmares?

We can find spiritual joy in the Buddha's awakening, in the

Dharma and in the sangha. It is like finding a key to a treasure trove of insights which a closed mind and ensnared heart have kept hidden. A feature of spiritual joy is its immediacy—beyond the comprehension of our mind. At times we may undergo a raw and painful event which arises and passes in time. Days, weeks, months, perhaps years later, we find a remarkable change of attitude. Often we are glad that we had to undergo the painful event because over time it affected us in important ways. We perhaps cannot explain satisfactorily why we are happy about the exposure to such experiences. What we do know is that we have grown as a person. We become a little wiser about life.

At times we may have the privilege of contact with those dealing daily with a life-threatening illness. We abandoned all hope for their recovery since no possibility remains for the renewal of their health. In spite of everything we see the sick person is sometimes unimaginably happy. People can manifest joy in the midst of dying, and we can feel gratitude, and spiritual joy for such people, who enrich our lives through their presence.

What is this remarkable capacity of the human spirit to see pain in a fresh light? When the Buddha spoke of spiritual joy as immeasurable he meant that this joy can emerge even in the midst of a painful event, that we do not even have to allow for the passage of time for the transformation of our perceptions to take place. There is an opportunity to find a transcendent happiness in the midst of any vicissitudes.

Joy reveals a mysterious power that suffuses consciousness in the most blighted of circumstances. This remarkable manifestation of joy can heal sickness, the pain of injury, loss and separation, and dissolve fear. Then the human spirit uplifts beyond the most dire of circumstances into deep emotional wellbeing and liberating insights. We may have met someone whose life appears to have been a tragedy, or a succession of them. Despite such travails they have not fallen into darkness. "How do you cope?" we wonder. For there but for circumstance go I. Perhaps we glean hints from such people to help us see the way clearly should our darkest hour come. Yet what we hear may sound trite, typical rhetoric common everywhere, the "take one day at a time" mantra. Joyful people, who have transcended personal tragedy, often cannot explain how.

Joy inseparably links to kindness, friendship, human goodness and love of the incidentals of life whether revealed in a dew drop or the play of children. If our hearts are not deeply familiar with these experiences, nor immensely content with the ordinary, we hamper our capacity to deal with the inevitable painful experiences. Joy is available to those unwilling to restrict consciousness to the narrow pursuits of self. It is rare for joy to flower in the midst of suffering for those who have a long history of indulging in egotistical whims.

Joyfulness, like other emotions, has an infectious quality, often triggering a similar response in others. The prevailing circumstances of the Earth do not have the power to intrude destructively into joyous consciousness. Those who have entered into realization of the nature of things do not grasp onto impressions. What reveals itself through the senses, or by information, need not necessarily bring dismay. Untouched by despair and cynicism, happiness and wisdom become powerful resources for changing the world. Cynics may interpret spiritual joy as a form of self-satisfaction that denies or represses the realities of the world, but, far from it, spiritual joy is available to those who are exceptionally selfless and who lead an authentically charitable existence. This joy and the capacity to laugh, to celebrate, to respond, has revolutionary undertones since it breaks down the fetish of materialism.

Equanimity

Be like the Earth. Just as when people drop excrement,
urine, spittle, pus or blood on it, for that the Earth is
not ashamed, humiliated or disgusted.
The Buddha.

Many religious leaders regard love as the core of the spiritual life; access to and application of this deep heartfelt feeling for others and the Earth, confirms the spiritual life. The Buddha certainly did not depart from recognizing the significance of love, but he understood the limits of the human capacity to generate love and compassion in all circumstances. We cannot always expect to engage in acts of selfless love for those with whom we disagree. Realizing this, he regarded equanimity ("upekkha") as equally as profound as love. Thus it takes its rightful place as one of the four divine abidings.

Equanimity receives scant attention in spiritual traditions compared to love, compassion and joy. In the spiritual life we often place unrealistic expectations upon ourselves and others. We imagine we should be loving and compassionate in the face of abuse and cruelty. We imagine we ought to have the capacity for forgiveness, no matter how vile the actions of others. These impractical hopes neglect the deep value of equanimity. On occasions when someone has hurt us or harmed someone close to us, when unable to forgive we wallow in conflict and resentment. We can neither forgive nor pursue revenge. It is in such contexts that the wisdom and value of equanimity become apparent. Equanimity challenges the bedrock of negative reaction when forgiveness is out of reach and, in some cases, an inappropriate response to brutal behaviour. Between the extremes of forgiveness and retaliation, stands the middle ground of equanimity for facing the savagery and cruelties of human behaviour. Inspired by saints and martyrs, some people do show a profound capacity to forgive others but forgiveness does not serve as the only criteria for a loving heart. Steadfast equanimity expresses equally the depth of heart and understanding.

Areas in which equanimity may be a profound spiritual response include:
1. *Circumstances*
2. *Obsession with information*

3. *Gain and loss*
4. *Health and sickness*

Circumstances: The Buddha never isolated knowledge from ethical considerations. He refuted our obsession with knowledge, and the belief that production of new forms of knowledge is always permissible. Many scientists admit that security of employment matters far more to them than other considerations. Some admit they do not relish working for government or corporate interests, nor feel particularly patriotic, but they want job security, a high standard of living and a good education for their children. To walk out of research in a nuclear arms factory, and say to peace activists on the other side of the high wire fence "I am working on the wrong side of the fence"—as one physicist did—takes not only courage but a degree of equanimity to the personal consequences of decisions.

The belief that we ought to love unconditionally, to feel tirelessly compassionate for political and religious regimes, exceeds the capacity of any human being, no matter how enlightened. The violence of politics and religion, and individual violence and corruption, prevents love from flowing freely to groups, individuals and the environment. Equanimity safeguards us from becoming downhearted at the cruelty, indifference and ruthless ambition widespread among sections of society. In the countless expressions of injustice, we may find ourselves stretched beyond our hearts capacity. Then we realize we have the power of mind to stay equanimous to the results of our actions though we have no guarantee of a favourable outcome, no matter how noble the endeavour.

The word "equanimity" in the English language does not convey adequately the spirit of "upekkha." Upekkha is a depth of steadfastness that is unshakeable. Untoward circumstances challenge our capacity to stay centred and steady, whether intensely pleasurable or painful. Upekkha is not born of suppression, or denial of normal human responses to situations; it is an even-heartedness, even-mindedness toward events which could otherwise be entangling. In unwelcome situations, we are liable to experience all manner of mood swings through lack of wise equanimity. We then launch into unsatisfactory reactions or withdraw into a state of inactivity, rather than stay present and aware.

Equanimity is a spiritual practice, not a blessing or good fortune, and so is a fruit of enlightenment. Though we may associate equanimity with painful events, its application is vital in pleasure, too. The temptation to seize pleasure in the form of goods, money, sex, status, power and dogmatic beliefs disturbs our values. We want to be somebody and we want to feel we are on the right side. Willing to sacrifice anything for the sake of illusions, we neither serve the deeper interests of ourselves nor others, nor express any kind of liberating vision. Equanimity is more than the ability to weather a storm in the face of defeat or failure; it is letting go of the thrust of selfish desire without suppressing our feelings. Otherwise hidden feelings of disappointment emerge that often produce biased actions or inactivity

Obsession with information: Western culture is obsessed with knowledge. An example is the pursuit of experimental science, a growth industry of the modern world. It reaches its zenith in the field of genetic engineering with scientists aiming for a complete decryption of the human genetic code—three billion units of information. Genetic scientists believe they will be able to identify hereditary, environmental and psychologically induced disorders. They believe their model of existence will permit a predetermined estimate of our genetic make-up indicating weaknesses in specific genes, brain skills, our probable life expectancy as well as prenatal diagnosis.

Medical scientists regard gene therapy, the replacement of defective genes with healthy equivalents, as a major key to future health. Experiments in gene therapy between the plant and animal world continue world wide with a limited number of experiments on humans. There are concerns that less scrupulous scientists will engage in gene therapy on embryos thus affecting future generations. Even the brain is not ruled out as an arena for genetic implants. Politicians remain largely uninformed about the ethical considerations of such gene therapy, part of a grandiose plan for the future, based on high-tech, elitist procedures.

For a scientist or science student, or for researchers or workers in any other field, who find ethical values in conflict with research, then equanimity around decisions becomes significant. When a qualified person resigns from a position on ethical grounds it requires equanimity since the personal costs may be:
1. *the sacrifice of a career*
2. *an uncertain future*
3. *financial insecurity*
4. *loss of prestige*
5. *the impact on lifestyle and loved ones*

Scientists often express doubt to loved ones about their work but are afraid to act directly due to these likely consequences. Ethical values and steadfast equanimity work together to support decisions respectful to life work together.

Genetic scientists do not consider how the right of access to our personal genome will generate the necessity for gene counselling because this new information may trigger fears and anxieties. Gene counsellors will be needed to work with people struggling to cope with the shock of opinions released to them about their genetic make-up. Patients will demand information from their doctors about their vulnerability from a damaged gene, a gene that might go out of control or have the potential for future ills. Others will live in fear of inquiring about the state of their genes. Recipients of such information will need much equanimity when facing the hard truths of their condition.

Governments will almost certainly introduce legislation extending the right of privacy to our genetic information to prevent its abuse, such as in selection for a career. Public opinion and insurance companies will make it difficult for prospective parents to bring deformed babies into the world. But legislation cannot guard against the emotional shock waves when individuals realize their genetic vulnerability. Honest geneticists admit they do not know what the widespread effect will be when this bank of information becomes available to the public. People must face the trauma of whether to know or not know what geneticists and doctors perceive as their future health. Without deep equanimity and a profound steadfastness, patients may torture their minds with anxieties.

Genetic engineering is moving along at an alarming speed yet lacks clear and understandable ethics. Genetic engineering on animals can make them fatter, slimmer or more productive. Scientists in the agribusiness treat farm animals as high performance machines to be made as efficient as possible. Genetically enhanced plants with inbuilt insecticides are released into the soil. There is a growing urgency to introduce ethical guidelines as engineered plants may have a long term impact on the food chain, people and the environment.

Manipulating the natural world sows the seeds for a situation to go out of control. Since a single cell possesses all the genetic material to grow a single plant, it means that hormones and nutrients can be fed into a cell until roots form to produce acres of genetically engineered identical plants. The effect of this is reduction of diversity in the plant world as farmers opt for the cheaper and more efficient crops that a major company offers. But when insects attack the new plant in unforeseen ways, it will result in a blight reaching epidemic proportions. Diversity and rotation of crops is a key to the welfare of the human and natural world.

The carrying of genes from one cell to another carries further risks for the long term health of plants, animals and people. For example, researchers in the University of Kentucky introduced a gene from the human growth hormone into a pig. The result was that the pig grew faster but emerged with an arthritic condition. The treatment of animals with artificial growth hormones is another example of gross intrusion into the animal world. It is not out of the question that unprincipled scientists, obsessed with the potential power gained from genetic information, will embark on "superman" biotechnology— switching their attention from the production of super nuclear bombs. Children, ignorant of and unconcerned with the consequences of their actions, should not play with fire.

Multinational chemical companies and the agribusiness give large funds to scientists to produce more efficient and profitable products. Some of the results of research appears in the regular journals. The popular media makes little attempt to inform the general public of the dangerous cutting edges of scientific research. Many methods of research remain confidential, except to reveal results that impress peers. Ethical standards must include the free flow of information about the type of experiments conducted with easy access to the scientists' hypotheses. When unacceptable experiments are taking place in the name of public interest, governments have a duty to pass urgent legislation to protect plants, animals and people, in both present and future generations.

The proliferation of genetic engineering and biotechnology are examples of our general apathy to dangerous experiments which could be damaging present and future generations. Equanimity in the face of information or challenging circumstances is not indifference but a steadfast inquiry as we inform ourselves, and challenge the sciences of abuse. Equanimity stabilizes the view that these experiments have gone too far when obsessive scientists push back the frontiers of knowledge and experiment into regions that violate natural life. Without stabilizing the view, we drift along in a meaningless spin of scientific rationalization determined to put patents on life and clones in the plant and animal world.

Medical and food production scientists have now opted for genetic manipulation, gene therapy and biotechnology to cure the ills of people and environment. Scientists propagate the social fiction that science is objective and unimpaired by personal value judgements. Every experiment carries with it a value judgement, even if it is only a subjective view that the work is important. Scientist work for desired goals—another value judgement. The consequences of these judgements significantly influences life on Earth.

Equanimity enables us to:

1. *make radical changes in values*
2. *leave behind without fear what is unsatisfactory*
3. *let go of activities intended to boost the ego*

In most professions personal ego satisfaction is an important factor. The degree of competition among scientists forces them to push on without reservations to impress their paymasters and peers. Awards, such as the Nobel Prize, sometimes fail to provide a service to humanity but affirm egocentric interests. They offer huge increases in personal status and large financial incentives, yet often do little for the genuine welfare of people and the environment.

Scientists imagine themselves to be detached observers of facts who remain equanimous to the results of their hypotheses and experiments. They spend years in painstaking research exercising their brains to surmount problems in the laboratory. Geneticists, physicists and biologists provide a legitimate view of existence, but it will always remain a view from a particular perspective. In the name of objectivity they cling to a programmed and narrow view of the human and natural world, i.e. they hold to the value of experimenting with and controlling life and matter.

The public imagines that scientists are clever people with concentrated, detached and equanimous minds free from personal investment in their work. This is a dangerous social myth. The warped values of scientists and others stand removed from the equanimity of the Buddha's teachings of divine abiding. Such equanimity embraces a strong foundation of ethics, a commitment to nonviolence and nonexploitation, an active reverence for the human and natural world, and freedom from various obsessions, including knowledge, egotism and blind pursuit of goals. Scientists abiding with spiritual equanimity working with a vision reverential to life provide a profound public service. They make a significant contribution not only to our understanding of life but to our participation in it. Such scientists are hard to find however, as job security, salary and prestige shape their work as much as their experiments.

The fastest expanding resource for information occurs through the information highways of electronic mail. Consumers of information are tapping into fibre optics at an extraordinary rate. Electronic mail enables invaluable (as well as warped) information to pass along the telephone wires thus converting the world into a global village. Barring language problems, people can communicate with each other regardless of the attitudes of their political leaders. Millions of computer literates have connected into electronic mail through the information technology. Membership of Internet, the most powerful computer network, increases by 80% per year.

Governments explore ways to monitor Internet while the corporate world, particularly telephone and cable companies, have expressed interest in the electronic network as a potentially profitable market. To join Internet, a thoroughly decentralized electronic network with a modest monthly rental charge, you need only a computer and modem. Avid users can get lost in cyberspace; the infatuation with ideas and exchange of information along the network distances people from the immediate world isolating computer addicts from friends, families, the local community and the natural environment.

Gain and loss: When a member of a board of directors of a multinational corporation had to step down, he put on a brave face. He had lost his seat on the board and had to move back into lower management. Emotionally, however, the decision of his fellow board members ordering him to step down crushed him. He could not hide his severe disappointment from close members of his family. It was not only defeat that hurt so much, but that a person he loathed had replaced him on the board. Unable to be equanimous, he felt compelled to find ways to undermine the new board member's authority at every opportunity. He bore a grudge for years, lived in a nightmare of power issues and the pursuit of revenge.

There are those whose sole interest is pursuing power. Once achieved, they cling to it; having once become leaders in their particular organization they may live in fear of losing their position of power. Equanimity saves us from clinging to our roles, and fulfilled or unfulfilled ambitions. An even-minded attitude endorses fair play and justice in the field of social relations whether at work, play or in the home. This view acknowledges the aspirations of others with the same interest as our own—without trying to relegate unsuccessful competitors to ignominious defeat.

Desires and lingering disappointments corrupt our natural capacity to deal with change, welcome or unwelcome. The Buddha exhorted us to make our minds steady as a mountain in a hurricane. The arrogance of the "I don't let it bother me" attitude does not convey equanimity but rather a hardness of heart and a refusal to allow feelings to get close to issues. At times, we need to let an issue bother us; we need to stir up our passions rather than deny them or harden ourselves to circumstances.

Equanimity has its place as one of the four pillars of a noble consciousness along with love, compassion and spiritual joy. The cross legged posture of the Buddha has passed down through numerous generations as a symbol of equanimity and steadfast wisdom amidst the heavens and hells of the world. One hand resting on the other in the lap, back straight, facing forward, has become an archetypal symbol of the wise person who faces the truths of life. Change and inner and outer events do not buffet the Buddha mind.

More important than scientific knowledge is the science of awareness, of relationships, insights and enlightenment. Knowledge from this profound science changes a person's life revealing wisdom and joy, freeing the heart and mind from ignorance, fear and obsessions. Wisdom reveals equanimity as a powerful presence of mind with an essential function to play in life. One frequent example is the relationship of parents to children. The Buddha once remarked that if we walked around the world with a loving parent on each shoulder we would still not repay their kindness.

Yet some parents criticize their children for the way they live—but the parent's concept of a worthwhile life may differ from that of their son or daughter. Upon becoming an adult, a son or daughter may choose to explore a free and independent life utterly different from what their parents imagined for them. Conflict of interests shows itself in the parent's attempt to control the lives of their children, even when they are adults. Integration of love with equanimity becomes vital for sustained harmony.

It is not unusual for parents to be kind to their children only to find that in adult life their children take directions the parents find painful. Parents then blame themselves for their children's lifestyle and problems. Some schools of psychotherapy have targeted parents as responsible for the suffering of their offspring in adult life. They have almost ignored the social and environmental pressures upon people of all ages. But problems are multifaceted. The finger that points to a single cause, such as upbringing, becomes accusatory. In such situations equanimity towards one's children or towards one's parents, becomes an act of wisdom.

Health and sickness: The Buddha's teachings on equanimity also apply to the dependently arising condition of body and mind. Once a young man named Subha approached the Buddha and asked him why there was such inequality in the world—healthy and sick people, short lived and long lived, beautiful and ugly, wealthy and poor, low and high caste, intelligent and ignorant. The Buddha explained that these differences arose according to actions and the fruits of these actions. Abiding in equanimity safeguards us from falling into conflict and anger over inequalities in the world. Equanimity with wisdom serves as a springboard for the direct expression of love and compassion, including the capacity to respond with determination to change the desires shaping economic and environmental injustice, a major factor in so many painful differences.

To be grounded in equanimity is to be free from obsessing about our health and the continuity of our existence. The mind easily succumbs to fear when dwelling on matters of life and death. We become preoccupied with health, fitness and physical prowess. Determined to live for a long time, we fail to question why we cling to the pursuit of a long life. Is one day so different from the next? The circumstances of nature ensure that the desire for longevity is a lost battle. In clinging to the marks of health, fear stalks like a sickness. Trapped in the world of life and death, gain and loss, health and sickness, we gloss over the opportunity to realize That which embraces all dualities. To experience insights into the human and natural world, to end suffering, to go deeply into the Here and Now—these values hold a significance greater than the value of trying to secure a long life for oneself. There is a high price to pay for the lack of values and wisdom due to the unexamined pursuit of knowledge, goals and longevity.

Finally, we may have to resort to a wise equanimity in the face of a deteriorating and dying world.

THE POLITICS OF EGO

The Political Mind

*The person abiding in a dogmatic view claims
'This is most excellent'
and disparages other views as inferior.
As a result the person is not free from conflict.*
The Buddha.

When people enter political and public life they declare their intentions are good. They work towards a prosperous society through their political philosophy, acts of Parliament and implementation of laws. We citizens also assume their intention is for the public good. It is not unusual for those in public office to reach the end of their career and despite the issues and struggles in political life, feel they have done their best for the country and for the electorate. They will report, too, how proud they are to have served their constituency.

Politicians think of themselves as elected public servants, who instil their values and systems of financial and social management into the public arena. They live in a world of dealing with the unsatisfactory effects of previous political decisions and promises. Prosperity for all is an impossible undertaking rendering many political pledges unrealizable, no matter how well-intentioned. Political assumptions go unexamined and the environmental and social consequences reverberate world wide, painfully affecting everybody, not only the underclass. The ideology of future prosperity leads to damage of land, water and air thus eroding people's health and happiness.

Self-deception pervades our society. The public often may form generalized pictures of politicians as comprised of the selfish and arrogant right, the humourless and angry left and the bores who fudge the centre ground. The present political spectrum has to go. We are fooling ourselves if we think that the present ideologies and personalities can produce a caring political economic system. Political integrity is born from the power of conscience and deep-rooted compassion while our present system is lacking in morality, generosity environmental democracy and global conscience. Our so-called democracy requires a profound clean-up as much as East European systems. East Europe openly admits its system is a failure—we refuse to. We must find comprehensive solutions to the failings of our political institutions and the manipulation of the public mind. We live in a violent and divisive society amid a savaged and polluted environment.

It is hardly surprising that in Britain, in common with other countries, the public regards political life, journalism, real estate agencies and second-hand car dealing as the most deceitful and untrustworthy professions. The common bond of public dislike for these four jobs is that those who work in these fields often engage in deception. Journalists serve the political interests of their employers. "Never let the truth stand in the way of a good story," is a common joke among journalists. Only newspaper owners can claim freedom of the press. Estate agents manipulate language and photographs to make property appear desirable. Commissions and omissions go ruthlessly hand in hand. Rather than serving people, politicians' primary intention seems to be preserving and expanding their power base. When it comes to the crunch, their personal political ambitions come first. Politicians manipulate voters to further personal aims.

No doubt, many people would add lawyers to their list. Lawyers have become high flyers and high spenders through exorbitant charges to their clients. They prosper on the backs of people's suffering, people's conflicts and disputes with each other or with the law. We give a vote of no confidence to these professions, yet their purpose is to serve society. There are notable exceptions amidst these professions, but they often keep a low profile rather than risk rejection from their peers or loss of their jobs.

The public has little opportunity to change or disregard these forces of social and personal power. We need to be much more aware of the degree of egotism at work among our career politicians and elected officials. Through their desire for power, they become alienated from the deep daily needs of ordinary people struggling to make ends meet. Their policies, all affecting people, animals and environment, demonstrate this. The self-centred behaviour of politicians, their affluent lifestyle and arrogant manner deserve widespread public concern.

Misled more times than we realize, we still vote for our politicians with the lingering hope that they will keep some of their promises. Yet only around 50% of the population turned out to vote in the USA, with only about 30% voting for the elected President. The figures show the gap between the rhetoric of democracy (government by the majority) and the fact: 70% of Americans did not vote the man in office.

One problem with Western democracy is our confused relationship with our leaders. Voters often unconsciously transform leaders into father figures under whom we live in awe and hostility. We invest our leaders with emotional and intellectual significance. Those with strong political opinions often engage in what psychoanalysts refer to as "transference": our leaders become idealized objects of love or hate around whom we repeat various forms of childhood behaviour. We then fail to mature in our relationships with authority figures.

At times of national emergency or ruthless political ambition, politicians' egos gather full momentum. We bind ourselves to the leader and nation and relying on this deeply ingrained sense of loyalty, those in power manipulate us. We perceive the nation and the leader of the nation as mother and father. So intense is this identity that parents are willing to sacrifice their children on the battlefield for Leader and Country. Young men and women are willing to kill on the orders of politicians, who would never dream of risking their own lives. Politicians visit the battlefront, before hostilities begin, to bolster the morale of the troops, then wait safely at home for victory and personal glory.

The Establishment, including the Church, politicians, judiciary and media, dismiss voices of non-violent protest about war as unpatriotic. The war-mongers wave flags and cheer on the leader's demagogic urges. War serves to get people behind the leader, and in a democracy victory in war can contribute to a successful re-election, too. Yet both sides in a war claim moral rightness. Countless numbers clamour to go to war; young men feel a sense of self importance following the orders of the father of the nation. Others resign themselves to their fate. Those who watch television, listen to the radio or read newspapers become indifferent to the traumatic suffering and deaths that destroy whole communities at times of war. Immersed in violence, real and fantasy, we hardly react when such film is broadcast. We have become used to violent images, pictures of dead, wounded and mutilated people.

Some months after the British-Argentine colonial war for control over the Malvinas-Falkland Islands, I met with a sailor, who had been on one of Her Majesty's Ships as part of the Armada that set off to war with the Argentinian armed forces. The sailor told me that, when the first missile hit their ship, there was utter panic and terror on board. They forgot the disciplined drills which they had rehearsed in case of a direct hit. Oil ridden sea water entered the ship and began to swirl down the corridors of the crew's sleeping quarters. He saw his best friend's head, severed from the rest of his body, drifting along the corridor along with other human flesh, vomit, possessions and abandoned meals.

Men were screaming with their clothes and skin burnt off. Minutes before they had been laughing and joking abut "showing the Argies a thing or two." Others were jumping into flame ridden seas. There were sailors hiding in cupboards crying for their mother, others were biting themselves with terror or were yelling profanities. Others became zombies utterly frozen in their tracks. Nobody seemed to know what to do or where to go. Then the electricity went out and there was nothing but darkness, terror and the most horrifying screams. He said he retched until nothing remained inside him.

The sailor told me: "They never mentioned any possibility of this to us during our training. I only joined the navy the previous year. I was fed up with Thatcher's England and the misery of unemployment. You cannot imagine until you are in a battle what absolute hell and horror it is. I am still terrified of going to sleep at night, and have to live with constant nightmares."

He added that when the fleet arrived in the South Atlantic it became apparent that the Admiralty arranged the ships in a specific formation which infuriated the sailors. They realized that the government had ordered the Admiralty to use the older ships to protect the newer ones. When the Argentinian navy or air force attacked the British Armada, the older ships with less sophisticated and less expensive weaponry would take the brunt of the attack. "We needed the most recent additions to the fleet to protect us but protecting these modern ships mattered more to the government than our lives," he said bitterly. Such accounts belong to the reality of war rather than the "theatre of war." Financial investments take priority over human lives. Yet we continue to justify this in the name of the nation, refusing to admit we are cogs in the great machine of nationalism, with inane notions of territory.

The grandeur, marketing of leaders, motorcades and state occasions are all part of a widespread public deception which reinforces those in power. The massive welcome home ceremonies, ticker-tape parades and 21-gun salutes cover up the horror of war and glorify the killing fields, killing skies and killing seas. In such times it is our duty not to believe in the declarations of our leaders; widespread public cynicism has become the reaction to years of deception.

The ego depends upon will, beliefs and selfishness for its survival, but sometimes this support system collapses showing itself in nightmares, anxiety attacks, depression, hostility and inability to make decisions. Decisions occur when the ego is in (or out of) control, but once politicians make certain decisions they are under pressure to follow them through—no matter how unwise or despotic the decision may later prove to be.

The public are dependent upon journalists for information. A single, well-researched, hard-hitting article by an investigative journalist—another rare species—can infuriate a powerful politician bringing desire for revenge. Politicians fear exposure of their dark secret decisions. They are afraid that any sinister truths behind their policies will be uncovered yet they are afraid to speak out against reports about their secret world in case they sound guilty. They are also afraid to remain silent in case the public demands further investigation. Fear haunts their lives and when these fears surface, their self deceptions around power show as arrogance or manipulation.

The two most common forms of gaining power are through clubbing one's way to the top or crawling, as much as through merit. People with power endeavour to control the flow of information to weaken threats to their position. The term for this is "safeguarding the public interest." When threatened, powerful politicians lean on those who own the media, issue threats or leak favourable information to other newspapers. People do not get the chance to make up their own minds due to lack of complete, accurate information. One small expose about a political event reveals a large truth.

In August, 1992, the New York Times reported that a Madison Avenue hair stylist has been flying every two weeks for the past eight years to Kinshasa, Zaire, to cut the hair of President Mobutu Sese Seko. First Class air travel, hotel accommodation at the luxurious Inter-Continental hotel and hairdressing fee cost Zaire citizens more than $5000. Mobutu has run Zaire, Africa's third largest country, for 27 years with an iron hand. A Zaire human rights leader says that "Mobutu treats the treasury as if it's his private purse." Abandoned by the West as having no strategic value, Zaire survives on subsistence level and is one of the world's poorest countries.

Our leaders act out their role as father figures and they play on the instinctive loyalties of their people. Their publicists present them as thoughtful, sincere individuals whose concerns are the real interests of society. They give their public speeches from cue cards to give the impression of spontaneity. Speech writers examine every word to ensure that their speech fits with the underlying aims, but there is often a cynical disregard for truth. Taxpayers cover the cost of promotion and marketing of the government's version of reality. We pay to be misled, and this strategy works. It is unheard of for politicians to admit to faults, failure and failed economic policies. They also cannot praise the policies or political insights of other parties. They compete ruthlessly for public respect at the expense of their colleagues, and the country.

For example, the former Prime Minister Margaret Thatcher, could not tolerate criticism. Her strategy for dealing with it was to attack back, to find fault and report the past political failings of her opponents. The publicists re-defined her intolerance as "conviction politics."

Politicians have become servants of political causes. They live in a world out of touch with compassion, honesty, investigation, or the needs of people. The politics of power and the forces of ego, play a substantial and irrevocable part in shaping policies. The claims and counter claims of the political, left, right and centre cloud urgent issues—their priority is winning the political argument. Politicians tell us to take responsibility for our lives while they refuse to take responsibility for their gross errors of judgements and the suffering their decisions bring. Our political leaders set an appalling example when they blame their opponents and everybody else but themselves for the state of the nation and the Earth.

Investigation of the inner life of elected officers and the well established often only involves examining their sexual behaviour, affecting only a handful of people. Through the clamour of journalists for hot stories, the public has developed a voyeuristic attitude to the sexual lives of the famous. When politicians break the law, or engage in mismanagement of state or personal affairs, or grossly mislead the public through a financial or information scandal then a public outcry does ensue. But we live in a state of denial when we refuse to acknowledge the bond uniting deception and our current political system. Cover-ups become a daily feature of political life through suppression of information.

The health and welfare of people runs secondary to the interests of our overpaid and privileged elected officials. Ideology frames their world view. While in office, the former U.S. Vice-President Dan Quayle said that being a homosexual is "a wrong choice that one makes." He might as well have said that it was wrong to choose to be black, poor or a woman since all these people are also frequently discriminated against. As one American columnist queried: "Why does Dan Quayle choose to be so stupid?"

Under pressure to conform to party opinion, politicians have little genuine freedom of speech. They compete for an influential position over their colleagues, the opposition and their personal staff. They live out their inner lives of unresolved personal ambitions, desires and fantasies on the world stage and we collude with them when we fail to question deeply their intentions and attitudes.

Media manipulators generate a view of our leaders which has little or no substance, highlighting a feature of personality, such as coolness or determination, until the public acknowledge it as an essential quality. The promotion people rehearse so-called "random" conversations on the street for a political walk-about before a senior politician or public figure arrives. Our politicians are living in a world of a marketable popularity and many voters cast their vote as much on personality as policies. The projected qualities of a leader's personality thus become more significant as it becomes more difficult to perceive fundamental differences in policies.

Politicians like to think they are realists rather than ideologues. The real world of suffering and its causes and resolution rarely merits interest among politicians. Our leaders show nominal regard for the poor, the sick, the disabled, the forgotten, or for parts of the environment which are dying at home or overseas. There are few references to world wide victims of a selfish society. Political beliefs reveal self interest disguised as pragmatic standpoints.

During campaigns, I received a letter questioning my motives for standing twice for public office for the Green Party when I have no chance at all of winning. One local voter wrote to me: "Are you caught up in power politics as much as those you criticize? I see the local media quotes you regularly. Are you clear about your intentions? Do you really have the interests of the Green Party at heart or do you just like seeing your name in print?" Such letters make me pause for reflection. The media is the main lifeline to the public for any political party but it can also become the main lifeline feeding notions of self-importance. Compensation for lack of self worth and the desire to be special can show itself in the pursuit of power to secure name and fame.

The pursuit of ego satisfaction at the local level obviously also applies in national politics. An elected leader must struggle to remain in power. He or she ignores, undermines or removes threats to his or her position. The leader will use any opportunity to marginalize individuals or groups to minimize their criticisms. Political leaders also worry about the will of the people. When Margaret Thatcher became Prime Minister she immediately gave the police substantial pay increases. She sensed she would need their support during her period in office, as police control social unrest against injustice. Political leaders will describe "an uprising" in poor neighbourhoods as a "riot." They employ the police, and occasionally the National Guard or army to quell an uprising. The government knows that public memory is short, so the underlying causes for social unrest can be safely ignored. Politicians employ a particular form of language to target protesters, describing them as "militants" to ensure the public has no respect for them.

In a factory, a handful of workers uncovered information that the board and management were secretly planning to close down factories and announce widespread redundancies which would destroy the local community. The workers decided to strike as part of their campaign. One of their first acts was to tip off the press. The story made a big splash in the local and national press. But it was not long before the public viewed the leaders of the strike committee as militants, because the press slapped this judgemental label on them. The board of directors and management used this label in every conversation with journalists and politicians. Any workers expressing doubts about the effectiveness of strikes were "moderates." The original issue receded into the background while the strikers were gradually and systematically undermined. The politicians, police and media acted as judge, prosecutor and jury.

The media will make a virtue of our leaders' desire to appoint and dismiss. Leaders like to appear tough and determined to stamp their authority on a situation. They like to give the impression of making hard decisions which lack compassion. Compassion then becomes equated with weakness. During her eleven years in office, Prime Minister Thatcher gave her support to the rich, the powerful and the ambitious while she treated indifferently the homeless, unemployed, poor, young, sick and elderly. "To get the economy moving" became her mantra.

The government then introduced the poll tax, a uniform tax for the rich and the poor. Once again, she fawned on the rich and snubbed the poor. The public conducted hundreds of protest meetings throughout the country. There were demonstrations and uprising of the people on the streets. Members of Parliament for the Conservative Party perceived the way the tide turned. They wanted to save their seats. Prime Minister Thatcher had to go.

After the Conservative Party metaphorically stabbed her in the back the Prime Minister had to leave her home at Number 10 Downing Street within 24 hours. They threw her out of office because of her bitterly hated and unworkable poll tax and her arrogance towards colleagues in the European Union. Angry letters filled the mailbags of Members of Parliament at the prospect that all people, no matter what their income, paid the same tax to local government. Her "Little Englander" mentality at meetings of European countries proved an acute embarrassment to the nation. Opinion polls show that what children hate most of all is to be embarrassed; she had treated her cabinet and backbenchers like children until the Conservative Party became tired of trying to explain away her arrogance. She had to go.

Leaving her home at Number 10 Downing Street for the last time a television camera managed to catch Mrs. Thatcher crying as she got into her car. The evening television news replayed those tear-filled moments in slow motion. Emotionally it was perhaps the most telling public moment in her entire political career. A homeless friend watching the television that evening remarked: "Serves her right. Now she knows what it's like to lose a job and be thrown out of her home." I have no doubt that many, many others had similar thoughts that evening.

In those moments of final departure, the camera caught Mrs. Thatcher in touch with feelings of insecurity, rejection and loss. The capacity to understand and respond to others who share these experiences expresses emotional maturity and lends itself to active work for the genuine welfare of others in similar circumstances. Such maturity has nothing to do with the ideologies of the left, right and centre, nor with rigid control over emotions and circumstances. Lurking beneath the force of control is fear—fear of touching vulnerability around insecurity, loss and unforeseen change. Mrs. Thatcher's worst nightmare came true—the people and her own party threw her out of office without waiting for a general election.

Mature relationships with others embrace freedom from superiority, inferiority or equality. With rare exceptions, political leaders only examine circumstances from their own position of privilege. They disguise their personal ambitions in the name of the party or the country. Those with wisdom empathize with the least fortunate in society; they legislate out of compassionate concern for others, animals and the environment.

Some public figures are as out of touch with their own children as they are with the public. Their children and close relatives cry for attention. Obsessed with career and the future, such parents neglect their children who miss the fullness of parental love. Expensive presents become the compensation for emotional deprivation. Abuse of children arises through neglect of them. Public figures may prefer to maintain marriages of despair rather than become an item in the gossip columns. The appearance of power impresses society so much that we give our influential people permission to live with a different morality.

With rare exceptions psychotherapists and psychoanalysts have been reluctant to turn their considerable insights to the political mind. As a result the public remains uninformed about the unhealthy psychological patterns of those who rule the nation. Such high profile of the leader's personality ought to provide the opportunity for psychologists to explain publicly typical patterns of leadership behaviour. The public would then come to understand that those that have unresolved inner issues of control, ruthlessness and arrogance.

Politicians' indifference to the environment is a further revelation of their alienation from the world. Senior politicians spend nearly all their time in the city, their lives buried in government papers and meetings. They live in the world of words. Holed up in the back of limousines, they read reports or use the mobile telephone. They see the world through a pane of darkened glass. Their relationship to the environment may only extend to a comment on the weather. They may spend their free time involved in blood sports such hunting, shooting or fishing.

The opposition likes to climb on its high horse and pontificate in a noble minded way about the policies it will pursue when elected to office. The rhetoric of heated exchanges is the political equivalent of American football; government and opposition forget the people's suffering in the charge and frequent clashing of heads. Watching the ugly spectacle of televised democracy, the public is left wondering who and what to vote for. Distinctions between the major political parties become less noticeable, leading to more argument and ferocious nit-picking. The struggle is no longer to reveal differences but to find them. There is a tenable argument that political leaders have hijacked their party, country and environment to avoid inquiry into their emotional lives. They do not realize the gap that exists between themselves and the widespread suffering around them. Politics attracts the ambitious and clever, but ambition and cleverness is no substitute for wisdom and compassion.

The Veneration of
Money

Lose the greed for pleasure. See how letting go is
peacefulness. There is nothing that you need hold
onto and there is nothing that you need push away.
The Buddha

Few things in the world generate as much emotion and thought as money. Like the agent provocateur, issues around money destroy individual lives, relationships, projects, societies and governments. Insidious desire for financial gain, despite the circumstances, eats away goodwill, generosity and kindness, invites hostility and violence and sets people against each other. Attachment to money is the breeding ground for corruption.

As a point for open, frank discussion money remains a long-standing taboo. The financial situation of individuals, particularly wages, savings, investments and bills, often remains hidden from the eyes of loved ones, friends and colleagues. We keep an air of secrecy around the value of certain possessions, the profit made out of a business deal, the amount paid in rent or mortgage. Repair bills, salary, income tax and gifts to worthwhile causes also remain undisclosed. Like sex, money belongs to a secret world of the privatized self. The wish to make as much money as possible and to avoid paying taxes instils fear of honesty. Financial status determines identity so bank loans, hire purchase agreements and high mortgages are employed to provide ready, unearned money.

Hardly a day in our life goes by without giving thought to money. We are afraid to inquire into the finances of close friends. Some find it easier to talk about the most personal details of their sex lives or reveal the most personal information they have about another's behaviour. But when it comes to a frank and honest disclosure about personal finances the mind clams up. Discussion of personal finance remains confined to meetings with the accountant.

Even in the bank standing near the till staring at our account statement we are afraid to let a passer-by glance at the columns of figures. The hand is likely to form an arch around the sheet of paper to stop a stranger from taking a peep. Apart from the bank manager or accountant, our financial world remains a narrow, petty one riddled with anxieties. The pressures around money, despite our actual financial circumstances, trigger selfishness, guilt and envy. One person will spend and spend. "I really wanted to do something nice for myself." Other people's unrest with money will manifest as meanness or gambling. Some people are fearful of disclosing their financial resources, or compulsively compare what they have with what others have. Our taboos around money hide widespread unhappiness and insecurity.

Money connects to pleasure and pain. The most often repeated single comment on money is that it is the "root of all evil." However, money is not the problem—our relationship to it is. When infatuated with money we deal with it through our pleasure and pain, whether suppressed or expressed. Four primary desires revolve around money: get it, spend it, hang on to it and increase it.

The self-centred dismiss concerns for the financial well-being of the less well off. "I got to where I am today through hard work. If they worked as hard as I do they (the poor) would not be where they are now." Arrogance and resentment undermine the capacity for generosity, eating away at goodwill. Many charities have benefited from a will where the deceased has left money to a good cause as an act of revenge against family members. Others racked with guilt treat money like a hot coal. It *has* to be given away, either on some reckless venture or as a massive philanthropic act. Some are afraid to appear tight, others to appear generous, others want to display their wealth, while some flaunt poverty. Money can be donated with emotional flourishes or quietly and regularly for the welfare of people and environment. Investment in money sustains pride, stinginess and guilt whereas awareness and insight express wisdom, generosity and compassion. How we relate to money reveals a great deal about our character.

The rationalization for holding onto money is fear of the future—often disguised in the name of common sense. No matter how much money someone has banked away it never seems enough. The compulsive need to see money grow is a defence against insecurity. Yet it is an illusion that money offers genuine security, or success in our own eyes or respect from others, especially those we think important. Compulsive needs show we are out of touch with ourselves and our environment. We are *unable* to recognize and investigate the latent insecurity that sparks off the desire for more money.

Given incentives and tax concessions, individuals and companies pursue profit with a single-pointed drive. Greed and clinging exaggerate the natural wish to provide necessities into an intensification of what the mind *thinks* it needs. Those who flaunt their affluence only reveal their inner poverty: the greater the external symbols of wealth the greater the internal barrenness. Privileged elite do not possess their capital, their capital possesses them. They surrender their existence to worship of money and ego satisfaction. Expensive restaurants, hotels, car showrooms, yuppie estate agents and sophisticated department stores become the church where money is the blessed sacrament putting the wealthy in touch with the God of abundance. Opulence imprisons lovers of luxury who have little appreciation of transcending mundaneness even though they may pay lip service to it.

Many of the wealthy want everything—an expensive lifestyle, to be loved and religious security: a hedonistic heaven on Earth and a happy heaven for eternity after death. Yet the pursuers of wealth deprive themselves of the genuine riches of life—liberation, realization of Truth, selflessness, humility and joyful discovery of the ordinary. Their accumulated wealth comes not only at their own expense but also at the expense of the unfed and the homeless. Those who aggrandize wealth often form a political ideology to support their compulsive patterns believing that:

1. *wealth is the priority*
2. *wealth trickles downwards (the trickle-down notion is the "piss on the poor" political philosophy).*
3. *everybody has the same opportunity to get rich if they work hard enough*
4. *a life devoted to becoming prosperous provides the family and the nation with a secure future*

Wealthy people often think of themselves as successful human beings. Countless others look up to them as the prophets of prosperity. As long as this thirst for money remains unquestioned we will maintain money as the Godhead of our priorities, competing with each other for a share of the spoils. The stock exchange has become a gambling casino demanding profit above ethical considerations and isolating society from an active reverence for life. It is easier to drive a BMW through a keyhole than for the self-centred to live with integrity. We would rather work ourselves to death than open up to expressions of deep human kindness, generosity and joy. We give little away, clinging to what we have and expecting more.

The wish to be *seen* as generous benefactors motivates some individuals or organizations to offer nominal donations to charity. Donations from the wealthy become signals to the public of success;

affluent people like to appear charitable. Such egotistic gestures of doing good have no spiritual merit at all. Of course, the money itself is beneficial to the recipients, regardless of the size of the donor's ego. But when such acts of signing cheques, spontaneous or planned, are a public relations exercise or tax avoidance initiative then there is no authentic generosity in the donation. From a spiritual standpoint it would be preferable not to make the donation in the first place since deceit pervades the underlying motivation.

Many want to be free from involvement in a self centred society but few have the boldness to act. Haunted by the desire for security, the middle classes remain chained to the pointless task of increasing their standard of living. Recognizing the futility of ambition opens the door to a re-examination of existence and our participation in it. Consumerism overshadows all the world's religions, it lampoons wisdom and compassionate awareness. Possessions, property, land and money become our main talking points. The idea persists that the consumer world represents the core of reality. When we realize the transparent falsity of this we discard the rat race and the pointless posturing of consumerism.

Some conclude that they have made their wealth through being lucky, but there is no such thing as luck. The "I was lucky, I made a fortune" individual arrives at a certain station in life through effort, ambition, information, competitiveness and neglect of other areas of life. The mind revolves around money, money, money. Fear and insecurity lurk everywhere, like unidentifiable shadows in the night. The old adage that you can't take it with you is repeated like a mantra, but few people truly hear it.

More than anything else, the preoccupation around profit contributes to the active consumption of the Earth, our prime capital resource. Spearheaded by desire and competition, the American-European-Japanese business conglomerate has become even more opportunistic in its determination to exploit the world markets. They are seizing the chance to make a killing in East Europe. It is only a matter of time before Eastern Europe finds itself dependent on Western loans and aid for its survival. Western capitalism receives raw materials from the Third World and profits from their crops. The profit from these materials, manufactured, packaged and marketed in the West will allow them to compete in the new East European market where millions are now thirsting to become consumers. The future of capitalism has never looked rosier and the state of the Earth has never looked more grim.

Western enterprise breeds resentment world wide, nevertheless intelligent and caring capitalism provides the opportunity for small, sustainable businesses to flourish which are of genuine benefit to people, animals and the environment. This allows people to go quietly about their business not assailed by competition and take-over bids. Thus caring capitalism is ethical when it supports small businesses, right livelihood and co-operation. Modern capitalism, however, is a corruption of the spirit of a thoughtful and friendly way of life in city and rural communities. Capitalism today lacks a conscience while modern communism and socialism appear to be cold, hostile and humourless.

The struggle against exploitation is expressed through spiritual values of right livelihood, reverence for the inter-dependence of life and conservation of resources. The religion granting dominion over the Earth is incompatible with reverence for life; these beliefs become locked in a holy war with each other, St. George and the Earth scorching dragon give a kind of mythical continuity to the struggle of good against evil, right against wrong, the God of love and reverence for life against the devil of consumerism and destruction.

Those engaged in heaping up profits and achieving success on the backs of others, and through legalized violence against nature, believe this is what the real world is about. We need to shake ourselves free of the arrogance of claiming to know what the real world is, as such claims only serve self-seeking interest. These views ignore investigation into obsessional behaviour and the hidden world of personal finance. Often, the ruthless and ideologically bound control the economic circumstances of individuals, the company or the nation. They hate the idea of opening up their private world of personal assets but they want to know everybody else's. Hypocrisy saturates the world of finance.

At the stock exchange, in an impersonal and detached manner, huge sums of money change hands through computer technology. Speculators can wreck the fragile economies of Third World countries, and a single takeover may cost countless jobs. The God of profit rules despite the harm caused to people and environment. The speculators and their underlings crouched over their computers alienate themselves from the real world of suffering, joy and interconnection. Not knowing who they are or what they are doing, the money dealers become mouth pieces for the shareholders. "Making a killing" is the name of the game. They succeed, but millions world wide may die.

Investment in the market place is a gamble not only with money but with the livelihoods, health, security and future of people who depend upon continuity of employment. Often it is not only a question of people losing their livelihood but, in the world of corporate interests, the very lives of working people are often at stake. Satisfying the profit motives of the shareholders and the demigods in the boardroom takes priority. The majority of shareholders know or care little about the way companies use their money. They do not meet the workers nor witness their working conditions or have knowledge of their health and safety conditions. Success is profit not ethical practices. Being a share-holder ought to require the willingness to examine the business practices of a company and to withdraw shares if its behaviour is unethical. Each time we refuse to invest in exploitive companies and opt instead for worthy projects we send small shivers through the business world. Refusing to subscribe to big business and big profit endorses the survival of the weak and vulnerable. Ethical investment is taking risks for people, not the aggressive pursuit of profit.

Self deceit knows no limits. We believe we are not in debt yet we have years of a mortgage to pay off, we distort the truth when we call such debt an investment; by changing the language we conceal the facts. We convince ourselves we are not in debt while accumulating bills on bank loans, credit cards and mail order catalogues. For everyone who questions a life revolving around profits and debts, countless numbers are eager to take up the banner of consumerism as the only show worth investing in.

In our obsession with money, we lose respect for ourselves and others. We relegate ourselves to pursuit of an ostentatious existence in which self interest suppresses our capacity to question, doubt and protest. We become a member of the church of consumerism, a follower of the cult of money worship, profit and privilege. We refuse to admit that our mind has become programmed into self-interest. The small mind has an immense capacity to uphold greed and selfishness through proliferation of an ideology with a religious or political fundamentalist tone.

One purpose of a contemplative religious life and free inquiry is to break taboos, including fixations around false gods, yet the veneration of money seems to have largely escaped such examination. Western society cherishes the view that it has nothing to learn from other societies and they have everything to learn from us. This perverse view and our pathological patterns of control need to change.

Hostility is no solution to the harmful and destructive financial forces in the world. Organized protest, campaigns and personal statements are a better challenge to profiteering and exploitation of the ecosystem since investors remain unwilling to acknowledge the harm their investments may be causing to others. Having little money, few possessions, no shares and hardly any involvement in the financial world does not prove that selfishness belongs to others. Given access to wealth our view of investments might change. After receiving an inheritance, we may abandon financial integrity.

Many people believe money is good, more money is better and are glad to pass on their wealth at death to their children. We resist revealing how much we have inherited, and rarely question what to do with inherited and unearned wealth other than spending it on an expensive house, car and goods. Yet inherited money can become a resource for exploring deeper values, an opportunity to express compassion rather than reinforcing the forces of selfishness.

Wisdom investigates both the worship and the God of our religion. But it is a greater act of faith to look the devil in the eye, to break the money spell, than to see God face to face. Like every other mental factor, greed does not occur by itself, nor arises independent of numerous conditions including insecurity, fear, peer pressure, the need to impress others and addiction. Unlike violence, a generally unacceptable form of behaviour, we treat greed lightly. Greed deserves to evoke as much concern as violence rather than being treated as foolish behaviour—like consuming chocolate biscuits.

Becoming a millionaire is probably the most popular fantasy in Western society. When our main enjoyment of life is making and spending money, we hide greed and aggression behind a mask of urbane civility. Genuine awareness recognizes the personal and environmental futility of self-centred ambition and the tyranny of money. Religious sects and cults have divested gullible individuals of their unearned inheritances. Only rage and bitterness remain; those hoodwinked often are left penniless. When duped out of money many people find it hard, almost impossible, to forgive or forget.

If we are to change our relationship to personal finances we must discuss our fears and daydreams around money. We need to discuss the amount of daily time we give to financial matters and explore our habits around money, the pursuit and the obsessions, the craftiness of behaviour. We need to talk about how much we hold back and how much we give. Communication needs to be in clear, specific terms of how money affects our lives. Rather than escape as we usually do into generalizations, we must be willing to focus on our personal accounts. Let us live without financial secrets.

Personal spending, savings, donations—and our attitudes— need to be exposed frankly and honestly to each other. Where there is insecurity there is fear and mistrust and it will take an immense amount of trust to break down the taboo. Small groups openly meeting together to share their concerns can develop honesty and break the spell of money. The personal accounts of elected politicians, civil servants and religious leaders also ought to be publicly available. After all, they are public servants with the electorate or faithful as their employers. Investors deserve to be informed of the salaries corporate leaders pay themselves otherwise we continue to live in the dark ages.

One response to the religion of consumerism, is to say: "NO. I DON'T WANT TO LIVE LIKE THAT." Integrity offers inner security. Awareness and contentment liberate us from the religion of consumerism so we can respond to the nature of life and be receptive to the plight of those less fortunate than ourselves. We can awaken daily to the artistry and loveliness of life. Allowing the heart to awaken requires probing beneath the patterns of insecurity and greed; the subsequent awareness shines like the sun through the menacing clouds. The heart's reverence for nature discriminates between necessity and excess, abiding in harmony with the natural world reveals joys of life inaccessible with the credit card.

Predictions And Prophecy

Dry up the remains of your past and have nothing for
your future. If you do not cling to the present then
you can go from place to place in peace.
The Buddha

Those who take the future of the Earth seriously leave themselves vulnerable. They alienate themselves from the Here and Now through getting caught up in speculation about what might happen to humankind and the Earth. What is the effect of this way of thinking and communicating? Does it make a difference? We have the capacity to examine and re-examine the three fields of time: past, present and future. We can draw upon information gleaned from the past, both distant and recent, as well as current events, using this information to predict the future. Yet despite the dire predictions of some global experts the future remains uncertain. Although the Green movement uses warnings about the future as a primary tactic to persuade people to change their ways, the priority for political awareness must be the desires and activities of human beings Here and Now.

Buddhism also has concerned itself with the future—merit making for the future, future results of past or present actions and future lives or rebirths. Though there is not a trace of real evidence to prove or disprove rebirth, millions of Buddhists base their religious beliefs on rebirth and what will happen to them when they die. Making merit, performing deeds of generosity and kindness become some of the means to ensure a happy and worthwhile rebirth in the human or heavenly realm. Prominent Buddhist teachers have used their belief in rebirth as an argument for conservation of resources. They claim that if people believed in rebirth then society would not be so indulgent in the Here and Now. Since people will be reborn, say these teachers, it is in their own interest to protect resources. It seems absurd to have to take on board a belief in rebirth in order to work to end the suffering and violation of the Earth. It is yet another example of obsessions with the future instead of acknowledging the modest usefulness of occasional references to the future.

The last decade established the credibility of the international Green movement. Society recognized that our lifestyle was abusive and damaging to the Earth. Green campaigns on issues such as recycling, waste management, conservation, global warming, pollution and hazardous chemicals gained street recognition. The demand for information, speakers and memberships of Green organizations multiplied overwhelming the staff of the Green Party and other Green organisations. In the late 1980's the Greens experienced a zany period that came and went. As Shakespeare says in "The Tempest":

"The cloud-capp'd towers, the gorgeous palaces,
The solemn temples, the great globe itself,
Yea, all which it inherit, shall dissolve
And, like this insubstantial pageant faded,
Leave not a rack behind. We are such stuff
As dreams are made on, and our little life
Is rounded with a sleep."

Those days had the quality of frenzied excitement, like Shakespeare's insubstantial pageant. Then the public's thirst for information faded as their attention, guided by the media, moved onto other matters. Green books stored longer and longer on the bookshelves were soon on sale at half the cost price. The belief that painful predictions would really make a difference to people's lives became the stuff of dreams.

The Greens resumed their role as one of the small pressure groups struggling for public attention. But one thing stood out— the international Green movement was in a crisis. Green issues were on the political agenda, were of concern to millions of people, but made little difference. Green thinking filled the air while the exploitation of the Earth carried on at the same relentless pace. Articulate Green speakers and writers were reaching large audiences, but basic government policies of the relentless pursuit of economic growth were not changing. The knowledge of Green experts failed to be translated into a comprehensive policy. Talking about the condition of the Earth in the year 2000 AD or the year 2020 AD came to appear irrelevant to the crisis Here and Now.

More than a decade of yearning for a breakthrough had passed and the fate of the Earth was again on the back burner. The stuff of dreams had hardly impressed itself on the so-called "American dream" of individualism, the personal pursuit of wealth and unlimited access to continuous pleasure. Simultaneously, the East European revolution led to expanded demand there for the market economy and a growing desire also to compete for the "American dream."

The major political parties still revealed their inability to see beyond their mandate to govern. Their ideology excludes long term vision, and their raison d'être has little to with insight, far more to do with perpetuation of their political system, no matter how inappropriate it is for life on Earth. Highlighting the future did have some value because people began to realize the relationship between spiritual values, of respect and reverence for life, and political vision. But emphasising the long term vision also has consequences, and through sheer repetition the international Green movement became associated with future thinking.

We have dutifully grasped onto every relevant piece of information released by the scientific community about the future state of the world, and used it to argue our corner. The motive for such a strategy was to spread concern, and alarm among the public, to get them and ourselves to change our ways, and our voting patterns. But the Green movement fails to grasp the futility of endless "futurizing." Every statement we publish about the future is a licence to postpone or delay change. With rare exceptions human beings are unable to think far ahead in time even when it affects us personally. We certainly cannot peep into the next generation, and long term projections seem far removed from the nitty-gritty of our everyday lives.

Both the Green movement and the public have imprisoned themselves by alleging to know what tomorrow will bring instead of concentrating on Here and Now. Even if speculations prove accurate, they neither serve genuine environmental concerns nor develop the inner resources of humanity. Many of the worst predictions will occur after most middle-aged people are dead. We go on about what a terrible legacy we are leaving for our children but, because such dire warnings sound vague and unreal, we do little about it.

To believe that we have a duty to protect the Earth for future generations requires an immense sense of responsibility. Such views are full of altruism, yet they lack the power to change the way we live. The response to such ideals will always be lukewarm from governments, corporations and the public, and the Green movement has a duty to end this game of prophecy.

In the history of the Green Party of Britain, one bizarre incident became an illustration of future thinking run riot. In the late 1980's, when the Greens were receiving massive public attention, a television sports announcer, David Icke, with a made-for-television face rose rapidly to prominence in the Green Party. Ironically, the Green Party in Britain and other countries harbours a long standing suspicion of prominent leadership, although unconsciously, it has looked for it. David Icke became a national spokesperson for the Green Party within six months of campaigning for it. Sincere and well-intentioned, Icke leapt to prominence as a party leader because he was a "face" not because of particular insights or vision, but the Green Party acceded to his rapid promotion.

About a year or so later he held a press conference in London to announce a series of rash prophecies about forthcoming global events. For the most part, he was wildly out of touch with the way events arise dependent on conditions. Nevertheless, his religious views challenged the orthodoxy of the Green Party, which avoids the significance of spiritual experiences upon environmental awareness. The press crucified him. The Green Party put its head in its hands when the concept "loony Greens" pervaded the public mind. I would go to give a public talk for the Green Party and hear such remarks as "Were you sent by God?" Prominent speakers in the Green Party tried to distance the Party from David Icke and his self appointed role as a religious prophet in purple with green credentials. Yet they had conspired to promote his prominence within the Party and now refused to accept their share of responsibility for the outcome.

In Britain, the Green Party itself struggled for credibility, if not survival. At the same time, the party entered a period of painful self examination. Leading party members, including Sara Parkin, Jonathon Porritt and Jean Lambert became involved in the Green 2000 organisation (more future labels) to reorganise the Party's structure. The party overwhelmingly supported their motions and elected two long standing, and active party members to be principal speakers with a nine-person party executive committee with specific tasks. These decisions led to greater accountability within the party. The Green Party entered its third decade with the decisions of Porritt and Parkin to be nonactive members. In September, 1992, in Bonn, Germany, a principal Green, Petra Kelly was found dead in her home. The consensus is that her partner, Gert Bastian, also a prominent Green, murdered her and then turned the gun on himself. No-one knows why.

At the same time, widespread inflation and unemployment in the West placed global and community issues on the back burner of mainstream politics. In its struggle to remain afloat in political waters, the Green Party in Britain faced the gargantuan task of getting the public and the government to undergo an utter U-turn in its economic, environmental and energy policies while committed to organisational change within the party.

Prominent party members had resigned themselves to sitting out that grim period of the Party's history waiting for a resurgence in its fortunes. To their credit, Party activists ignored the internal wrangling of different factions among the Greens and focused their energies on an active concern for the welfare of the Earth, and for some this period of turmoil produced political maturity. With much relief, the Party has moved on from the pain of its internal warfare.

We only have to examine the harsh realities of the Here and Now to realize that society and the environment are in a severe state of daily abuse. Democracy works for the few and deceives the many. Yet to question its present form invites a wrath of reaction from those identified with this system of government. We must distance ourselves from trying to convince the world of the marvel of Western democracy. In Western democracy ill health plagues numerous families, adults abuse children, children become aggressive. Adults live on a diet of alcohol, cigarettes and pills for insomnia and depression. Crime and violence haunt our streets. Crisis centres and advice bureaus operate in cities and towns trying to help people cope with nightmare situations. Banks and businesses hassle everybody to buy more, to get into debt and thus take on board more anxiety.

The business community, entertainers and sportsmen and women employ agents to grab as much money as possible from their deals. City air is thick with fumes damaging our delicate organic tissues. Excessive pressure on our body invites cells to run amok, the start of cancer, the curse of Western "civilization." Hospitals, mental clinics, schools and prisons are overcrowded while staff and residents alike hate these institutions. Chemicals and preservatives riddle the public's food; chemical pollution destroys the land. Local rivers are dying; the seas are polluted and unfit for fish and swimming. Every week the Water Authorities in Britain permit the dumping of more than 2000 million gallons of sewage into our coastal waters. There are more than 400 endangered species in Britain of wild animals, birds and butterflies. Profit hungry farmers, developers and road builders extinguish our beautiful meadows. Farm animals and birds spend their lives beneath the electric lights of farm factories, and, significantly, weather patterns appear untypical.

Time passes, the future becomes the present. Nothing significant seems to have changed despite immense efforts by well meaning organisations and individuals. Both people and organizations become disillusioned, and for some the need is to work harder. More work builds up pressure and stress until there is the inevitable burnout. For others dwelling on the future leads to anxiety, which infects the perceptions of tomorrow producing feelings of insecurity in daily life. We then begin to feel depressed about the condition of life itself.

Campaigns can adversely affect activists' personal lives including relationships, finances, diet and sleep. Some activists experience anger or even hatred towards those who do not perceive the seriousness of the situation. They think of ways to retaliate against those who violate life for profit and prestige. They condemn other campaigners who do not appear as committed or as radical. Frustrated, they form themselves into small groups thinking of themselves as guardians of the truly Green approach that will protect the Earth, while others compromise their political vision to gain influence until they have conformed to the prevailing view of the market economy. The ideologues and the compromisers live in a world of extremes at the expense of deep awareness and compassion.

Posturing about the next decade or two obscures our present misery and confusion. The Buddha refused to predict the future and expressed caution abut the validity of rebirth. He said: "If there is rebirth...." He regarded such predictions as unreliable; nobody can safely read causes and effects and the myriad number of unknowable and unforeseen circumstances that weave events together. Religious teachers, past and present, have frequently made fools of themselves when they make rash prophecies that have proved to be wrong. The Buddha told spiritual seekers not to be concerned with the how, what and when of the future.

Future thinking can produce harmful results rather than positive ones. We imagine people will wake up through highlighting the collective fate of future generations. But predictions become self-fulfilling prophecies, i.e. they lead towards the events they are trying to prevent. Obsessing about the global future feeds into dangerously high levels of fear and anxiety already present. People then engage in self obsessed pursuits to feel secure, the very tendency which has led to our present mess. The obsession with the future, both personal and global, accelerates the deepening of the nightmare which has already befallen the Earth.

The roots of this mania for "futurizing" rest in the values of our culture. Competitive examinations, making money, career, pensions, retirement, breakdown of relationships and fear of loss or change grab our attention. We have no sense of what it is to realize a depth of intimacy with the Here and Now, and live cut off from day to day life by focusing on future worries. When we do actively experience the Here and Now it is often only through getting what we want or losing what we have. The ego's self interest obstructs a direct and enlightening access to the Here and Now.

Based on environmental understanding of the 1970's, the Green Party accurately predicted environmental life in the 1990's. In 20 years, the world's population has increased by nearly two billion, the number of cars on the world's roads has more than doubled, accidents have occurred at nuclear power stations, destruction of tropical rain forests and hazardous chemicals have damaged the protective ozone layer. The gap between the *have* and the *have-nots* has increased sharply between the nations of the overdeveloped and underdeveloped world, as well as the gap between the rich and poor within nations.

Most reasonably well informed people have access to some alarming figures about what might happen if we continue like this, but that's no substitute for inner and outer change. Today the Party and other Green movements are still making predictions. Unlike religious prophets, the Party has grounded its concerns for the future in scientific analysis, but it is still a form of prophecy. The future has become an escape from reality not a contribution to changing it. If we are willing to abandon our apocalyptic messages we can conserve more energy and inner resources for transforming the state of affairs Here and Now. From a spiritual standpoint, the egos, lifestyles, income and greed of the powerful must be challenged. We must work to find ways to enforce their public and environmental accountability. Faith, devotion, renunciation have an important function in safeguarding the Earth and its peoples and we must dig deep into ourselves to find wisdom about today's world, not tomorrow's.

The Marriage of Liberalism and Fundamentalism

The sage has ceased to associate with dogmas
for such a person no longer requires
the solace that dogmas offer.
The Buddha

The forces of politics and religion have always had a potent hold over individuals and society. Consciousness appears remarkably vulnerable to persuasive influences. We identify with influences and adopt them into our own value system. Beliefs, concepts, experiences and memories can conspire to consolidate a fundamentalist standpoint that seems irrational and bizarre to liberals. In turn, liberals often adopt a patronizing position, regarding themselves as upholding the intelligent viewpoint. Convinced of the correctness of their own viewpoint, neither liberals nor fundamentalists comprehend the other's world. Not able to understand each other, through lack of genuine communication, each becomes antagonistic to the other.

Liberals may immerse themselves in cerebral and condescending ideas about dogmatists. Drifting along in a sea of analysis, they dissect every issue until all that remains are swirling complexities. Their eclectic views lack the boldness of the fundamentalist, while cleverness is no substitute for wise conviction. For liberals, repulsion from fundamentalism is never far away from attraction even though they continue to engage in a bitter struggle for supremacy over fundamentalists. Fundamentalists have what many intellectuals lack—direction, a clear set of beliefs and certainty. They revile liberals for drifting along in the world of books, the arts, humanities and serious newspapers. They rush to the defence of their standpoints with all the reasoning their views can muster. Expounding the rhetoric of rights, freedom and tolerance, liberals attempt to counteract the vigorous proclamations of fundamentalists' views.

Neither can meet the other eye to eye, heart to heart. Liberals and fundamentalists rarely associate with each other, viewing each other only from a distance. Convinced of their personal positions, neither recognizes the insidious way their beliefs contribute to the position of the other. "If everybody were like us there would not be these conflicts" is a view that both camps share, along with unresolved hostility and anxiety.

They are prisoners of their own ideologies. Fundamentalists repulse many liberals but there is no shortage of liberals who become fundamentalists when security and conviction come to outweigh all intellectual considerations. A religious experience, or political conversion can enliven the emotional life, and pierce through the vacuity of "living in one's head." The intensity of these experiences sweeps aside a lifetime of rational thought; it is not at all unusual for a well educated, well qualified, reasonable and articulate person to start proselytizing a fundamentalist belief system.

The Buddha dismissed excesses of human behaviour in political, religious and social settings as well as the personal. Issues around extremism were clearly on his mind when he delivered his first talk to his five friends in Saranath after walking from Bodh Gaya, the place of his enlightenment. He highlighted the significance of the middle way making it a central platform of his teaching. As with all views and standpoints, the middle way has no inherent existence, other positions define its relationship. The Buddha adopted a pragmatic approach to the spiritual life when he explained that the extremes of self indulgence and self rejection lead nowhere. He endorsed a life of morality, meditation and wisdom as that which provided the most suitable inner environment for the full emancipation and realization of a human being. Despite initial misgivings, the five men listened to him since they knew the Buddha had experienced the extremes of sensual indulgence as a prince and self rejection as a hardened ascetic.

The strong commitment, exclusivity of view, intense group identity and the presence of a charismatic leader, typical of fundamentalism, can expose all that is lacking in the life of a liberal. Having taken on the fundamentalist views, certain liberals begin to regard their old clinging to various eclectic viewpoints and their inability to experience religious certainty as failings. The liberals lack of passion for a cause may be one factor of attraction to fundamentalism. Converts have overcome their fears of commitment and seen the light: "There is no other way" is a common statement of the convert to fundamentalism.

Fundamentalists have no time for what appear to be the perverted values of liberals including permissiveness, indulgence and disrespect for traditions. It is often forgotten that the tradition of the liberal mind is as old as the fundamentalist. Just as liberals may swap sides after exposure to fundamentalism, so some fundamentalists also undergo a change of belief. Again, sustained contact with the opposing view is often a key to dissolving standpoints. Exposure to a spacious, tolerant climate contributes to a quiet meltdown of tenacious ideas formerly adhered to as truth itself.

The circulation of thoughtful analysis and diversity of views holds a particular attraction for an alert mind. Freedom from absolute conviction may appear threatening at first, but after a time inquiring fundamentalists become alarmed at their tenacious clinging to views and intolerance of others. Instead of perceiving truth and nothing but the truth, changing fundamentalists begin to abhor the intensity of their ideology and their expression of unresolved aggression in the name of passionate belief. Reasonableness becomes the hallmark of intelligence and the application of intellect has a quietening effect on the excesses of emotional certitude. The fundamentalist experiences is attracted and moves towards liberal ideas.

However, for others, contact with opposing beliefs may reinforce conviction in their own. Clinging to particular views then strengthens a psychological and physical separation from disbelievers. In maintaining the status of either ideology, the "never the twain shall meet" dictum becomes a key condition for holding rigid views. Without intimate communication, neither party has much chance of understanding the other, thus they keep their ideological swords drawn.

Perceptions and misperceptions characterize each viewpoint. The two opposing lines share a common ground of conceit and arrogance and trap themselves in the belief that *their* view is the correct way of seeing things. Their mutual adversity binds them into a relationship that feeds extreme standpoints. Criticism of one end of the spectrum by the other end offers an illusory security of position. They proclaim a position as though it had some inherent significance and forget that any standpoint depends upon another's views.

The Buddha's concern is quenching suffering and conflict, not the promulgation of views. In his celebrated talk to the Kalama people, the Buddha urged them not to accept or believe anything immediately. He gave ten examples.

Do *not* accept anything because:
1. *It is stated*
2. *It is traditional*

3. *It is widely believed*
4. *It is written in books, such as scriptures*
5. *It seems logical*
6. *One has a liking for the view*
7. *It has been thought out*
8. *It agrees with preconceived opinions*
9. *The speaker appears believable*
10. *You identify with the teacher.*

These illustrate ten ways that we become slaves, intellectually, emotionally and spiritually, to standpoints. In his later talks, the Buddha investigated the mutually supportive dualities of extremist views to challenge the mind's tendencies to cling to standpoints. The Buddha went further than support for the narrow goal of a well reasoned and balanced life, though this might seem a natural outcome of his teachings. He challenged believers to give up their claims on Truth, as well as the suffering bound up with lifestyle and attitudes. The Truth is to be lived, not to be claimed nor organized. The Buddha realized that defining Ultimate Truth through language is ultimately misleading. Truth is one without a second he once said.

For some people, emotional and intellectual conditioning influence particular views. Others cling to a detached viewpoint conveying an "above it all" mentality. The realization of the emptiness of standpoints frees us from the duality of clinging and rejection. No position or nonposition is worth holding onto. Judging others from the position of "self" reinforces the ego and the ego of others, which fuels controversy and the continuation of old conflicts. A wise view recognizes that both self and other share much in common—the desire to feel secure, possession of views, condemnation of others and the feeling of being right. Insight into all standpoints negates the tendency to become entrenched in any position or nonposition.

Wisdom examines impartially views recognizing the ways we support and reinforce others' beliefs. Without realizing it, we conspire to perpetuate the problem of liberal and fundamentalist positions through the patterns of attack and defence. Attacking one position and defending another reveals the underlying interdependence. Clinging to our views and beliefs *directly* encourages others to cling to their views as well. The challenge is to see into the interdependence of all views and beliefs.

The inability to comprehend the emotional experience of fundamentalism may have its roots in the emotional disconnectedness of the liberal minded intellectual. The intense feelings of the flag-waver—"my religion right or wrong"—frequently baffle and outrage liberals. Feeling misunderstood, fundamentalists may find little alternative but to shout out even louder to the world. They are seeking respect and acknowledgement from those who define themselves as liberal minded. But the more they shout the more others judge them and continue to dismiss them. Feeling undermined, they seek to strike back. This emotional strategy protects their deeply held religious or political beliefs.

It is worth noting that the Buddha also spoke of two other extremes that the conventional mind falls into—that everything exists or that everything does not exist. The Western mind has engaged in dispute for centuries between the "eternal life" position of the Church and the "extinction at death" of science. Adopting either of these views borders on the absurd since there is no practical proof available. Having heard countless meaningless debates on life and death, the Buddha regarded them as a complete distraction to understanding the nature of life and Ultimate Truth.

Both sides endeavour to arouse as much support as possible. Liberals consider themselves champions of free speech, a term they hold sacred, no matter how insensitive its expression. Champions of adherence to moralistic beliefs are unable to grasp the sensibilities of the liberal tradition, highlighted in so-called educated societies. Some causes of the liberal tradition, such as tolerance for pornography and video violence, are crass and distasteful yet the rhetoric of free speech continues. But the fundamentalist fails to comprehend the liberal tradition supporting individuals' right to express themselves, to criticize and present sensible and well-grounded cases for alternative views. The application of thought and reason does not necessarily undermine deeply held religious or political beliefs.

On the other hand, "free speech" exists in context and does not possess inherent value itself, otherwise it becomes a licence for the perpetuation of views and beliefs at the expense of others. Taken out of context free speech can become arrogant, patronizing and sensationalist leading to harm and exploitation of others. But fundamentalists must learn to appreciate that liberals have worked for generations to establish a tradition of tolerance and open-mindedness to prevent dogmatic views from crushing the spirit of freedom in people. Liberals perceive themselves as guardians of a certain kind of intellectual and creative tradition constantly under threat from fundamentalists.

Both fundamentalists and liberals protect their beliefs. Identification with either strong religious beliefs or free speech makes any person susceptible to aggressive or patronizing reactivity. Through attachment and clinging to views, their respective standpoints become an ongoing mutual threat. The "adversary" reveals the same degree of investment in security as the "protagonist." When mistrust and aggression accompany our views it is a clear signal that insights into the need for security are vital. Experiences, images and language give some sense of stability to extremist views. Past, present and future come together in the strident effort to make unequivocal pronouncements on the truth of things. Objectivity-subjectivity distinctions blur in this interdependent situation. Blind to the degree of our indulgence, we live and act as though we had special access to the Truth. Our "truth" becomes another hammer to beat down the standpoints of others.

Wisdom is neither clinging to any extreme position, nor grasping onto the middle way. Realizing the emptiness of hostility to others, the cessation of pride and prejudice opens consciousness to a comprehensive awareness. Clinging to views reinforces ego-centred perceptions and dogmatic grasping by the "self that knows" makes possible the equally dogmatic rejection of "others who don't know." Both claim to know, and that the other does not know. Both are party to the same basic view without admitting it!

In later talks, the Buddha discussed with Kassapa two other extreme positions that frequently arise whenever suffering appears. One extreme is to blame oneself for the causes of suffering, the other extreme is blaming others. In a state of reaction, people target themselves or others as the cause of suffering rather than wisely adopting the teachings of the middle way of dependent arising. Suffering arises because the conditions are there for it to arise: taking total responsibility is one extreme, not taking responsibility another.

The wisdom of the middle way acts to reduce suffering rather than getting lost in reactivity. Reluctance to express views is often born from a reluctance to challenge others. Viewpoints need to be considered in context; intentions, values, social conditions and objectives are not separate from the view itself. We often take up a standpoint which deep down we could not care less about. Like scaffolding for a nonexistent structure, we build an edifice of opinions braced with generalities and assumptions that may even appear intelligent. We deceive ourselves and others when we imagine our views are objective, even if quoting an authority.

Views that work to end suffering serve the interests of all. If wisdom and compassion are to take priority there is no room for loyalty and identification with liberalism or fundamentalism. We realize the origin of views, bound up with past and current perceptions, and see the ending of views through insight into clinging and cherishing. Opinions no longer spellbind awareness. This swirling swamp of desire, conceit and clinging leads to anguish and dejection, particularly when we feel misunderstood. Attachment to our perceptions and beliefs gives rise to negativity and fear. As a result there is neither awareness nor insight into the patterns dominating our perceptions.

Awareness and insights into extremist views have a three-fold purpose:

1. *They safeguard us from clinging to views which distort either the general appearance, or the details*
2. *We do not become entrenched in an irrelevant ideology that only serves to perpetuate suffering through conflict*
3. *The application of wise restraint protects us from inflicting violent pressure on others.*

The "inner" establishes the reality of the "outer," the "outer" establishes the reality of the "inner." What was loved dearly and intensely can later become a despised belief—we can spend much of our life promoting and defending a belief only to react equally vigorously against it later. Without inquiry and wisdom, believers of one extreme or another submit to views but their feelings, thoughts and perceptions are unreliable. The murmurings of inner and outer doubts are suppressed to preserve the core beliefs.

Emotions and thoughts consolidate our perceptions into a reality that becomes a burden. Beliefs are nothing in themselves but are codependent on the state of mind of the believer. The clear mind aims to dissolve duality and division not intensify it, thus ideologies of liberalism and fundamentalism are not the concern of spiritual wisdom. When we shape our existence around an organized belief system we obscure the interconnected relationship of everything with everything else. Ending infatuation with concepts of Truth reveals compassion for those trapped in belief systems. Liberation from certainty and uncertainty refutes extreme views, then we can work to resolve conflict and respond wisely to the hostility of opposing views.

Free from dependency upon views we do not dwell obsessively upon the generalities and particulars of existence. Not finding a foothold in consciousness, our views do not act to limit our understanding and heartfelt responses. Through the centuries, the diverse body of Buddhist insight has been a "pointer" to that "Realization" of the emptiness of views. In that "Realization" everything naturally and effortlessly falls into place.

The Truth does exist as we know it.

The Truth does not exist as we know it.

The Truth does exist in another way.

The Truth does not exist in another way.

The belief that I cannot rise above beliefs perpetuates self-deception.

The belief that I can rise above beliefs perpetuates self-deception.

We cannot elevate the "Earth" nor a "beyond" into a metaphysical reality.

We cannot deconstruct the nature of things into a nothingness.

We cannot regard the Ultimate Truth as that perceived through the mind.

Ultimately, liberalism, fundamentalism and the message of the middle way are all ways of words.

All this is worthwhile meditating deeply upon so that we realize all things are empty of inherent or self existence—including liberalism, fundamentalism, the world, beliefs and Truth. We then realize our heartfelt salvation requires no viewpoint to cling onto, nor metaphysical category for its expression.

TEACHINGS OF THE BUDDHA

The Message of Awakening

By realizing it (the Deathless) yourselves Here and Now, through direct knowing, enter upon and abide in that supreme goal of the spiritual life.
The Buddha

The teachings of the Buddha offer an ethical basis for the spiritual life, a range of tools for working with emotional and mental processes, the transforming resources of insight meditation and a profound practical philosophy applicable to daily life. The teachings also offer direct heartfelt insights into the nature of dependent arising of mental-material phenomena, expansion of heartfulness and the cessation of suffering. Insights into the conventional world and the Ultimate Truth of phenomena are indispensable to the Buddha's message.

Translated into English from the original Pali, the talks (suttas) of the Buddha consist of about 20 volumes. Every talk is an in-depth exploration and expansion of the Four Noble Truths. The Buddha said that a worthwhile life attends to these Four Truths: there is suffering in the world, conditions for that suffering, the end of suffering and the factors for the end of suffering. By referring to them as noble truths, he highlighted their significance, which dawned upon him on the night of his awakening. The Ultimate Truth reveals the cessation of suffering. Its timeless nature is free from characteristics and unconditioned. Realization of the Ultimate Truth of things, which makes everything possible, is liberating. The Buddha realized that the mind cannot get a hold or grip on Ultimate Truth, thus it brings a natural humility to the mind. Realizing the Emptiness of inherent existence of anything exposes this Truth, one without a second.

Sometimes the teachings formulate into easy to remember groups. This way the mind can understand, with relatively few concepts, the diversity of what the Buddha communicated. The main groups are the Four Noble Truths, the Eightfold Path, the Four Foundations of Awareness, the Three Gems, the Five Aggregates, the Five Precepts and the Four Divine Abidings. The value of these groups of themes, all discussed in this book, reveal insights into the Here and Now. The teachings consummate in awakening to the Truth of things.

The Buddha dispensed with various beliefs that might seem integral to a religious life. Beliefs in a soul, Creator, Saviour, worship and rituals were dispensable if they did not stand up to the light of inquiry and experience. He did not consider it necessary in the spiritual life to cherish prayers, sacred meals, rituals, traditions, gurus and dogmas. He endorsed a liberating wisdom in the midst of religious and secular life.

He directed his teaching to all manner of people—royalty, the rich, the powerful, the poor, the sick, gurus, fundamentalists, the secular and ordained. For the first time in the long history of the Indian religious tradition, he formed a sangha (literally, a gathering) of both men and women committed to spiritual inquiry and liberation for the welfare of everyone. The Buddha took no interest whatsoever in gaining converts to a set of beliefs. He had no regard for the powers of manipulation or charisma ("One who touches my clothing but does not understand the teachings does not see me.") He described spiritual gatherings for awareness and inquiry as one of the Three Gems of life, along with awakening (buddha) and the teachings (dharma).

He diagnosed everyone as free from inherent or special existence. Teachings which question ruthlessly the whole structure and concept of self do not leave anything, anyone or anywhere to grasp hold of, to cling onto as special, or worth identifying with, including the Buddha. Yet the teachings pay immense respect to people, animals and the environment. The heart of the teachings is applicable to all generations of men and women who express interest in cutting through the superficial formations of life.

But this does not mean to say that the teachings of the Buddha cannot be criticized. The Buddha welcomed criticism as a vital feature of the spiritual life. Some aspects of his teachings are clearly designed to serve particular cultures and times in history. A number of the precepts for those ordained into the sangha seem only relevant in certain climates for certain cultures. He only permitted change of minor rules of the 227 precepts and rules (vinaya) laid down for men in the ordained sangha. This has led to some confusion over the centuries in adapting the rules to different cultures and climates. For some Buddhist traditions, protection of every rule mattered more than living with wisdom. His one speculation about the future of ordained women was unnecessary and unhelpful when he commented that ordination of women would contribute to the decline of the order—assuming that he actually made such an uncharacteristic opinion.

He condoned eating flesh, detailing what animals to eat and what must be avoided. He overlooked the pain caused to animals, birds and fish who end up devoured on the table of householders or in the begging bowl of the homeless sangha. The only form of spiritual exercise the Buddha seemed to value was going on long walkabouts. The Buddha ignored yogic exercise though it was familiar to him. There is insufficient analysis by the Buddha of the relationship of privilege to poverty. He encouraged generating good karma to be reborn in a rich family, yet he himself ran away from such a privileged environment. The consequences of these oversights have been extensive for the Buddhist tradition and for the world.

Throughout the centuries the Buddhist tradition has remained on the political sidelines during times of war and exploitation. Most Buddhist traditions have neglected diet and exercise as a vital feature of the spiritual life. The Buddhist tradition has concentrated on the ordained sangha, development of the mind and voluntary simplicity while neglecting householders and the body. The primary interest in the West in Buddhism is also development of mind, with much less interest in the Buddha's message on lifestyle, consumption and the Ultimate Truth.

The determination to cause a fundamental change in awareness and values in society is evident throughout his teachings. In that respect the Buddha's teachings embrace spirituality, religious experiences, psychotherapy, philosophy and ecology as well as having a social-political dimension. He perceived that self, particular selfish desire, brought about corruption and denigration of the fabric of society. He communicated his concerns to householders and the voluntary homeless who practised his teachings.

The Buddha certainly emphasized relative truth—there were fewer references to Ultimate Truth. He endorsed the uprooting of clinging to conditioned beliefs. He told seekers after Truth not to cling to his teachings. This has saved many a Buddhist from going into the missionary business, and the Buddha had no interest in ramming his spiritual insights down the throats of others. To a considerable degree, his expansive and tolerant approach to the religious life has inspired Buddhist teachers through the centuries to communicate a generosity of spirit. There is a high value placed on tolerance in the Buddhist tradition. Undoubtedly, the heart of the teaching is the Four Noble Truths. It is very improbable that any Buddhist of any tradition would deny this. The Buddha stated:

1. *there is suffering in the world*
2. *there are conditions for suffering to arise*
3. *realization of the Ultimate Truth ends suffering*
4. *there is a way to end suffering, namely the Eightfold Path of right understanding, right attitude, right speech, right action, right livelihood, right effort, right awareness and right meditation*

Examination of the Four Noble Truths in purely personal terms is a narrow understanding. These truths also apply to all aspects of social, national and global life, including political-economic standpoints. In contrast, the Four Truths of our political leaders are:

1. *there is consumerism*
2. *personal desire is the central purpose of existence*
3. *there is the maximization of consumerism through economic growth.*
4. *the way to it is through the market economy, exploitation of the environment and becoming a workaholic.*

The Four Truths of politicians world wide increase suffering as much as help alleviate it. As a result the Earth and countless millions slide towards the hell realms. Out of the Buddha's fourfold statement, which analyses the primary concerns of existence from the standpoint of wisdom and compassion, he devoted his life to serving the Dharma. His teachings are concerned with the Ultimate Truth of the nature of things as well as the conventional world of mind, body, and environment. The Buddha gave numerous talks, answered questions, engaged in dialogue and asked questions of seekers after Truth, but he endorsed his teachings with his lifestyle, one tailor-made for the message and for a sustainable and peaceful world. Meditation and reflection certainly play a significant role as part of an expansive approach to the spiritual life. Realization of the truths of existence come to those who listen wholeheartedly to teachings on enlightenment. A life of wisdom and compassion emerges from these realizations.

The Buddha formulated two main guidelines for living the spiritual life. One is the three fold training, namely ethical guidelines (sila), meditative awareness (samadhi) and wisdom (panna). This training, accompanied with teachings on liberation, contributes to our ultimate welfare. The Buddha said Nirvana is the peace found in liberation from suffering. The second guideline is explained in his talk on the four foundations of awareness (Satipattana Sutta), namely body, feelings, mental states and dharma. It is quite often forgotten that the Buddha emphasized in this talk that liberation is not necessarily a matter of arduous spiritual practice for seven years or more, but accessible in this very week of our lives.

Some schools of the Theravada tradition of Buddhism uphold a long term view of the path to liberation. Some Mahayana schools conceive that liberation and the accompanying awakening insights will take numerous lifetimes. Both traditions could learn from Zen which has highlighted the immediate accessibility of liberation. Some schools of Zen though seem to have a preoccupation with special experiences, the ability to answer koans or certain forms of realization—all being viewed as proof of attainment. Zen could benefit from the practical skills of working with mind states available in the Vipassana (insight meditation) tradition. Both can learn from the Mahayana tradition, which emphasises compassion as much as meditation. None of the Buddhist traditions deserves to claim pre-eminence over the others.

The experience of life takes priority in Buddhism. But its preoccupation with special experiences, and their subsequent interpretation, is another area which, I believe, has led to widespread confusion. The wilful pursuit of a transcendent experience can reinforce the ego at the expense of a liberating wisdom. Claims and counterclaims about the significance of particular spiritual experiences abound in the Buddhist tradition today just as they did 2500 years ago. Fully realized teachers can confirm the authenticity of transforming insights and realizations of students. Yet some teachers misunderstood their own experiences, or their own teachers made an error of judgement; and certain teachers have got themselves into an immense mess in their personal lives, or behave with a degree of arrogance that would not be tolerated outside the spiritual life. Such situations have led to doubts and confusions among sincere spiritual seekers.

The Judeo-Christian religious tradition has relied heavily on theological seminaries and book learning to produce rabbis and priests instead of spiritual teachers. Many teachers in Buddhism dismiss or even ridicule any significance given to book-learning in the spiritual life. My Vipassana teacher, Ajahn Dhammadaro of Thailand, forbade reading in his monastery and loved to poke fun at scholar-monks. Only one thing mattered and that was full spiritual realization.

The Buddhist passion for insightful experiences challenges the intellectual view which has been predominant in Western circles. Owing to its attractive and reasonable philosophy, the Buddhist tradition pays respect to direct experience while exercising caution about the value of intellectual interpretation. Profound experiences are a feature of spiritual practice, but the authenticity of experiences must be revealed in our relationship to ourselves, others and the environment. Jesus put it succinctly when he said: "You shall know them by their fruits."

In a conversation with Sariputta, a life-long friend, the Buddha disclosed at length what happened to him the night of his awakening. and in the subsequent weeks. His enlightenment had three phases. First there was full realization, which he summarized as the Four Noble Truths; second there were the reflections and insights into Dharma teachings; and, third, was the application of those teachings.

On the night of his enlightenment the Buddha *understood* what really matters to humanity; such realization was liberating and he *responded* to what he saw. I believe that he did not advocate spiritual experiences for their own sake: he told Sariputta he experienced a whole range of them before the night of realization. Nor did he advocate an intellectual understanding. He realized that liberation has no special marks nor signs to it. A Mahayana text quotes the Buddha as saying: "I achieved nothing from complete unexcelled enlightenment." Such statements only make complete sense to liberated beings.

Throughout the Buddha's teachings there is a precision in his communications that is rare and precious. For example, the Buddha made clear statements about the First Noble Truth. Yet these statements frequently have been misinterpreted. The Buddhist tradition, particularly the Theravadins, conveyed the impression that the Buddha regarded all life as suffering and the only thing to be done was to escape into Nirvana. This traditional view has deterred many spiritual seekers from taking a serious interest in the Buddha's teachings. Yet the Buddha's teachings do not present an antilife viewpoint. He investigated the presence of suffering, but he did not agree with the view that all life is suffering.

Buddhist commentators and detractors of the Buddha have claimed that the Buddha declared that "life is suffering." The Buddha did not make such an unqualified universal statement, which would have been inconsistent with the precision of his teachings. He wisely avoided falling into such a trap. To do so he would have had to have stated "all life is suffering" (sarvam dukham) or "all phenomena are suffering" (sabbe dhamma dukkha). Nowhere in 20 volumes of recorded talks of the Buddha does such a statement appear. If all phenomena are ultimately unsatisfactory, as certain Theravada teachers claim, then it means there is no way out. The initial reaction of some people to hearing the claim of Buddhists that "life is suffering" is to experience a genuine inner doubt about the validity of this view. It does not stand up to our experience or understanding. I suspect, though, that some Buddhists and others grasp onto this extreme view to justify their depressed or unhappy personality.

Others, unfamiliar with the words of the Buddha, will assume that the teacher or the tradition has a thorough knowledge of the Dharma and is reporting accurately the message from 2500 years ago. Those who claim that "all is suffering" do an immense disservice to the Buddha Dharma, for this communicates a pessimistic message and reinforces negative universal viewpoints. If life is to be regarded as miserable, then the outcome will be to want to get out of it as quickly as possible—a mindful suicide would be a serious option. What is unsatisfactory is taking up the various formations or constructions of existence as Ultimate Truth. In Pali, the language in which the words of the Buddha were written after several generations of oral tradition, the text reads *sabbe sankhara dukkha—all formations* (mind, body, world) *are unsatisfactory* from the standpoint of Ultimate Truth.

The formations deceive perceptions. We then participate in a warped view of life believing in a divided existence. The environment and self appear as separate events and as independent and unique constructions. Realization of Ultimate Truth reveals the unformed, unconstructed, unmade nature of things.

Some traditional teachers have promoted a detached view of life. They themselves have striven, possibly successfully, to dwell like this and remain utterly unaffected by events. Some Buddhists view Nirvana as a detached state. They then engage in dogmatic views about life and Nirvana in a dualistic mode.

As explained in the chapter on the Four Noble Truths, the Buddha inquired deeply into the nature of suffering and unsatisfactoriness *when* it arises, the ending of suffering and conditions which contribute to its arising and cessation. He was certainly not proclaiming an absolute state of unbroken suffering or unsatisfactoriness. He regarded suffering as an expression of relative truth. Ultimate Truth reveals the emptiness of suffering and the formations it depends upon. Even at the relative level, our daily experiences show we are not living in suffering from moment to moment. The Buddha was asked: "Why do we live the spiritual life?" He said because "it is such a happy life to live."

In a conversation with his son, Rahula, The Buddha said:
"Develop meditation on kindness to banish resentment.
Develop meditation on compassion to banish cruelty.
Develop meditation on spiritual joy to banish envy.
Develop meditation on equanimity to banish hate.
Develop meditation on the nonbeautiful to banish lust.
Develop meditation on impermanence to banish pride.
Develop meditation on mindfulness of breathing to bring great fruits."

The Buddha specified these fruits as awareness, inquiry into the dharma, energy, happiness, serenity, meditative depth and equanimity. He said that enlightenment is the flowering of these seven factors at the expense of dwelling in greed and grief in the world. The Buddha endorsed the significance of the experiences of kindness, joy, happiness and serenity. He disputed the orthodox religious view that deep down we are all hiding unresolved personal problems or that we are all sinners. In the depths of meditation we become absorbed in happiness, joy and reflection; a happy psyche asks little of the world. As deeper meditations develop we experience a state free from reflective thought with further refined depths. Through the depth of insight meditation and wisdom we shake off the grip of addictions and unsatisfactory behaviour.

The infatuation with the material world drops away. Employing people and situations to boost our ego become empty. Inner contentment, not imposed morality or the use of will power, ends the abuse of people and environment. Having touched a depth of joy and realised the power of kindness, the interest in the needy self fades away. Spiritual seekers sense that fulfilment of the spiritual life is close. Each of the seven factors of enlightenment exposes the grossness of worldly pursuits and a possessive or imperial attitude to life.

The Buddha said:
"Whose mind is calmed, who sees the dharma,
the Truth with insight brings such a happiness,
and this joy transcends that of ordinary minds."

In the much-loved opening verses of the Dhammapada, the Buddha said:
"If one speaks or acts with a pure mind,
Happiness follows one as the shadow that never departs."

Spiritual life has acknowledged the importance of mystical wonder. Some claim saints and mystics have the capacity to have personal power over the environment—producing something out of nothing, walking on water and having power over the minds of others. He did not deny certain powers but he said that they "vexed" and "disgusted" him. The Buddha gave practical teachings to awaken our hearts to the nature of life and our participation in it. The first duty or Dharma of a human being is realization of an enlightened life. All other considerations are of peripheral importance.

Four Noble Truths

What is the Noble Truth of Suffering? Birth is suffering, ageing is suffering, sickness is suffering, death is suffering. Sorrow, lamentation, pain, grief and despair are suffering, being tied to the unloved is suffering, separation from the loved is suffering, not to get what one wants is suffering: in short the five aggregates affected by clinging are suffering.

What is the Noble Truth of the causes of Suffering? It is desire which renews existence and is tied to pleasure and lust, relishing now this and now that, pursuing sensual stimulation, desire for existence and nonexistence. And where does this desire establish itself? Wherever in this world there is anything agreeable and pleasurable, there this selfish desire arises and establishes itself.

What is the Noble Truth of the Cessation of Suffering? It is the utter fading and cessation of that same desire, the rejection, relinquishing, liberation from it and letting go of it.

What is the Noble Truth of the Way of the cessation of suffering? It is this Noble Eightfold Path that is to say: Right Understanding, Right Attitude, Right Speech, Right Action, Right Livelihood, Right Effort, Right Awareness and Right Contemplation.

Of these Four Noble Truths, the Noble Truth of Suffering must be penetrated by full insight into suffering, the Noble Truth of the Origin of Suffering must be penetrated by abandoning selfish desire, the Noble Truth of the Cessation of Suffering must be penetrated by realizing the cessation of selfish desire, the Noble Truth of the Eightfold Path must be penetrated by commitment to it.
The Buddha

The Buddha devoted his life to expanding on the above statements which he proclaimed after his awakening. He made wisdom, and insights into existence, the foundation of his teachings. The diversity and wealth of his teachings and the subsequent history of the Buddhist tradition hinge on the Four Noble Truths, and this message has as much application today as it did at the time of the Buddha. Desires maniifest as the three poisons of the mind: greed, hate and delusion.

Politicians, educators and the business world function so as to cultivate the desire to produce and consume. Even compared to a generation ago the multiplicity of items available within the hallowed grounds of the shopping mall is mind boggling. Homo Sapiens has become Homo Shopiens. The manufacturers of goods attempt to satisfy every conceivable desire of hungry customers. The sheer diversity of colours available for a single shirt or blouse reflects the conspiracy between producers and consumers to cultivate desires. The shopping mall endorses ever changing fashions in order to lure endless streams of customers. Even a strong minded customer, who keeps a close eye on the purse strings, often leaves the mall or supermarket with more goods than he or she needs.

The eye sees an attractive object sparking a pleasant feeling in the mind, often simultaneously the desire to possess arises regardless of needs. Customers become walking time bombs of desire, sometimes fretting from one object to another owing to a fixation on a particular colour, size, shape, sound, taste or touch. Goods on display exert a pull on the senses, particularly the eyes, so that homo shopiens reaches, sometimes regretfully, into the wallet or purse for cash or credit card.

The board of directors, management, advertising agencies and sales staff aim to transfer the maximum amount of money from the hands of the shopper into the hands of the shop staff then, eventually, to the management and directors. Business people employ every conceivable strategy in their advertising to ensure this transaction takes place. The marketers of goods persuade the public to go into debt so that goods can be purchased with unearned money. In some cases, poor families owe money to the credit companies for Christmas presents bought for their children more than a year previously.

The public spends more hours shopping than any other activities except work, television viewing and sleep. Television, itself, is a primary medium for the exploitation of suffering, an abuse of the First Noble Truth. The news, documentaries, films and soap operas indulge in endless accounts of human and global suffering, numbing the minds of nearly a billion people on Earth night after night. Movies end with the triumph of good over evil, a massive form of public deception. 2000 years ago an enlightened human being said: "Let the dead bury the dead," a response to a life of social numbness instead of spiritual liberation. Today he would say: "Let the dead watch the dead." Television reduces countless numbers of intelligent and perceptive people to a state of infantile immobility, paralysed in an armchair existence. Images are no substitute for reality, and even the most penetrating documentary can become a form of escape.

The power of advertising and the subtle pressure of social norms, persuades shoppers to work hard to raise income to pay for goods born of easy credit. This vicious circle of producing and consuming forces people to owe money to the banks, the building societies or the creditors to pay for the mortgage, the car, the children's education or household goods. Paying off debts becomes a way of life and few escape the web of debt. Whether in or out of debt, even fewer escape the money anxieties that accompany the clutch of consumerism. The ugly shadow of personal debt becomes the consequence of enchantment with goods, knowledge and money. Government and business endorse infatuation with production and consumption rather than participation in a creative way of life that supports our genuine well being. No wonder there is so much unhappiness.

How do these contemporary issues, the substance of our daily life, fit in with a body of teachings that were given more than two and a half millennia ago? The money world appears to seep into our lives awake or sleeping but this world offers little in the way of peace of mind and contentment. Participating in this world we may become clever but we do not become wise. We have become so clever that we are destroying the world with our cleverness. The Buddha would remain unimpressed with our obsession with knowledge, personal gain and control over matter as he upheld the Four Noble Truths as the core of his teachings. The primary duties of politicians, the Church, business people, scientists, philosophers and the privileged are dedication to insight and action to eradicate the suffering but too often the ego of self-importance gets in the way.

Practising psychotherapists have acknowledged the problems of the dysfunctional family. Instead of placing blame upon the individual for his or her behaviour they have wisely attempted to make the individual concerned take responsibility while pointing out the contributions that others make to reinforcing personal problems. Politicians consistently fail the people they represent for they prefer to blame others rather than challenge their own unexamined political beliefs. They have led people to believe they are entitled to all forms of self-gratification and prosperity. Few feel satisfied with their situation. Aggravation, cynicism, complaining and feeling victimized are the common currency.

Community life has broken down into various fragments of the victim culture. Social problems such as smoking, alcohol, gambling, compulsive shopping, working long hours and anxiety become defined as diseases, an addictions or due to hereditary factors. People find this attitude convenient since it lets them off the hook; they are victims so they don't have to take responsibility. But when responsibility is placed exclusively on the individual it lets politicians and the privileged off the hook. Politicians and Church leaders whine on about individuals lacking discipline. Yet we only have to look at their lifestyle, or waistline, to remember the adage "don't do as I do, do as I say."

For the past 2500 years Buddhism has applied the Four Noble Truths to the condition of the individual rather than examining the Buddha's insights from the standpoint of political, social and environmental realities. This preoccupation with the individual, despite the countless insights of the Buddha into the emptiness of a "self" existence, has undermined the social, political and environmental concerns of his teachings.

At first glance, the Buddha's teachings of "nonself" can appear a cold analysis of existence rather than an authentic inquiry into the nature of things. The solidification of self separates oneself or one thing from another generating a fetish of self interest and obsession with other things. A well integrated human being examines this metaphysical belief in separate existence and the supremacy of self interest. The teachings of nonself challenge the basis of contemporary politics, rooted in the belief in the marketplace, and that people exist independently and in competition with each other for control and access to goods and the environment.

In the reification of self and other, the differences between a holistic perception and profit obsessed perception stand out:

Holistic and expansive	Profit-based and narrow
Awareness	Selfish pursuits
Causes	Effects
Change	Progress, evolution
Community	Central control
Compassion for the poor	Support for the Establishment
Compassion for the world	The real world
Cooperation	Competition
Cycles	Growth
Diversity	Control
Environment	Private Ownership
Genuine self-worth	High salaries for executives
Health and safety	Efficiency
Heartfulness	Cold logic
Interconnection	Objectivity
Interdependency	State, the
Intimacy	Rationality, metaphysics
Job satisfaction	Cheap labour
Kindness, generosity, understanding	Arrogance, aggression, blame
Local Community	Self, nuclear family
Love of animals	Exploitation, experiments
Love of artistic endeavour	Creation of megastars
Making love	Having sex
Making things last	Obsession with changing fashions

Holistic and expansive	*Profit-based and narrow*
Natural happiness	Pursuit of pleasure
Nutritious diet	Alcohol, smoking, rich food
Quality	Quantity
People as people	People as consumers
Pilgrimages, nature	Holidays in the sun
Play	Winning
Prevention	Cure
Resources	Profit
Respect for legislation	Manipulation
Sharing	Taking,
Spirituality, culture	The modern world
Wisdom and compassion	Knowledge and gain

The Four Noble Truths can serve as the basis for radical social and political change since the Buddha gave no indication that he thought of suffering in purely personal terms, as he emphasized the dependently arising condition of suffering. It is equally true to say from the overview of the Four Noble Truths that:

1. *The Earth with its numerous inhabitants is suffering. Submission to the megamachine contributes to it.*
2. *The Earth's suffering arises according to the way we live our lives. Selfish living which perceives the world as an opportunity to fulfil personal desires contributes to suffering for all beings and the planet.*
3. *The Earth's suffering will end when selfishness, fear and aggression end. All our institutions—political, economic, social and religious— require a revolutionary change.*
4. *By concentrating our hearts and minds on all facets of daily life, we derive collective insights and wisdom to overcome suffering wherever it arises and in whatever form.*

Active commitment to practical and heartfelt investigation into the Four Noble Truths transforms the painful circumstances of society. Identification with unsound beliefs and social conditioning obscures this vision for ending human suffering. Devotion and meditation exercises must be regarded as a part of the spiritual life. Liberation is the emancipation of humanity from suffering.

During the 45 years that the Buddha gave teachings, from 35 to 80, he consistently put forth his insights into the human condition, and revealed endless depths of discovery about the Four Noble Truths. He perceived that society can penetrate through the desire-suffering cycle so that people dissolve the painful wheel of becoming.

On the one hand, Buddhism can claim to have given some measure of protection to the teachings of the Buddha. But Buddhism also become a religion, thus often obscuring the profound significance of the teachings. In this way, Buddhism has sometimes inhibited society's opportunity for the realization of the Four Noble Truths. The teachings survived not so much because of the religious and cultural forms, or the wide ranging beliefs, but through the remarkable presence of certain wise men and women within the religion who have had a transforming impact on peoples' lives. They have carried the essence of the teachings—awakening to the end of suffering—from one generation to the next. The significance of wisdom stands far above religious beliefs and Buddhism's degenerate ritualistic traditions.

The teachings refer to suffering as not getting what we want and separation from the loved and the desirable. In Buddhist terms, desire is defined as the pursuit and craving for experiences, roles objects, and relationships which produce suffering in the past, present or future. There is desire, too, for continued existence or nonexistence. There is an element of unsatisfactoriness, if not anguish, in such pursuits born from blindness and a lack of wisdom. The teachings point to a life of wisdom where the mind is not oppressed with such desires. The cessation of such desires releases a creative and spontaneous life, free from the grip of the conditioned mind.

The nuclear family suffers through household pressures, too, frequently a major characteristic of home life. Two people, or more, who began by loving each other come to hate each other. In the imprisonment of conflicting personality structures and mutual misunderstanding, little opportunity emerges to break the spell of those negative forces. Neither person wants to listen to the other, or bridge the gap in communication. Partners live in despair over the state of their relationship, parents and children fight each other and grandparents fret over their children's conflicts. People often no longer wish to live together;   those that continue to prefer to lose themselves in front of the television, in alcohol or in sleep.

The 50-year-old U.S. oil executive proudly earned $750,000 a year. He described himself as a company man, a loyal and dutiful servant of the company. Married for 24 years, he and his wife had moved 10 times in the course of their marriage—each time at the request of his company. His wife suffered his arrogance and self-opinionated diatribes night after night. He said he "loathed Greenies" and regarded multinational companies as the "most environmentally conscious organizations on the planet." The oil executive didn't realize that his home environment was an utter mess.

He bolstered his self-esteem through an obsession with materialism. If he had understood the strategies of advertising, including his own employers, he would have realized how advertised products link to the self-esteem of potential purchasers. But he imagined he was master of his life instead of realizing he was a slave to the company machine. He believed in the notion of free will as a way to deny this servitude. His plight was similar to millions of others, all unable to take charge of life due to unresolved feelings of inadequacy. The executive constantly compared himself with his colleagues and to overcome his inadequacies he drove himself hard—to the company's satisfaction—to reach the top of the corporate ladder.

His wife felt progressively unhappy, bored and unfulfilled. The last straw came when he persuaded her for the umpteenth time to attend yet another special auction—this time an auction of furs and jewellery—for the wives of the executives. After the auction, she telephoned the wife of another executive and asked her tentatively what she thought of the event. Neither woman wanted to commit themselves to expressing their true feelings. She took courage and said: "I hated it. The company is my husband's mistress. I hate this shallow and crass lifestyle." Twenty years of suppressed hatred burst out. She refused to tie herself any longer to what she hated. She left.

Her husband thought she had gone mad and needed a psychoanalyst. He absolutely refused to admit that his attachment to his career and ever increasing income were significant factors in her departure. "I have been good to you," he shouted at her. "I have given you everything you wanted. You're just an ungrateful bitch." The wife moved to another city, found a one room apartment, took up yoga and meditation and worked in a small office. "I have never been so happy in all my life," she told her husband over the telephone. Unwilling to change, her husband came home at night to sit at the head of an empty table.

Such sad scenarios are frequent. Lifelong marriages often begin in heaven and maintained in hell. Fear of separation becomes the glue that keeps a marriage together. There is no special virtue in lifelong marriages. Virtue reveals itself in wisdom and love. The obsession with self interest denies relationship and there is a painful deprivation of shared contentment and joy. Lack of opportunity to share and discuss everyday personal experiences reduces marriage to ritualized meals and 10 minute conversations. As the Buddha pointed out suffering arises when there are the conditions for it to arise; separation between loved ones, even when they live together, invites despair and sadness. Yet the capacity of two people to meet each other can transform the pained heart into one of contentment and joy. Overcoming selfish desire gives access to the deepest recesses of our being revealing insights into interconnection. These perceptions remain hidden when we are tied to self and things, to "me" and "my."

The political-economic view holds that striving for material success will improve the quality of our lives. We imagine we will become happier people by owning more things. Our parents, politicians, and educators coerce us in to pushing ourselves as hard as we can to get on in life. Not only is the personal cost high (One in three men has a heart attack before the age of 60, one in six women will seek professional support for emotional problems) but the stress and pressure placed on people of all ages is paralleled by the same demands placed on the environment. As a result, we live an unwise and superficial life on an eroding planet lost in the rhetoric of an advanced civilization.

When society promotes selfish desire at the expense of human and environmental relationships we are indulging in the pursuit of a heaven of our own making, and thereby invite hell—social, political and environmental. The Second Noble Truth dealing with the causes of suffering is ignored again and again, as though it were irrelevant. Our society makes no effort to gain insight into desire, nor to understand the relationship of desire to suffering. Our consciousness remains trapped in the notion of struggling for survival to make ends meet and productivity.

Even when smothered by desire, rebellious thoughts will still arise "What am I doing this for? I am going to die anyway." Doubts often haunt the most successful overachiever. The teachings address those who are willing to turn their back on the pretensions of the conditioned mind. The freedom to question success offers the opportunity to shift away from conventional and banal pursuits. It is at this point that the Third and Fourth Noble Truth have significance. Setting out on a pilgrimage of discovery makes every act count, every factor of the Noble Eightfold Path matters, so that the fusion of these truths becomes clear.

We take no time to reflect on our day to day desires, how they inform our views, and the connection of desire to the harm of others. To put this in crude psychological terms, we might say that desire rules the rich nations and fear rules the rest of the world—fear of the tyranny of their governments, or fear of not securing the next meal. The Four Noble Truths deserve greater attention, not only from a personal position but equally within political and economic arenas.

The Buddha's willingness to define his terms eliminates unnecessary confusion about what suffering meant for him. This is clear in the Four Noble Truths. There is a tremendous amount of suffering in our world through birth, ageing, sickness and death. Even with our sophisticated technology and within clinically white walled hospitals, mothers and babies may find the birth experience a traumatic time. Elsewhere birth can be a matter of life or death, or a new baby can bring suffering to a large family straining their meagre resources. Acknowledging the presence of ageing, sickness and death is taboo, so we relegate elderly people to humourless homes, and sew the seeds for our own fate. We make every effort to avoid facing suffering. As a rap song says, *denial* is more than the name of a river in Egypt.

Our ability to deploy technology to cope with the harsh facts of life offers little compensation for our lack of wisdom necessary to deal with the circumstances of existence. Yet warning people about debt, or persuading couples to give more time to their relationship than their careers, or suggesting people live with moderation often become fruitless endeavours. Many people respond poorly to preachers and warnings, or to grave predictions about the future. Change requires not only a rebellion against the old selfishness, but realization and vision intuitively connected with a practical daily wisdom. The opportunity for profound insights into life, daily happiness and love represents the cutting edge of consciousness and commitment to awareness. Realization of the Third Noble Truth extinguishes the mind burning with egotism. There is a blessedness that pays full respect to life, a depth of peace an active concern that puts birth, change and death into perspective.

It will never be enough for people to work exclusively for the preservation of the Earth, few people even feel concern for future generations. From time to time parents of young children wonder what the future may hold for them, and if they have done the right thing in bringing children into the world, but such thoughts rarely make inroads into the main stream of social conditioning. People rarely change through feeling guilty about their lifestyle or worrying about the future. Discovering authentic values in the Here and Now vitalizes the process of social change. Consumerism is the religion of dead spirits, conditioning and habit, the product of the cold impersonal nature of market forces and government policy. Awakening is the discovery of authentic life after ego death, dissolution of fear and the freedom from preoccupation with consumerism.

At times, cause and effect analyses result in a useful belief system. However, but an enlightened wisdom realizes that ultimately we are not products of conditioning, not bound to cause and effect. Realization of Ultimate Truth dissolves the superficial pattern of investment in pleasure and control. This is the vision of the Third and Fourth Noble Truths which eradicates manipulative organizational structures and our illusory self-obsessed existence.

The Buddha revealed the *"fading away of desire, extinction of craving, letting go and liberation."*

With realization there is abandonment. With letting go there is realization. Each of the Four Noble Truths relates to the other three, none of the Noble Truths have any independent self existence. Liberated from the desire-suffering cycle, the insightful teachings of the Four Noble Truths become established in our hearts. We then experience an enlightened life and abide with active reverence for all people and the Earth.

Five Ethical Guidelines

If one speaks or acts with a pure mind,
happiness follows one as the shadow
that never departs.
The Buddha

Crying out against any nation's crude disregard for sentient life and the violence inflicted upon the Earth, despairing Greens have expressed the crude view that humankind are a "cancer of the Earth," We do not know when to stop, when to let go or how to change our ways. This compulsive attachment to getting what we want desecrates life. At every level of human organization, from the individual to international business, there is an aggressive thirst to get at the spoils of the Earth, but we are scarcely aware of it. Nothing is precious, nothing is sacred, everything is up for grabs—except what "I" own. Denial of deeply rooted personal and national behaviour affects our perceptions of responsibility. We are losing the capacity to express moral outrage against wanton greed and aggression.

Governments claim individuals are totally responsible for their own lives, yet ministers in office refuse to take responsibility for disastrous policies. When governments cause suffering and hardship upon people they evade responsibility. Governments like to blame previous governments, other politicians or market forces, while criminals blame their actions on financial or emotional deprivation. No one is willing to own up. Denial and avoidance become the norm.

The privileged look down on the underclass who live in fear of worsening hardships. The despair of the poor cripples their potential to change their lives. The establishment, a minority, dominates the majority through power, greed and fear. These conditions, which cause destructive behaviour and harm, operate within a legal framework. The legality or illegality of decisions often obscures the consequences; how we make decisions, such as through acts of Parliament, can obscure the motives and the painful results. Arguably, denial reaches its zenith at times of crisis when the jaundiced views of politicians and military leaders launch a war. To imagine there can be war without immense suffering to civilians, animals, centres of population, a nation's infrastructure and the environment is a denial of staggering magnitude. When the political establishment feels uncertain of its morality, it can safely call upon the Church to support its decisions. Moral theologians fashion for the political establishment four solid reasons for a "just" war:

1. *a war is launched against an unjust government or army, not civilians*
2. *it is for the defence of citizens*
3. *the cause is just*
4. *there is no alternative.*

Ironically, all political and military leaders employ the same rationalizations. They believe what they are doing is good and right. They have convinced themselves and others that military action is necessary because there is no alternative. The world's religions often support these actions or remain mute. Persuaded by the State and Church, most people dutifully acknowledge the concept of the just war. The establishment, largely consisting of the old, rich and privileged, sends into the battle the young, poor and underprivileged. Few religious or moral voices uphold nonviolence against the call to arms, the crudest form of conflict resolution. To campaign against the export of any arms to any foreign nation expresses global awareness and interdependent responsibility.

At any moment in time, the military of the USA and other powerful nations is ready to go on the offensive. The West floods every region of the world with arms. The U.S. continues to be the number one arms dealer world wide selling more than $30 billion of arms every year, including to poverty stricken African nations. The U.S. alone sells weapons to 140 countries including more than 50 authoritarian governments. The U.S. military stands as the biggest employer in the world with more than 9,000,000 employees at an average cost to taxpayers of $50,000 per year. Fearful of increasing unemployment, the US government considers only most modest cuts in defence expenditure. US taxpayers' money spent to defend Korea, the Persian Gulf and the Philippines equals the amount of money spent for the environment, education and infrastructure in the USA.

When politicians realize they are out of their depths in their international conflicts, they call upon the military to bomb and destroy their opponents. Thus lack of morality and imagination inhibits conversion of military factories into plants for peaceful uses. Morality does not enter issues of defence. Public concern around causes for violence in the home and on the streets often turns to violent television and video films while avoiding challenging the power and promotion of military might—often the inspiration for such movies. Nations actively pursue the minds of the young for a military career. The young's obsession with war video games serves the interests of the military complex. Through clever and manipulative advertising, the military romanticize war to attract the attention of the adventurous young. In their advertisements, they leave out the screams of those whose flesh is burning.

Buddhism first began to take root in the West in the years after the First World War. The battlefields of Europe had exposed the shallow depths of Western civilization. Both sides launched into a war of unimaginable cruelty and environmental desecration under the guise of the four principles for a just war. The socialists' cry of "workers of the world unite" had a hollow ring to it. The workers of the Western world had united—in hatred of each other—at the behest of the Establishment. An entire generation of Europeans heedlessly suffered in The Great War; the age of global reasoned violence was upon us.

In the years following the First World War, a handful of thoughtful individuals looked elsewhere for spiritual insights and for teachings resolutely committed to nonkilling. The Christian Church had lost its connections with the nonviolent teachings and exemplary life of Jesus. Spiritual seekers read that the teachings of the Buddha began with five basic precepts. The first one said loud and clear: "I take upon myself the rule of training to abstain from taking the life of living beings." Respect for this first precept marked initiation into the spiritual life. It means much more to the spiritual practitioner than questions of national boundaries; every person has a duty to observe the first guideline. Barbaric responses such as war for dealing with conflict violates this precept. We render spiritual values meaningless if we justify the wilful killing and suffering of other people for the sake of the nation state. There is no more serious act in life than to take away another's life.

The Buddhist tradition pays respect to all forms of life, yet the majority of Buddhists eat animals, birds and fish. For all the inquiry in Buddhism into cause and effect, the majority of Buddhists ignore the relationship of the killing of animals to the eating of them. However, it is taking it too far to equate eating of flesh with responsibility for the killing of animals.

Buddhists frequently teach, practise, chant and pray to "save all sentient beings" but this determination has a hollow ring to it when

Buddhists are eating the animals they wish to save. Authentic vegetarians, that is those who refuse to eat animals, birds or fish under any circumstances, have long since recognized that the eating of meat raises questions of morality and health. Every year more than 600 million animals and birds are consumed on British tables. *The British Medical Journal* reported a twelve-year study revealing that vegetarians are 40% less likely to die of cancer than meat eaters. That means that the eating of meat not only kills animals but people as well. Like cigarettes, serious health warnings need to accompany all meat products.

The Buddha recognized two forms of relationship through this guideline. First, there are those who recognize the wisdom of a code and who observe it despite the circumstances. Secondly, there are those who are vulnerable to abuse of these guidelines owing to latent tendencies of mind and external pressures, actual and imagined. The Buddha endorsed concentration in daily life on five guidelines until they mattered more than the violent thinking of political ideologies and abusive forms of self-interest. He made it clear that those who ignore them, or encourage others to do so, reveal their lack of spiritual wisdom. "Conduct makes wisdom shine, wisdom makes conduct shine." These guidelines to spiritual practice offer support the welfare and protection of ourselves and each other. They are:

1. *I undertake the training to abstain from taking life.*
2. *I undertake the training to abstain from taking what is not given.*
3. *I undertake the training to abstain from sexual abuse.*
4. *I undertake the training to abstain from false speech.*
5. *I undertake the training to abstain from careless use of intoxicants.*

The Buddha regularly referred to these guidelines, reminding us how much we share common human experience and wishes. He said: "Consider oneself as similar to others and others as similar to oneself." If we were to take this single phrase of the Buddha to heart there would be no need to train ourselves to fulfil the guidelines of ethical living.

The Buddha spoke specifically of the importance of deep reflection when he said: "Here am I, appreciative of my life, not wanting to die, fond of pleasure and averse to pain. Suppose someone should deprive me of my life, it would not be a thing pleasing or delightful to me. If I in turn were to deprive him of his life, one appreciative of life, not wanting to die, one fond of pleasure and averse from pain, it would not be a thing pleasing or delightful to him. How could I inflict that upon another?"

There are five conditions which must be met to constitute violation of the first precept:

presence of a living being, human or animal,
knowledge that it is living,
intention or resolution to kill,
action which destroys life and
the resultant death.

All five conditions must be met for an action to break this guideline—it only requires the absence of one condition for the guideline to be protected.

The five guidelines are not exclusively concerned with the individual. They recognize that our "self" exists in relationship to other "selves." Our actions have consequences for ourselves and directly influence the course of action of others. In respecting the five precepts, we acknowledge that others matter and that our life is interconnected with others. In disregarding the precepts, we live in the darkness of ignorance with minds polluted through the forces of attraction, hatred and addiction. We then damage the very framework of human and environmental existence. Until this personal and national blindness is wisely resolved, suffering of immense magnitude will continue to arise.

In exploring these five guidelines the clever mind, with all its rationalizations for the situational response, finds endless cases of abuse:

1. *abortion, euthanasia*
2. *manipulation for profit, cheating*
3. *pornography, indiscriminate sex*
4. *lies for personal gain*
5. *irresponsible use of drugs and alcohol.*

Skirting these guidelines upholds self interest above wisdom and kindness. Respectful and sensitive insights into our values and decisions provides a safe environment. We obscure deep values intended to contribute to our welfare through excessive intellectual analysis of unresolved problems. At times we need rather to listen to ourselves, to others and beyond ourselves and others. Our awareness and application of values will determine the continuity or discontinuity of life on Earth.

Buddhist texts, like other Eastern religious texts, proclaim the doctrine that we reap what we sow. Human life is compared to a wave on the ocean, where the forces in the ocean give shape to the wave: until we discover depth in life, then the wave of our self rises and falls again, endlessly reborn into the world of appearances. Buffeted by circumstances we crash into other waves adversely affecting their welfare, our health and our feelings of security.

Wilful disregard for the five precepts invites a nightmare existence. The Buddha commented that even if there were no rebirth those who ignore these ethical guidelines would suffer in many ways in this life. They deny themselves genuine joy and happiness while dissatisfaction fills their days and nights. When we make other people's lives miserable we simultaneously make our own lives miserable, whether we realize it or not. To build a wise and contented environment as a community supports the total rhythm of our life and the lives of others.

Reflection on each of the precepts enables us to see the relationship of ourselves to our social environment. Some harmful actions occur owing to unresolved personal problems, including self-doubt and insecurity, rather than the deliberate intention to inflict suffering. Traditionally the judiciary has viewed punishment as the solution to the criminal mind; many judges have failed to see that the criminal mind is in acute need of self-understanding. In order for the mind to change, it first must be motivated; there must also be a clear intention to resolve problems and opportunity to cooperate with those skilled in the field of self-knowledge. Locking people up in prison is not a long-term solution to crime.

There are criminals, political extremists and certain military personnel who show the depth of evil in the world. When caught and convicted they show no remorse, contrition or expression of self-reproach. Such people show an unimaginable degree of hatred, which finds its outlet through desire, extreme political beliefs and inflicting the maximum suffering upon others, including innocent people. Their pervasive hate means they cannot listen to the voices of wisdom. Society must be safeguarded from such criminals and terrorists until they can acknowledge the horrendous results upon people and environment of their actions. Occasionally such people find their way into power treating the lives of people at home and abroad with utter contempt. Their pathological behaviour brings hell on Earth.

Prison life gives temporary protection to the public from those who abuse the five guidelines. For change to come it requires cooperation from the criminal mind, counselling skills and an appropriate environment. The mind adapts continuously to the environment it participates in (or was subjected to in the past). It is not so much "I think this way about..." but rather "the environment thinks" one way or the other. For example, men or women who are detained enter the prison environment where they mostly begin to think like other prisoners. When the atmosphere of the prison environment is hostile, the mind of the inmate concentrates itself on exclusive self interest, negativity towards others and dwelling in fantasies about life after prison. These reactions and projections become the common currency of prison life.

Worthwhile exceptions to identifying with environmental thinking occur through insight. This enables another type of expression, one that is ethical, creative and not tied to addictive self interest. We evolve through the motivation to understand ourselves and our relationship to our social or natural environment. The judiciary, politicians, prison staff and the public often overlook the hard truth that the current prison environment perpetuates problems, rather than resolving them. Overcrowding, daily hostility, poor living conditions and savage punishments make a person fit for crime. Prisons are training centres for further abuse of the five precepts thus perpetuating the criminal mind.

The decision to honour the second precept is no easy task. The most common crime is theft of private property. Numerous factors contribute to such behaviour, and greed, poverty, unemployment, alienation, desire, envy and insecurity may all be present. The law and its officers concentrate on this type of crime, namely theft from places of work, people's homes and cars. These crimes generate much distress for its victims. With so much public attention directed to these kinds of crime, it means that the criminal acts in the city, in the stock exchanges and the wheeling and dealing in the business world get largely ignored. Environmental justice hardly ranks in the considerations of the judiciary system. The police force is often out of its depth in dealing with such kinds of criminality and society deserves an additional police force to concentrate on crimes against the environment. This will need highly trained lawyers and police who understand intimately the methods of businesses to maximize profit at the expense of the environment and people's welfare at home and abroad. The judiciary and police must confront those who profit from human suffering; the greedily ambitious business and political world reduces the quality of life of all people and their environment.

The third precept concerns sexual behaviour. Buddhism has adopted a liberal attitude towards sexual experiences. Marriage consists of a social contract rather than a religious vow. Sexual experiences between adults before marriage are not regarded as acts of immorality. Practical and sensitive forms of birth control for women and men can express the wisdom of a discerning mind. Thus it adopts a different viewpoint from other major religions. Buddhists concern themselves with actions that generate suffering for themselves or others, not with religious moralizing. The danger of the Buddhist approach is that on occasions it has confused tolerance with permissiveness. Permissiveness generates suffering through lack of clarity and kindness.

The advertising industry relies heavily on the raw emotion of sex to promote products. Some advertisements symbolise a penis entering a vagina or show violent images linked with sex. Magazines, newspapers and television advertisements assault our minds everyday with subliminal messages. The impact of sexual exploitation in mass media upon an individual's unresolved sexual problems can help spark sexual abuse. Everyone is vulnerable to abuse, thus our commitment to nonabusive sexual behaviour is necessary to generate a zone of safety. Others will feel comfortable and assured in our presence. Men and women will be able to trust each other, and know they or their loved ones, including children, are safe from the infliction of sexual abuse.

In sexual issues, abortion is a sensitive and emotionally loaded social debate. The conflict between those who believe in the right of the pregnant woman to choose and those who believe in the right to life of the foetus generates mutual hostility, if not rage. As a result, conflicting views neither serve the genuine interests of the pregnant woman nor those of the foetus. Groups with vested interests have opted for confrontational standpoints with condemnation and abuse paramount. With or without termination suffering can ensue. We do not have to cling to either ideology of right to life or right to choose—whether at the beginning or end of life. But there certainly needs to be greater awareness that our society obsesses over *choices, sex, violence and death*.

It's no wonder that such extreme emotions and arguments emerge. Spirituality and psychotherapy have cultivated the rhetoric of "listening to ourselves." But in delicate life issues we may be listening to two conflicting inner voices, and the one we finally listen to may not be reliable. The voice within does not possess any unique existence, nor necessarily an intuition of the right thing to do. Our mind consists of the absorbed environment, past and present and latent tendencies, and none of these are reliable sources of insight.

Pregnant women sometimes exclude their partners from the decision making process, but also far too many men faced with an unwanted pregnancy wash their hands of the situation. Many men, who do not want to be fathers, express relief when their lover aborts. They will nod approvingly at the concept of the woman's individual right to make her own choice. It's a view which fits in very comfortably with the desires of men who do not wish to be held accountable for their actions. Apart from a few comforting words at the time, men often feel they don't have to concern themselves any further with emotional or material support. They are then able to get on with what they want—namely their own emotional and material self interest.

Differences around the concept of choice accelerate conflict. The more we dwell on the issue of choice the more likely it is that our conditioning determines the choice, but we attempt to disguise this by calling it independent choice. We react to external control through belief in personal choice, so highly prized in a neurotic culture. Yet it requires forgetting that external forces also define choices. Our so-called choices often ignore surrounding circumstances and the subsequent impact of our decisions on others and the environment.

A theme of spiritual life is expanding the heart's capacity to embrace the "world of 10,000 dharmas." Life and death are not personal issues, but community matters which ought to involve the cooperation and concern of all. It is this neglect of each other, the brutal aspects of individualism, that forces individuals into supporting the ideology of destruction. In unconscious terms the termination of life, or being an accessory to such an act, generally cuts off an area of ourselves that seeks expression. There are indeed circumstances where the duty of wisdom and kindness is to terminate the process of life. However, in our brutal society, these exceptions rapidly become the rule—often due to the lack of emotional and material support, thus the "choice" is no real choice at all.

Decisions might appear to be the sensible choice. But our social environment contributes as much as the individual to insensitive abortion, euthanasia, and other examples of terminating life. The attention needs to switch from fixed beliefs to the development and renewal of community so that we give care and support to each other. But the best interests of all concerned require spiritual realization beyond the immediate pressure of circumstances. We need to discover a liberating vision where skilful action emerges from our state of being, rather than our own conditioning, so that we generate no long term harm.

The fourth guideline concerns language. What we say and what we write influences the decisions of others. Trust and truth go hand in hand but we lie, condemn and dismiss others as we trumpet our views. Truth is rejected; getting our own way takes priority. We become cynical at the expense of Truth and trust, instead of developing so that what we speak what is true and useful. When wisdom underlines our words we are aware of the short and long term consequences of what we say or write. Then when we speak we will consider the time, place, person and subject matter skilfully, and be aware of the intentions that support what we say. What we say about a third person we can say face to face, or we observe noble silence rather than speak to cause harm or suffering to another.

The qualities of mind that give support to the observation and application of the five guidelines are awareness, vigilance and discipline. When under the influence of intoxicants all the guidelines are vulnerable to abuse. We are prone to believing that short term gain, or relief, is preferable to anything else. This hedonistic mentality sacrifices a vision and celebration of life that sees beyond short term interests. Addiction contributes significantly to violence, theft and paranoia. The alcohol and drug trade gradually erodes the welfare of the abusers life. Those that experience drug addiction often find initially they were unable to cope with inner problems or society and its regimented 9 to 5 values. Yet the medical profession often attempts to use other drugs to socialize the addict back to the kind of existence they already recoiled from. Medical professionals in the West ignore intensive herbal treatments to cure addiction. For some, drug problems occur as an escape from conventional life or inner torment but also as misguided attempts to contact spiritual experiences. Whatever the conditions for drug use and abuse, they contribute significantly to the violation of each one of the precepts for wise living.

If we look at the significance of the fifth precept in this way we see it needs to be expanded further to include abuse of toxic substances. There are major industries who maximize profits through manipulation of one or more of the ethical guidelines. The defence industry, market speculators, people with power, and alcohol, tobacco and pharmaceutical industries have much soul searching to do. The entertainment industry, whether video horror films or Bangkok pimps, also ignores these guidelines thus contributing to further fear, abuse and violence. Working in these trades isolate the mind from clarity and kindness so that harm and destruction can snowball from ourselves to others.

Respect for the five ethical guidelines ensures that others matter as much as we do. These five precepts serve as a foundation for community life, both locally and globally. We must relinquish forms of livelihood, behaviour and vested interests that violate our relationships with each other and the environment. Integrity, wisdom and kindness for all life reveal a wholeness of perception and values undiminished by the unsatisfactory forces of social or personal pressures.

We do not need to identify ourselves with some higher principle or universal ideology; our concern is with the arising of suffering and its cessation. The archaic belief in God as a loving father has lost all credibility with the extensive cruelty, hatred and self interest practised today. People cannot reconcile the paradox of a Loving God that permits such obscene behaviour or such environmental devastation from the forces of nature. Living with wisdom, as the Buddha commented, makes our values shine. The social environment matters because we belong to it. A considerate human being respects the five guidelines and sees how they contribute to a wholesome inner life and are indispensable features for environmental justice. But they are never to be taken up as religious dogma. By establishing the five guidelines through meditative awareness and insight, we have the capacity to enter deeply into experiences of authentic spiritual realization; to become self-righteous about the guidelines is an extreme reaction, a moralistic intolerance.

The Buddha compared painful existence to being struck by darts, which he named selfish desire, hate, delusion, pride, false views, indecision and regret. In examining the five guidelines we recognize that intentional abuse attracts unsatisfactory, if not fearful mind states. We may be haunted with regret for years as a result of our actions or carry on with hardened indifference. Those who wilfully bring harm to others through their actions suffer a harshness towards life that denies them the opportunity for joy, happiness and love. Who can reach them?

Environmental Ethics

The real mystical wonder is the noble power of transformation that frees the mind from the desire to harm. It is revealed in the capacity of the human spirit to transform abusive conditioning and a manipulated environment. We can discover an expansive sensory awareness that opens up our eyes and ears to another existence. Profound wisdom sees into the interconnection of social and natural environment and the self. This ensures noble ethical standards. Our liberating exploration dissolves the notion of an independent environment, not our efforts to uphold it or live in harmony with it. In the space of a few years we have rammed home the concept of the "environment" as though it had a genuine self existence, absolutely independent of our description. We imagine that we are talking about something that is out there worth keeping. Spiritual enlightenment sees through the dualistic world of self and environment, that neither self nor the environment has any inherent existence.

The realization of the Ultimate Nature of things transcends notions of self and environment. It is thoughtful and caring human beings who conceive an inherent value for the environment, and the protection of the environment is positive. But it is not the consummation of the spiritual life. To realize the Ultimate Truth is to end all ways of conceiving, to go beyond positive and negative conceptions. Green manifestos, campaigns and our deep ecology belong to the conceived realm, the world of relative truth. What matters is the embrace of the Inconceivable, the Non-Dual.

We have built up reputations and knowledge out of our environmental expertise, but this can tie us to our notions of and beliefs in the environment as a primary truth. This way of thinking says little about the extraordinary emptiness of these views, and even less about what truly matters. Those who deeply love the Truth have realized the cessation of name and form, self and other. In Liberation, there is this vast web of interconnection that effortlessly generates an ethical life.

Four Foundations
for Awareness

Meditate.
Do not delay, lest you regret it later.
This is our instruction.
The Buddha.

The Buddha concerned himself only with the enlightenment of humanity. This was his priority. Again and again, he told people to meditate diligently on the Here and Now. He urged people to stop in the midst of their personal circumstances and meditate to come to genuine insights and understanding. He urged us to go deeply into all forms of experience, including the relationship of our senses to sense objects, that is the environment, both social and natural. He exalted wisdom and compassion above cleverness and related the ethics of human behaviour to events in the environment. When there was greed, lust and perverted values the Buddha said "timely rain does not fall."

The Buddha said when rain does not come the crops become affected through various kinds of pests and plant diseases, and then people die from famine. Science has attributed famines, floods, earthquakes and epidemics exclusively to natural causes, but now we recognize that human behaviour is a significant factor. We make unwarranted intrusions into nature, devastating it, enslaving it to our demands, and by not relating to the world as a moment to moment partnership, we upset the balance. This intensifies the frequency, range and severity of environmental and human tragedies, and we reap the consequences of ravaging this delicate ecosystem. Some religions have tended to regard such tragedies as punishment by a supreme deity for immorality. If that were the case there might be more room for hope. We could collectively seek to say enough prayers to this wrathful deity to assuage His temper. We must remind ourselves that responsibility is the ability to respond. We ignore exploring the codependency of morality with personal, national and global priorities. Morality remains excluded from the political agenda.

Our generation and all future generations must confront the impact of circumstances, of cause and effect, known in the East as the law of karma. Karma means the unsatifactory influence of the past conditioning upon the living present. There is no wrathful deity to assuage, nor a loving God who will reward us for our devotion to Him. We created a God into whose hands we put all that we could not explain, and dispensed with this God when we believed science could explain everything. But we have also become tired of endless scientific explanations. Ignoring ethical concerns, we experiment with cellular life, blowing up atoms and interfering with DNA structures. Having made God, we play at being God. The Buddha endorsed moral awareness as a basis for inquiry. Science without morality is like a speeding car with a drunken driver. Upon the foundation of ethics, awareness and meditation, we perceive our interdependence with the environment and guard against harm and destruction.

Through our lack of meditative depth, we have undermined respect for life, demoralized other self sustaining cultures and provoked an ecocrisis. We live in spiritual darkness, lacking awareness of:

1. *physical life*
2. *feelings*
3. *states of mind*
4. *Dharma.*

The Buddha called upon spiritual seekers to focus on these four foundations for awareness.

The depth of our blindness reveals the arrogant notion that we think ourselves civilized, intelligent and at the forefront of evolution. Mesmerized by brain power in an industrialized world, we are absorbing ourselves, and the minds of the young, into an intolerably compressed world of mechanization and computerization. We have now progressed to the point where we are in danger, through genetic science, of risking the release of dangerous viruses, which can only further our collective self hatred and destructiveness. We have no love and appreciation of the Buddha's middle way for we have become creatures of extremes. We move deeper into a minefield of pleasure and pain. The fit will not survive because the fit are making themselves and the Earth unfit for existence. Abuse of the Earth is making us fit only for extinction.

Through our collective blindness, we have allowed ourselves to be led along the destructive "path of progress." We have refused to stop, be still, and be deeply aware of the Here and Now, of the living present. This willingness to be still, is meditation. To sit and be still, conscious and spiritually attentive in the immediacy of the

Here and Now is a beloved feature of the Buddha's teachings on spiritual practice. It is an indispensable feature for inner renewal and for the welfare of the environment. Without profound insights from a meditative silence within ourselves and our immediate sensory world we do not know which way to turn.

Similarly the walking, standing and reclining posture demand sustained meditation on the Here and Now. We stop to listen to life, the beauty of life, the cry of the neglected and the nature of existence revealed in the process. In this way we renew our relationship with ourselves, each other and with the earth and air. Moment to moment meditation is a key to awareness and direction. Whether alone or with others, indoors or outside, we can commit ourselves to the embrace of the Here and Now, to allow a full receptivity to our sense of interdependency. The demands upon us have numbed our deeper sensibilities so that we respond with mechanical obedience to the state, manufacturers and television. The voice that rebels against all this can contribute to a post-consumer culture, and a turning point in life. For some that may mean participating in a meditation retreat, or going to a monastery for spiritual renewal, or spending time alone in nature instead of with books and endless words. The Buddha regarded meditation as indispensable to the spiritual life. Meditation develops a depth of insight and uncovers resources for an active participation in compassionate action.

Such spiritual practices release us from clinging, aversion, and frantic and irrational lifestyles. When silence and stillness permeate our being through a depth of meditative awareness there is a renewal from within. This makes way for realization of our original nature—uncontaminated by inner and social conditioning. Exposure to a palpable silence, supported by enlightening teachings, acts in a profound way on consciousness while the impact of ego interests on consciousness and the environment stands out clearly, sometimes painfully. Awareness of clinging and aversion trigger a determination to examine the conditioned mind, that is the karma, and the associated harmful views that form unsatisfactory ways of relating to life. Such views inhibit creative and healing insights and the power to follow them through.

Moment to moment awareness—sustained mindfulness of body, feelings, mind states and dharma—touch deep places within us. Revelations and deep responses enable us to deal with the most challenging situations, and have access to a wealth of inner potential which we usually neglect. Those concerned with the fate of the Earth can find the potential for wisdom that dissolves despair and anxiety about the present or future. Depth of meditation integrates the inner with the depth of environmental life. Absorbed in silence, the human spirit finds itself receptive to insights and joy unobscured by personal and social pressure. Just as there is diversity of sentient life because nature has made space for it, we have to inquire deeply to find space within for the diversity of liberating and compassionate insights.

Evolution is not so much a matter of sophistication of language and technology; evolved human beings are not necessarily those with cerebral knowledge. They show their state of being through their presence in the world. It is the whole person that belongs to the nature of things, not the tiny part called the brain. The Buddha's teachings address the whole person—body, feelings, states of mind and relationship to the nature of things.

While other religions regard faith as the core response to the spiritual impulse, the Buddha designated awareness and meditation as the vital features. He made it clear that first we must become aware of a situation and understand the process; then once grounded in awareness we can act. Endless thoughts about a situation are no substitute for awareness and wisdom. Action follows an ethical awareness whereas thoughts may not bring an iota of change: they may even add to the problem. We become attached and caught up in beliefs about results, including the results of well-intentioned activities. In the Ultimate Nature of things, there are no such things as results. "Results" arise through thoughts isolating and interpreting aspects of the interdependent nature. We get lost in human belief systems, such as action and results, cause and effect.

In a talk by the Buddha called the **Four Foundations for Awareness**, he begins his talk with the statement:

"There is this one (only, direct, unique) way to purification of beings, for the destruction of suffering, for finding wisdom and realization of Nirvana—namely the Four Foundations for Awareness."

He said that the spiritual practitioner abides with energy, mindfulness and clear comprehension of the *body, feelings, states of mind* and *Dharma* (nature of things and spiritual teachings). Wholeheartedly bringing awareness to each of these four foundations supports transforming insight for "purification of beings, the cessation of suffering, the attainment of wisdom and the realization of Nirvana." The consequences of being out of touch with any of these means we identify with inner unsatisfactory forms of conditioning and social forces. We then become subservient to desires and pressures, overlooking the liberating significance of insightful meditations. The neglect of this significance leads to the secularization of the teachings of the essence of Buddhist meditation. There is a danger in the West of the Buddha's deep and expansive teachings becoming reduced to the practice of mindfulness in daily life.

The Buddha explains the significance of **"seeing the body in the body."** All too often we preoccupy ourselves with *seeing the outer body*, the body of appearance—size, shape, age, race, colour, gender, complexion. Ego feeds massively on such concerns. Large international industries exploit our vulnerability over our physical appearance around matters of gender, sexuality and the use of cosmetics. All depend upon the outer appearance. The suffering of people and environment entailed in these forms of clinging and aversion cuts across the face of existence. So the Buddha's statement in the Four Foundations for Awareness is a challenge to self-made preoccupations and their consequences, namely belief in the duality of self and other as the Ultimate Truth.

By connecting meditation to the bare experience of body—vibrations, sensations, pleasant and unpleasant experiences in the simple acts of sitting, walking, standing or reclining—we cut through ego investment in appearances and impressions. We become anchored in body nature, harmonized with the bare life force and realize the emptiness of grasping onto the outer body. In this realization there emerges a natural wisdom which acknowledges care for the *outer body*; clinging and aversion to it then has no meaning.

A Buddhist text says it is a rare and precious experience to be born a human being. It uses the analogy of a turtle which surfaces in the ocean once every thousand years, and by chance places its head in a yoke floating on the surface of the ocean. Of all the sentient creatures, human births are that rare in the universe. Taking so much for granted, including birth as a human being, we have come to live in a controlled environment with awareness of organic life relegated below identification with self-centredness. We often remain stuck with a dissatisfied image of our body; women and men must develop an awareness and understanding of the changing process of bodily life. The Buddha said we need to reflect on the process of *birth, ageing, pain and death*. Practising Buddhists in the East repeat these conditions of life, as a kind of mantra, to counteract the constructed self-image imposed by commercial interests and unresolved latent tendencies.

Practising the Buddha's teachings reveals to us that meditating on the body, feelings, states of mind and the Dharma opens our world. Organically, we begin to go deeper into the nature of things finding the opportunity to realize for ourselves the undivided Truth. The four foundations for awareness are the keys to liberating insights, and present a different spiritual message from many other religious beliefs.

The Buddha said one meditates on the body by sitting erect, mindfully experiencing the breathing process. One is aware when the in and out breath is long or short, and engages in this meditation until the breath becomes calm. One is aware of the arising of the breath and the passing (i.e. changes, impermanence) of the breath. One sees "there is the body" so that "awareness is established to the extent necessary for wisdom." He added "one abides clinging to nothing in the world." The Buddha further said that this meditative awareness is also established while "walking, standing, lying down, looking ahead or around, bending, stretching, eating drinking, chewing, tasting, answering the calls of nature, in speaking and in silence." He thus explained that such a mindfulness covers every activity repeating "to the extent necessary for wisdom. One dwells clinging to nothing."

One also reflects, he said, on the state of the body and the various unsatisfactory aspects of physical life. Included in his list are excrement, sweat, fat, spittle, snot and urine. One also reflects on the different stages of a corpse decomposing and on what will happen to our own bodies: the Buddha stated that the purpose of these reflections is to end clinging and aversion. For the Buddha the spiritual life could not be divorced from the truths of everyday existence. One reflects on the body as a composite of elements—earth, air, heat, water and space. The Buddha said that the body, like the environment, consists of the interplay of these elements. Knowing about these elements of the body reveals our deep, natural connection with the surrounding world, and questions the notions of a detached "I" not formed of the natural world.

Throughout history people have viewed these elements as the basic constituents of existence. Pollution and destruction of the environment means inflicting harm upon each of these elements. Damage to the Earth, global warming or the invasion of space violates the practice of mindfulness of the elements. Our culture invades and desecrates everything it can get its hands upon. Hindus attempted to declare sacred the Himalayas, the River Ganges and perceived the cow as holy to protect the elements and animal kingdom from the compulsive drive of human beings. But consumerism and industrialism are overrunning religious perceptions, even in India.

The Buddha turned his attention to feelings. One is aware when there is a pleasant feeling, unpleasant feeling or feeling neither pleasant nor unpleasant in the body or mind, whether a worldly or spiritual feeling. One sees the arising and passing of feeling. Again he repeats that "awareness is established to the extent necessary for wisdom. One dwells clinging to nothing."

What does it mean to see **"feelings in the feelings?"** For the sake of swelling the brain with knowledge, we can lose contact with our feeling life or get lost in outer feelings without touching a depth of feeling. We then experience superficial feelings about situations or interpret the world exclusively through thought. We divide the world into separate issues, including the environment, instead of experiencing and understanding interdependency. We neglect feelings which played such a vital role in our early formative years. Or, alternatively, we regard ourselves as the emotional type—a range of different emotions buffet our consciousness, so that we lack peace and contentment. To either neglect our deeper feelings or to be harassed by outer feelings or emotions prevents moment to moment meditation which acknowledges "feelings in the feelings."

To experience "feelings in the feelings" is to taste the subtlety of feelings, whether pleasant, unpleasant or neutral. It is to be aware of their influence on perceptions, thoughts, consciousness, speech and action. Touching the depth of feeling realizes an intimacy with the nature of things that is not accessible through thought. The Earth and oneself come closer and closer together, everything wondrously meets in the depth of feeling. I realize I do not belong to myself but I belong to the environment, and I realize that our environment does not belong to itself, but belongs to humanity. In that depth of feeling there is a dissolution of the differentiation of self and environment: a deathless dimension reveals itself.

The Buddha then turned his attention to the next foundation for awareness—states of mind. He pinpointed numerous states of mind.
"One is aware of the mind with selfish desire and aware of the mind without such desire,
with anger and without anger,
with blindness and without,
the tired, dull mind and without,
the restless mind and without,

the uplifted mind and the mind which is not uplifted,
the developed mind and the undeveloped mind,
the contemplative mind and the scattered mind,
the free mind and the unfree mind."

The Buddha told those committed to spiritual practice to watch the arising of these states of mind, their passing and arising and passing. One sees "there are mental states." "Awareness is established to the extent necessary for wisdom. One dwells clinging to nothing."

At times we exacerbate our painful states of mind instead of resolving them—without realizing it. When unsatisfactory states of mind occur we may enter the fight or flight syndrome. We take flight through alcohol, drugs, food, sleep, music, denial, or running away. Or we fight the mind state through rebellion, laying heavy judgements on ourselves, using will power to force our way through or directing blame outwards. Escaping from difficult states is postponement and fighting ourselves is the equivalent of trying to put a fire out with wood.

To **see the mind state in the mind state** is to bring a wholehearted attention to the situation, take an interest in its expression and to see what can be learnt from its manifestation. Insights into the package of feelings, thoughts, perceptions and intentions that form a mind state become possible. By seeing the "mind state in the mind state," we pass through the *outer mind* and beyond any oscillation between unsatisfactory and satisfactory mind states to those resources born of depth of meditation out of reach of conventional mind. Hot and cold mind states are forms of the *outer mind* upheld through clinging and aversion. Seeing deep into the heart of the mind reveals insights that decimate unsatisfactory patterns. We are then open to a receptivity not available in conditioned reactions of the outer mind.

Finally the Buddha turned his attention to the **Dharma**. No concept in the teachings is as wide in meaning as this one. It means:
1. *Ultimate Truth*
2. *teachings (concerned with enlightenment)*
3. *relative truth of things*
4. *all events of dependent arising, interconnection, subject-object existence, including sense objects and states of mind*
5. *duty (to live with wisdom and compassion).*

To **see the dharma in the dharma** is to go deeply into the teachings of spiritual enlightenment, into the nature of things. Intellectual understanding shows a superficial response which ties us to the *outer dharma*. To see the dharma in the dharma is to be transformed by the teachings, by the nature of things.

The Buddha was fond of classifying the teachings for ease in remembering themes. This is particularly apparent in this talk where he organizes his message into groups. Since he assumed the teachings would be preserved in an oral tradition for at least several generations, he felt that they would be most easily remembered in this form. To understand the depth of the teachings, the spiritual seeker should apply the heart of this talk to daily life, or focus wholeheartedly on any one of the themes to awaken the whole being.

When we speak of concern for the environment we mean the **sensory world**, that is the relation of eyes to sights, ears to sounds, nose to smells, tongue to taste and body to touch. The Buddha said the spiritual practitioner "knows well" this relationship and the mutual impact we have on the environment and the environment has upon us. The harm and pollution inflicted upon the environment through our actions enters back into our lives through all five sense doors. One is aware, says the Buddha, of the "fetter" or unsatisfactory condition that "arises dependent on eye and form, ear and sound" etc.

The Buddha spoke of **five hindrances** or unresolved problems, namely the range of selfish desire, anger, apathy, agitation and inner doubt and the absence of each of them. He said that one knows "there is sense desire" and one knows "there is no sense desire." He says that "one knows how this comes to be, and how it ends, and one knows its nonarising." He spoke in the same way of the other four hindrances.

He then referred to the dependent arising of the **five aggregates**, namely form, feelings, perceptions, thought formations, and consciousness. One meditates on the appearance and passing of these aggregates and the factors that contribute to their arising and passing. He spoke in the same way of senses—eyes, ears, nose, tongue, body and mind consciousness—and their content or object. The Buddha referred to contents of consciousness and contents of the five senses in the same way. The surrounding environment and the psychological environment can be regarded in a similar light.

Next he highlighted the **seven factors for awakening**, namely awareness, inquiry into the Dharma, energy, joy, serenity, meditative mindfulness and the deep peace of mind when one is equanimous to the cycle of events. The factors all express the joy of the spiritual life.

When the Buddha investigated the **Four Noble Truths**, he pinpointed what contributes to suffering. He repeated himself by saying that one sees the arising and passing of the Dharma. "Awareness sees there is the dharma. Awareness is established to the extent necessary for wisdom. One dwells clinging to nothing."

Finally the Buddha posited the question as to how much time one needs to apply the **Four Foundations for Awareness** to experience unshakeable realization of the Ultimate Truth, or the liberation in which there is hardly any falling back into patterns of blindness or conceit. Six years, five years, four years? he asked the men and women listening. He concluded with a message of immediacy in terms of liberating insights by saying this unexcelled liberation can be realized within a week. At the end of the talk the sangha were "delighted" with what the Buddha had said.

Noble Eightfold Path

One insight is that clinging is the basis of all suffering. The other is that by complete cooling and cessation of clinging no more suffering is produced.
The Buddha.

The Buddha (along with Marx) shares the rare distinction of unwittingly generating an "ism" after his name. If he were alive now, he would probably not appreciate the name "Buddhism." The Buddha would regard many contemporary forms of his teachings as far removed from the original liberating spirit of his message. In the Far East today, Buddhism is an endangered species as consumerism and political conflicts overwhelm religious faith. The Buddha may even have approved of the funeral of Buddhism, but not of its replacement with worship of the market economy and cultural decimation.

The Buddha is more like a physician than a prophet or philosopher. He does not ask us to believe or accept anything on faith, but offers instead a diagnosis of the nature of human life and a prescription to heal its ills that we are free to follow or reject. He abandoned the prospect of his privileged life and chose instead a life with an extraordinarily moderate living standard. He did so because of a profound commitment that emerged from his analysis of the human condition. The Buddha's compassionate concern meant that the welfare of people mattered far more to him than personal security. Fortunately, the Buddha lived in a cultured society where support and appreciation for spiritual seekers was widespread; hence society treated the Buddha and his companions with deference and hospitality.

The Buddha's main concern was liberation from the suffering and alienation which he perceived as common to all people's lives. He traced suffering to the ego's ignorance of the nature of the processes of life. He rejected religious approaches and the existence of a divine power, or God, who could help or could be turned to for consolation, assistance or empowerment. He said the way out of suffering lies through realizing the Truth and insight into the realm of conscious activity. He believed in the capacity of human beings to be happy, and that the way to deep happiness and contentment was experiencing liberation, inexpressible through language. He stressed the importance of community rather than individualism. Such views committed the Buddha to action. He would have warmly supported Marx's dictum on the pointlessness of philosophizing about the world when the task is to change it.

The Buddha pointed the way for people to change the world by changing their responses to it, and their experience of it. By changing their assumptions, beliefs, values and attitudes they could meet the world's suffering. He said that full release from suffering is *only* through realization of the ultimate nature of things. It is insights from the realization of the sublime Emptiness of birth, change and death, mind and matter, that distinguishes the Buddha's message from any political ideology. The Buddha's teachings primarily focus inwardly which logically result in nonviolence and compassion.

The Buddha spent his life living his enlightenment and the Way, called the Noble Eightfold Path, teaching all who came to him. The Buddha summarized his teachings as the Four Noble Truths. According to the first, to live in a "normal" or conventional unenlightened consciousness is to suffer or abide in unsatisfactoriness. However, the message of the next three truths is that this is not inevitable, nor must we wait for any sort of afterlife to find genuine happiness. The second noble truth is that suffering has definite origins, namely ignorance of external and internal factors. The Buddha rejected the idea that we generate and create our own suffering entirely by ourselves: this would deny the social, economic, political and environmental factors that influence individuals. But he also denied that external factors are exclusively responsible for the unsatisfactory aspects of the human condition, for this would deny the capacity of people to change inner factors—the basic assumptions, values, beliefs, and attitudes—that shape our experience of the world. Adopting the position of "the middle way" the Buddha developed his doctrine of dependent arising:

"When this is, that comes to be
With the arising of this, that arises
When this is not that does not come to be,
With the cessation of this, that ceases to be."

To understand through observation, meditative awareness, reflection, dialogue and action, the nature of dependent arising of suffering—or of joy, or of any other feeling, experience or thing for that matter—is the key to understanding the teaching of the Buddha. "One who sees the Dharma sees dependent arising," he said.

According to the Buddha, people become trapped in conditioned pursuits and the thirst for possessions, privilege, property and profit. This state of mind permeates society and creates the breeding ground for envy, competitiveness and violence. The result of such desire is not security—either for individuals, society or the Earth. Clinging to assumptions accompanies thirsting for one thing after another. Beliefs confirm people in their experience of suffering and alienate them from each other. This leads us into ideas and actions that wreak untold pain upon the world.

The way to liberation from suffering lies not in belief in a God, prayer or sacred book but in ethics, awareness and wisdom. The first step of the Eightfold Path consist of right understanding of the factors that contribute to suffering. The implication is that if we explore the spiritual life the result becomes a community living with integrity and wisdom.

The Eightfold Path that ends suffering is:
1. *Right Understanding: of suffering, its causes, its extinction and the way to end suffering*
2. *Right Thought (or Attitude): thought free from exploitation, oppression, cruelty and abuse*
3. *Right Speech: speech which abstains from lying, backbiting, harsh language, gossip and vain talk*
4. *Right Action: not killing, stealing, engaging in sexual abuse, lying or abuse of alcohol or drug*
5. *Right Livelihood: not dealing in arms, slavery, meat or poison*
6. *Right Effort: to avoid or overcome what is unwholesome and unhealthy and develop and maintain what is wholesome and healthy*
7. *Right Awareness: of body, feelings, states of mind and the nature of things*
8. *Right Samadhi: depths of meditation free from unhealthy states of mind.*

The Buddha's Noble Eightfold Path was his prescription not only for the individual but also for society. He urged us to commit ourselves to exploring each factor of the Path because, to ensure a sustainable world founded in wisdom, each link must be attended to. To ignore or reject any of these factors contributes to suffering in ourselves and in the world. Each link challenges the unsatisfactory nature of human existence whether selfishness, aggression, confusion or fear. The willingness to cultivate each link turns consciousness away from egocentred activities towards a life of liberating awareness, insight and selfless action.

The Noble Eightfold Path embodies respects for life and pro-

vides the opportunity to live with integrity. By not identifying ourselves with the Buddha we pay respect to his teachings, which
refute conventional religious beliefs. Spiritual life is inseparable
from direct penetration into our vulnerable existence. He said:
"Free from pain and torture is this path, free from groaning and suffering. This is the path for the purity of insight. If you follow this
path you will put an end to suffering. Give ear, then, for the Deathless is found. So act! You will in no long time make known (the
Deathless) to yourself and realize."

A source of suffering, or alienation, lies in the notion of self—
the erroneous notion that the self, ego or I, is the essence of a person,
or exists independently. For it is from this notion of inherent self
existence that the selfish desires that lead to suffering arise. The privatization of "self" leads to an egocentric lifestyle at the expense
of communal and global awareness. The Buddha reminds us that
notions of self or ego, are dependently arising, and that awareness
of the relative appearance of "self" opens the way to the last six
steps of the Eightfold Path. Each step represents a different aspect
of the process of breaking through ego as the determinant of our
thoughts, feelings and actions.

The steps focus both outwardly, on our relationships with the
external world placing attention on our speech, actions and means
of livelihood and inwardly on effort, awareness and deep meditation. For example, if determined to end suffering, we will consider
carefully what trade, profession or vocation to pursue or abandon.
Happiness arises when our work accords with social harmony and
justice, more specifically, when it is lawful, nonharmful and free
from blameworthy acts.

As a result the Buddha addressed the issue of right livelihood
as one of the key factors in adopting the Eightfold Path. He expressed clearly the kinds of livelihood which are unacceptable for
those who wish to live in harmony with themselves, others and nature. He regarded dealing in arms, animals for slaughter, slavery,
intoxicants, poisons and exploiting children or adults as unacceptable. The Buddha warned people, including rulers, of the dangers
of "luxurious living," "self indulgence" and "intoxication with authority." "If rulers do not live according to the teachings (Dharma)
then the whole country suffers." There is a responsibility, he said,
to provide everyone in the community with four basic requisites—
food, clothing, a home and medical care.

The result of breaking through egotistical activities and attitudes
fills us with an awareness of the interdependence of life. From this

follows a profound compassion, fellow feeling for everyone and everything else. Thus the Buddha's teachings are essentially ecological, egalitarian, nonviolent, antimaterialistic and committed to peace, justice and ultimate realization. It is no wonder that a wide range of people acknowledge the supportive voice of the Buddha in their lives.

Right Livelihood and the Farmer

The thirst for profit enters every conceivable area of human activity including the once noble livelihood of farming. Numerous farmers in the western world want to maximize production through using the most efficient machinery available to them. They hardly lay hands on the land through spending countless hours in tractors and combine harvesters, soundproofed through ear plugs or head phones. They have become servants of political bureaucrats, the agribusiness and chemical industries who persuade them to use chemicals on the land to compete with other farmers. Thus farmers endanger their health, the health of the land and the public. Factory farms treat farm animals and birds with the same roughness as inanimate products crammed together when efficiency of production matters more than care and compassion. Not surprisingly the incidence of depression among farmers is high. Alienation, suffering and their causes are themes which the Buddha returned to again and again.

Numerous Western farmers have earned themselves a reputation for claiming their survival is at stake when they are only referring to a dip in profits. Their livelihood has become a source of much public criticism because the public sees such displays of wealth in the farming community. Large farms have been subsidized, farmers have been told to stop thinking of their farms as a way of life and to be business minded adopting models of efficiency and competition. Farmers have responded to the desire of the agricultural lobby by making their farms highly intensive. They invested much money, went into debt, intending to make substantial profits through intensive use of chemicals and artificial substances to boost output. Farmers wanted to grow fat off the land. Some were successful, some failed but many small farmers, who loved their work, were driven off the land.

Often the result of ambitious efforts to maximize production was over production, food mountains, endless waste through storage and an utterly confused agricultural policy. Farmers have been forced to go cap in hand to banks and government. No wonder they became so depressed about whether or not they would lose their land and livelihood. The same family had often farmed the same piece of land for a dozen generations or more. They had weathered many storms, but the desire to maximize production and profit brought them to bankruptcy, or its edge.

Accepting the urging of governments, the bureaucrats and the agrichemical business to fashion intensive farms has left more and more farmers on the razor's edge of survival. The big farmers, who are always looking to increase returns by increasing acreage, buy up the land of the small farmers who are desperate to sell. The licence for greed, no matter how much the agribusiness rationalizes it, is harmful in the short and long term since it generates unnecessary suffering and hardship. Right Livelihood, the fifth link of the Eightfold Path, thus not only includes the type of work, but also the motivations and intentions that support the work.

Environmental degradation threatens small farmers world wide. The loss of land in the last 20 years is equivalent to the amount of land devoted to crops in India. Deserts are expanding into once fertile land. Tree coverage of the Earth has diminished in 20 years by roughly the size of the USA east of the Mississippi River. While about 2 billion people have been added to the Earth since 1970— more than the world's population in 1900—thousands of plants and animal species are disappearing. The Earth is in an energy crisis through the desire of Western politicians and the corporate world expanding their energy demands to increase production and to keep consumers on the treadmill of desire. Consumers appear to have little real idea of the widespread suffering generated by current economic policies. How on Earth are they going to find out?

Once the Buddha was staying among the Magadhans near South Hill at a village of brahmins, the highest caste, at Ekanala. The equivalent in England would be visiting the landed gentry who like to wear tweed coats and drive Range Rovers. The Buddha stopped to observe Bharadvaja, a wealthy farmer who had 500 ploughs in yoke during sowing time. The Buddha went to the man for alms. The farmer turned to the Buddha and remarked contemptuously: "I plough and I sow and so I eat. If you ploughed and sowed you could eat too."

The Buddha, with his shaved head, bare feet and worn cloth, said: "I too plough and sow and then I eat."

The farmer said: "I can't see your plough or your oxen."

The Buddha replied: "Trust is my seed, self control is my rein; wisdom is my plough, modesty is my pole; mind is the strap and awareness my goad." The Buddha described himself as well guarded in his actions and speech and moderate in his diet. Truth destroys the weeds and pollutants of the mind, he told the farmer, and such a person experiences security through freedom from suffering. This kind of ploughing sets a person free.

Touched by the depth of wisdom of the Buddha and realizing that there was another dimension to farming, Bharadvaja offered sweet rice milk in a large copper bowl to the Buddha.

The Buddha on religion:

The Buddha's critique of traditional religion and his atheism is evident. He would not have been impressed with a farmer raising his hands to heaven for manna to fall. He told people not to rely upon traditional religious texts and practices, even if society had for a long time unquestioningly followed them. The Buddha insisted that essentially we are all alike. "All people tremble at punishment; all people fear death. Likening oneself to others, one should neither slay nor cause to slay." The Buddha also denied the existence of a Creator who loves his creation. He warned that speculating about the beginning or end of the world would contribute nothing to efforts to end suffering, it might even lead to "mental derangement." He considered metaphysical speculation to be irrelevant to the pressing spiritual and existential problems of life on Earth. He focused on the Noble Eightfold Path as the true expression of the spiritual life, rather than adherence to a set of unworldly beliefs.

Once people were grounded in the Path, the Buddha encouraged spiritual practitioners to look deeper into the nature of the Here and Now. The religious thought of the Buddha's time elevated the Self to a transcendent metaphysical entity, spelled in English with a capital "S" Such teaching led to a strong hierarchical view in which the highest caste, the Brahmins, claimed to have realized the Self as one with God (Brahman) while those of lower caste could have no hope of anything of the sort. He exploded the notion that the "self" has any inherent existence. He classified the constituents of a human into five aggregates: body, feelings, perceptions, thought formations, and consciousness. Subject to dependent arising, change and transformation none of these can be considered essential or real in any metaphysical sense. According to the Buddha there is neither inherent substance in the notion of self, I, my, ego nor inherent existence in any of the five aggregates of body, feelings, perceptions, thoughts and consciousness. He left no room for such beliefs, infatuation with self interest or for an unexamined life filled with egotistical and divisive attitudes and activities. He dismissed the worship of and devotion to saviours, gurus, religious leaders and other public figures. He reminded everyone that a human being consists of five aggregates.

The Buddha exhorted people to look into the factors that contribute to the dependent arising of conditions, including the strength and frequency of "I" and "my" and to take a life-long resolve to change the unsatisfactory factors. The Buddha explored the patterns of ignorance, desire, self-cherishing and aggression. He did not expect individuals to sort out all issues on their own, but rather highlighted collective responsibility and action. He formed the sangha—a spiritual community inviting everyone to take refuge in it. The sangha of homeless ones, known as bhikkhus and bhikkhunis, was classless and democratic, making decisions through wise attention.

On his death bed, the Buddha refused to appoint a successor. He also refuted any tendency among followers of his teachings to make him into an object of veneration. He perceived that any such religious endeavour only reinforced the myth of an independent self existence. Awareness and insight into the nature of existence are the keys to salvation, a salvation that can be experienced in this life. The sangha must find out what is beneficial and what is harmful for themselves and for society. Those in the sangha who merely have faith in him, the Buddha stressed, may experience satisfaction but will not discover liberation. The Eightfold Path thus serves as an unshakeable foundation for spiritual practices and as a springboard into the depths of realization.

Through such statements the Buddha shifted the focus of attention from the charismatic religious leader to the practical day to day application of the Noble Eightfold Path. Sacred books and holy teachers were of no concern in the Buddha's message. Devotion to a guru or saviour was not the measure of commitment to the spiritual life. There were two considerations; realization of Nirvana in the midst of life and living in accordance with the Path. The former reveals the latter and the latter reveals the former. The teachings expressed a radical departure from conventional notions of religion which depended almost entirely upon faith and devotion for survival.

Every factor of the Eightfold Path is significant for those who wish to lead the spiritual life. They touch upon every aspect of our existence, every expression of body, speech and mind. Instead of a religious life expressed as worship, the Buddha spoke of a spiritual life committed to bringing fullness of awareness to life experience. Recognizing the significance of what he was pointing towards, spiritual seekers for generations have felt a profound relief at not having to surrender or devote themselves to a religious authority. The Buddha told followers of the teachings that he was their friend not their Guru, discouraging an adolescent devotion to himself as a religious leader. He insisted that spiritual seekers relate to him as adults to an adult.

Spiritual practitioners, wisely, continue to place the emphasis on his teachings rather than on the Buddha himself. This approach places the various expressions of Buddhism, and Buddha worship, firmly in its place. Exploration of the spiritual life, the support of his teachings as a guide and the transformation of consciousness, pay genuine respect to the Buddha. Worship of his name distracts from the teachings. The Buddha regarded teachers as a distraction to the teachings. In an uncompromising manner, he pointed out that spiritual insights included piercing through notions of personality, the self and fixations about authority so the teachings could reach fulfilment for humanity. Dharma teachers today are fond of telling their students: "Become a buddha not a Buddhist." Siddhartha Gautama, a Buddha, would approve of such an exhortation.

The Social Conscience
of the Buddha

He does not falter when he comes before a high assembly;
He does not lose his thread of speech,
Unhesitatingly, he speaks out.
The Buddha.

At the time of the Buddha, India consisted of numerous small kingdoms which had developed an advanced culture of philosophy,
theology, psychology and social awareness. Its political, economic
and religious tradition had both breadth and depth. Organized
trade was commonplace; the iron deposits in the region of the Sakya
kingdom provided the raw materials for tools. Society used money
to purchase goods and valued precious metals. These kingdoms
were self supporting under the influence of the lord of the region.
The wealthy built their homes of baked brick, and there were extensive rice paddies, livestock, fruits and vegetables. Tropical forests, woods and vegetation featured in the countryside while in
several cities and towns, trade took place with a commercial infrastructure. There were also accounts of social problems from gambling to mugging associated with city life. The main towns or cities
in this region of North India were Kapilavatthu, Rajgir, Savatthi,
Kosambi, and Varanasi.

Brahmin priests in cities, towns and villages dominated religious life. Writing was used mostly for Vedic texts, observation of
laws and for keeping accounts. This increased the population's reliance on the Brahmins who claimed their authority by birth, and
from their religious tradition, both oral and written. Brahmins were
critical of town dwellers probably due to their diminishing influence in the towns. As urban dwellers became more involved in production and distribution they turned their backs on religion.

It is clear from the texts that the Buddha spent his time teaching
in cities as well as travelling on foot in rural areas. He invited people
to drop out of the activities of production and reproduction to become homeless. Householders, who committed themselves to the
dharma life, had to examine the quality of their daily lives. The Buddha insisted they had to change their livelihood if their work con-

tributed to the suffering and harm of themselves and society.

This approach flew directly in the face of the Brahmin tradition which valued the social order of the caste system, sharing some parallels with the British class structure. The Buddha and the sangha renounced caste so his teachings were an ongoing threat to the orderly system of caste and ritual attendance at religious services and sacrifices. Despite a relative degree of sophistication in society, the class structure confined people to their particular domains, Brahmins especially considered it unthinkable to change their particular caste. Having no regard for the privilege of birth, the Buddha sought to dissolve the social barriers of a rigid system which did not allow social mobility. In the 20th century in Britain and other Western countries, the underclass—namely the destitute, homeless and the unemployed on the edge of survival—have no real opportunity to join the middle classes. The working class have no chance of associating with the upper class of royalty, the titled, landed gentry, the judiciary and city financiers. In that respect nothing much has changed in India in 2500 years or in Britain in 2000 years. It is the exception in both countries when any person moves between the underclass, low paid working class to the middle and upper classes. Economic segregation dominates the social outlook.

When the Buddha addressed privileged and well-educated people, he told them that no matter what their social status, they led a "vulgar" life if they devoted themselves to pursuing pleasure and profit. Businessmen and women tend to use profits for their own pleasure and for the pleasure and advancement of close family members. This keeps wealth within the hands of a privileged few. For those who could not realize liberation in the Here and Now, he advocated daily spiritual "practice" as a way to transform the lifestyle, live with integrity and become receptive to the joy of an enlightened life. He explained in detail the practices of the middle way lying between the extremes of selfishness and self rejection.

The Buddha also questioned the unwritten social agreement between the clergy of Brahmins and laypeople. The priests claimed to have sacred knowledge, to have a significant relationship to the divine and claimed authority from their religious tradition and the transcendent. The Buddha regarded these beliefs as social myths, and dismissed such claims. He said those who engaged in genuine spiritual practices had given up their identity with the class structure and all notions of being born special.

He was not explicitly critical of the role of a lord or king as the Buddha did not see these as inherently damaging the social structure. But the actions and attitudes of the person in such a powerful position mattered. He took this to an even more subtle level and said that intentions behind the actions were significant, so intentions must be brought into spiritual awareness. Yet the Buddha did not endorse privilege. He talked of the danger of indulging in conversations about "kings, thieves, ministers for war, politicians and terrorists." By lumping kings with others known for their desire to control or exploit he indicated concern about misuse of these roles and their power.

The Buddha also switched attention away from roles to the underlying psychological motives that influence behaviour. The Buddha did not create a religion for personal salvation, but worked for liberation and justice for all. He campaigned for the welfare of everybody, including animals and the environment. By giving equal priority to all, the Buddha destabilized the caste system. He wanted to replace it with people working together as a community to end suffering, establish the Eightfold Path and realize the Truth. He dismissed privileges born of birth, or desire or both.

The Buddha specified that the issue of right livelihood is the most important element causing social upheavals or revolutions. In the Kutadanta Sutta, the Buddha proposed an economic policy for the primary purpose of eliminating social problems. He warned rulers on seven occasions of the dangerous consequences of maldistribution of wealth and said the duty of government is preventing poverty. He said that the institution of private property and family came into existence initially with the desire to accumulate food for personal use.

In a healthy society, leaders act as wise judges that the people designate to ensure fairness and justice. His willingness to ascribe social responsibilities to those with powerful positions in society, his questioning of authority, and his emphasis on deep spiritual practice expressed his commitment to social change. He welcomed those willing to abandon their involvement in the forces of production and reproduction. He perceived the danger of staying within a small circle of social or class contacts where the mind easily becomes habituated into a narrow, rigid, structure so the community is interconnected and mutually supportive of the spiritual life. The Buddha said that "depending on the oil and wick does the light of the lamp burn; it is neither in the one nor in the other nor anything in itself; phenomena are likewise."

In India fixed social patterns and enclosed family units meant that people moved almost exclusively within the same circles throughout their lives. This compares similarly with the nuclear family and fixed working week of today, where figures show that the vast majority of people have only one or two close friends in whom to confide their deepest thoughts. For those who felt restricted by this social structure the Buddha made available an alternative way of living with spiritual practices and deep communication at the heart of community life. He, himself, was born into a noble family, the transformation of his life from nobility to simplicity has been a source of inspiration for centuries. His disregard for privilege aroused much interest among wealthy social groups of the time. He preferred to wear cast off clothes, but more importantly, he received affection and respect from the poor for he lived as a homeless, penniless wanderer.

The Buddha spoke to the business community, advising them to work within strict ethical guidelines, saying the consequences of ignoring such considerations would be widespread suffering. He said those who truly consider others will prosper. Profit from business must contribute to the welfare of employees, relatives, friends, the people and organizations working for the welfare of others. He said that profit had no value if it led to the use of "alcohol, gambling, idleness and foolish company."

The Buddha dismissed all notions of a powerful and omniscient God regarding God as the stuff of superstition. He directed his attention to the realization of Truth rather than the perpetuation of self-serving beliefs. As recorded in the Agganna Sutta, the Buddha traced the formative influences of society, including its religious and political institutions, without reference to a supernatural agency. He replaced the issue of God as the central matter of spiritual life with the issue of suffering and its resolution. He refuted notions of divine intervention as well as claims of God-given roles and responsibilities for religious or political leaders. He treated such claims with disdain and treated them as projections of mind.

The Buddha classified human beings into two categories—householders and voluntary homeless ones who support each other. Householders are a part of society with the duty to engage in noble forms of livelihood. Homeless ones are those not engaged in producing either children or goods but dedicate themselves to spiritual realization and service for all. Both groups must inquire deeply into their lives and their social and natural environment. Homeless ones maximize time to share their wisdom wherever they have contact with people. The combination of these two wings of society, interconnected through awareness and service, contributes to the welfare, happiness and wisdom of society.

Those engaged in spiritual practice must examine the methods they employ to make profit and the subsequent use of profit. The Buddha referred to six groups of people, comparing them to the six directions. All of whom deserve to be beneficiaries of profit. The East stands for parents, West for partners, children and relatives, the South for teachers, the North for friends and companions. The Nadir stands for employees, and Zenith for those concerned with spiritual values and service. Duty, one expression of the Dharma life, was not to caste, family or country but to all those in need whether related through blood or not. Ignoring this Dharma took the meaning out of the spiritual life. The image of the four cardinal points, nadir and zenith served as a powerful reminder to those who made profits from business to support as many as possible. For the Buddha community took priority over family.

The Buddha contacted the kings and lords of the various regions. On one occasion the Buddha met with a Brahmin King in a village called Khanumata in Magadha. Law and order was breaking down in the region so a rich Brahmin named Kutadanta planned a major animal sacrifice hoping to quell the violence. Visiting the area, the Buddha related a story from the past. He told of the time when the country of King Mahavijita was "beset with thieves, towns and villages were plundered by gangs of armed robbers and the countryside was infested with terrorists."

Wisely, the religious advisor of King Mahavijita said that to increase the length of imprisonment, confiscate goods, make threats, banish or execute criminals would not bring the situation under control. The break down of law and order would not end through those means. The religious adviser told the King that, if he wanted to restore law and order so the people of his country could live in safety, he had to do three things. First, he had to distribute necessities to all those in need; secondly, he had to assist all those living on the financial edge in the business community; and, thirdly, he had to assign people a decent living wage. The adviser told the king that if he followed his advice peace would be restored and joy also would be felt in the hearts of his subjects. He said people would play with their children and houses would not need to be locked up. The Buddha then advised the Magadha people to adopt the same measures.

In another talk the Buddha recalled a region where ethical values declined. There was less and less regard for nonviolence. Stealing, sexual abuse, lying, alcohol and drug abuse became the norm. So said the king and his ministers came together to discuss the situation. They decided to increase the size of the police force to guard property. The Buddha criticized this decision, saying the King failed to give financial support and homes to the underclass who lived in poverty. The story continued that one thief told the King that he stole because he and his family had nothing to live on. Instead of imprisoning him, the King provided him with his needs plus enough for the thief to share with the poor and make offerings to priests and those committed to spiritual values.

But then another thief appeared expecting the same reward. The king thought that if he gave support to every thief thefts would increase even more. So he told the police to tie the man up, shave his head and publicly execute him. The Buddha said poverty stricken people began to follow the example of the king when they caught thieves. So the number of murders increased. The Buddha said: "Thus from not giving support to the needy poverty became rife. From poverty came theft. From the increase in theft came the increase in weapons. From the increase in weapons came the increase in the taking of life." He concluded that when a situation has deteriorated to such a degree then "fierce enmity will prevail one for another, fierce hatred, fierce anger and thoughts of killing, mother against child and child against mother, father against child and child against father, brother against brother, brother against sister and so on."

Here the Buddha does not attribute the causes of suffering to personal evil or the work of the devil but to economic factors and the relationship of the political ruler to the people. By not doing anything to relieve poverty the King allowed social relationships to deteriorate so that people lived in violence and fear. The Buddha said the King must relieve the suffering of the poor to stop the disintegration of society. The Buddha said that King Sankha, who inherited his palace from King Maha-Panada, listened. He gave the palace away to beggars, the unemployed and people of spiritual practice. The King's loving kindness for his subjects served as an example for them to do the same, and he thus restored peace and justice to the land.

On another occasion, the Buddha told a mythological story about the beginning of human existence. Two people living the Dharma life told the Buddha that Brahmins ridiculed them for leaving the caste system. The Buddha responded with a story that at the beginning of time life was an original blessing with beings "feeding on delight." They were "luminous and living gloriously."

He said the Earth looked like the skin of warm milk rich in colour, smell and was sweet like the taste of pure wild honey.

One person tasted the delightful Earth and began to feed on it and others followed in the same way. As greed took hold of them, they began to lose their luminosity and their bodies became much more coarse. Differences in appearance began to develop between them; they were considered handsome, beautiful or ugly. They began to compare themselves with each other. They became arrogant and conceited about their looks, the beautiful Earth began to change. As the beautiful Earth began to change so did human beings until the differences between people became even more coarse. He said their bodies began to "burn with lust." As their bodies became coarser people began to build dwellings and made love under covers. Cow dung was thrown at those who made love outdoors.

As time went by people become even more gross. The Earth was now producing rice as the primary food; they had long since stopped feeding on delight, so people began to store it up. They divided the land with boundaries. One farmer would rob another farm of its piece of land and then stones, sticks and rocks of the land would be used for violent retaliation. The Buddha said this is the origin of today's society. Initially there was the original blessing, then came contact, pleasant feelings, desire, greed, theft, violence, lying and punishment.

As a result, certain people gained power. They began to rule, censure other people and establish laws. In exchange the leader received a share of the rice. Thus kings, ministers and the military took control. A minority went to live on the edge of towns, living in huts and meditating to overcome greed and aggression. The Buddha criticized those who instead studied religious texts but did not meditate. He said they were not followers of his teachings. He said the origin of the Brahmins, the priestly class, was those who studied and neglected meditation. Such priests revealed the decline of the spiritual life while conspiring with the powerful to implement and uphold the hierarchy of privileges. As on other occasions, he tells a story to make a point.

The Buddha showed through the story that the class system is born from selfishness and leads to rich and powerful rulers. Secondly, though the priests wish to convey the impression they are born from God, they are a product of employment by wealthy benefactors. Throughout history, the ordained clergy, East or West, has rarely challenged power and privilege. The members of the Establishment gained a certain self satisfaction from attending religious services and from spending time in the company of religious leaders. This has helped to give a sort of legitimacy to their privileges, priests likewise have taken comfort in the belief they are bringing God's word to the upper classes, imagining they are influencing the corridors of power. Thus the relationship between the powerful and the priests ensures continuity of the status quo. The Buddha's story of the journey from purity to corruption was a sharp criticism of these privileged elites.

The homeless sangha, initiated by the Buddha, was a constant reminder to the rich and powerful of their excessive lifestyle. The sangha lived with the minimal basic items, which they shared to dissolve further the notion of private property. They expressed their wealth as health, happiness and the awakened mind. When they visited wealthy patrons, the Buddha told them not to sit in a seat at a lower level than the privileged and insisted that dignity rests with the servants of the Dharma not with the servants of the ego.

The social conscience of the Buddha was an integral part of his teachings. However, as Buddhism developed through the centuries, devotion took hold of the hearts and minds of millions at the expense of the quest for Truth, justice and an active compassion. But currently there is a spiritual renaissance taking place in Buddhism amidst religious decadence, as individuals and organizations realize they can apply the Buddha's teachings to personal, social and global situations.

For example, the Dalai Lama has received the Nobel Prize Peace. Another Nobel Prize winner, Aung San Suu Kyi, has been incarcerated in her home in Burma since 1989 by the military dictators. She spends hours daily engaged in insight meditation (vipassana) and reflection on the Buddha's teachings. Three members of the international board of the Buddhist Peace Fellowship—Ven. Thich Nhat Hahn from Vietnam, Sulak Sivaraksa, the human rights lawyer and activist from Thailand and the Ven Maha Ghosananda, the Supreme Patriarch of Kampuchea—have been nominated for the Nobel Prize. Ven. Ghosananda has led peace pilgrimages right across Kampuchea to unite warring factions. Another member of the same board and international award winner Dr. Aryaratna of Sri Lanka, directs the world's largest village self-help project involving thousands of villages. He has received numerous threats to his life as the civil war in Sri Lanka continues.

One Thai Buddhist commentator wrote: "It is impossible to look at the roles of monks in contemporary Thailand without looking at the life and works of Ajahn Buddhadasa (1906–1993) whose six decades of religious reform has laid out a common conceptual framework and language for 20th century Thais to work in. His influence is evident among the monks active in community development and conservation in the wake of increasing rural poverty and environmental degradation." Ajahn Buddhadasa lived for more than 60 years in the forest giving profound Dharma teachings while rejecting the religion of worship.

Despite the massive exploitation of Thailand at every level, there is also a minor spiritual renaissance occurring in Thai Buddhism, the country with the highest concentration of practising Buddhists in the world. One monk in Surin province teaches insight meditation retreats to villagers leading them to question greed and aggression. Other monks have set up village rice banks, communal rice farming, saving schemes and food cooperatives. Village people are tackling their debts to become self sufficient. One monk in Nakorn Rachasima opened a buffalo bank. In Chaiyaphum a monk began a nursery and started reforestation; one monk ordains trees to protect them from the loggers.

The West must learn to adopt such methods used in other cultures for the welfare of the individual, community and nation. In a Thai monastery, Ajahn Chamroon of Wat Tharm Krabork Monastery, Saraburi and a team of co-workers have cured more than 50,000 drug addicts both Thais and foreigners, through a ten-day intensive purification process of traditional herbal medicine and meditation. Sadly, the patronizing attitude from colonial times still dominates Western perceptions of other cultures so the proven Thai method of ending heroin and cocaine addiction remains unavailable in the West.

In Buriram Province, a monk teaches the village people to resist being uprooted by military-led relocation schemes. In Nonathburi, jobless migrants and employers meet in a monastery to discuss their plight. In Lopburi province a monastery has become a hospice for Aids workers. Ajahn Chah established several monasteries in the West as models of austerity, simplicity and wisdom. Ajahn Dhammadaro's monastery in Supanburi accommodates 600 monks, nuns and lay people for the practice of insight meditation (known as vipassana in the Buddhist tradition) during the traditional three months "rains retreat." Ajahn Yantra leads thousands of Buddhists on pilgrimage through the hills and jungles of Thailand. Phra Dhepvathi, wrote the best-seller, *Buddhadharma*, a systematic explanation of the Buddha's teachings and its relevance for contemporary society.

Such monks apply essential Buddhist themes of ethics, tolerance, mindfulness, nonviolence, kindness, insight meditation, moderation, wisdom and compassion to local, national and global situations. Student radicals recognize that this renaissance in Thailand points to a post-consumer culture. The Buddha's teaching are also applied world wide to campaigns for disarmament, respect for nature, psychological and physical health, conservation, ethical sciences, education, human rights and death and dying issues. Since Buddhism is free from obsessive concerns about birth control, divorce, the priesthood, the beginning and the end of the earth and irrational dogmas, it is free to concentrate on issues of direct human and environmental concern.

Japan boasts the largest Buddhist sect, known as Soka Gakkai society which offers a compellingly simply message, namely to chant *Nam-myoho-renge-kyo*, a mantra they claim will enable a follower to achieve whatever he or she wants. Part of the attraction of the sect is that followers are encouraged to chant for anything they desire—a car, a lucrative salary or success on the stage or sports field. In recent decades, Soka Gakkai, founder by Nichiren, has actively engaged in proselytizing to increase their membership. World wide membership has gone past the 20 million figure. Behind the mantra lies an aggressive Buddhist sect that seeks to convert entire nations. They believe that one third of the world will convert to Soka Gakkai by the next century. Thus Soka Gakkai International seeks a pre-eminent position for itself. Power struggles and internal conflicts have been a constant feature of Soka Gakkai. Leaders within the organization have shown a history of intolerance towards other Buddhist traditions, which has not endeared the society to the world-wide community of Buddhists. The Nichiren tradition has more in common with Christian fundamentalism—a mixture of gross materialism with spiritual power—than traditional Buddhist teachings of nonviolence, tolerance, kindness and Ultimate Truth.

The Buddha's teachings explore deeply the interconnection of all events and recognizes that the movement of the butterfly wing in the Amazon forest affects the weather in France. Using the resources of awareness, meditation, inquiry and action, the Buddha points the way to break the mould of addictive personal and social patterns to discover the nature of things in a fresh and liberating light for the welfare of all.

THE BUDDHA AND OTHERS

Jesus,
Son of the Earth

There is an Unborn, Unmade, Unformed.
If there were not, there would no escape known
here for one who is born, made, formed.
The Buddha.

In his teachings, Jesus moved frequently and freely between Ultimate Truth, which he referred to in many ways—the Law, God,
Life, the Kingdom of Heaven, the Lord, Light, the Father—and relative truth. His teachings on relative truth covered our relationships with other people (our neighbour), ourselves, our actions and
their results. When he perceived that many did not comprehend
his teachings on Ultimate Truth, he said: "You do not understand
but one day you will."

Jesus adopted the same position as the Buddha, summarily dismissing attempts to disregard the Ultimate Truth or the Law of Dependent Arising. The Law shows the conditionality of everything
that arises in the world of mind, body, spirit and language. All
things and events occur due to the Law of Dependent Arising which
is timeless, unchanging and all embracing. No person or thing has
any existence outside of God, namely that which makes all things
possible. A human being depends for his or her existence on body,
feelings, perceptions, thoughts, consciousness, environmental support and the Law of Dependent Arising. In the absence of any of
these conditions there is the absence of what we call a human being.
Jesus also said that we can do nothing without the Law. He said
he gave "knowledge of the mysteries of the Kingdom of God."

Jesus and the Buddha spoke again and again in thoughtful and
poetic ways of this Law that makes all things possible. We are encouraged again and again to meditate and reflect upon this all embracing Truth of life and its profound significance. All other
considerations take second place to insights into the Law of Dependent Arising. Ananda, the Buddha's attendant thought it was

easy to understand the Law, but the Buddha told him: "Dependent Arising is profound. It is through not understanding, not penetrating this Law that this world resembles a tangled ball of thread. Who understands the teachings (the Dharma) understands the Law of Dependent Arising."

Jesus said: "Do not think I have come to abolish the Law. Until Heaven and Earth pass away, not the smallest letter or the smallest part of a letter will pass from the Law." He urged the people to follow these teachings on the Ultimate Truth to realize the Kingdom of Heaven.

Fearless and compassionate, Jesus attempted to bring profound spiritual awareness and full realization of Ultimate Truth into the daily experience of the people of Palestine. With bold and uncompromising statements, Jesus walked the land, a message of liberation and God pounding in his heart. He was a threat to the religious and political Establishment with his message of spiritual fulfilment, the significance of the Here and Now and realization of God. Within the space of three years, the political and religious authorities had had enough so they tortured and crucified him. Jesus knew the risks and the consequences of proclaiming his teachings; a spiritual teacher is "not without honour, except in his native place and among his own family and in his own house."

To understand fully his message, three considerations are vital:

1. *one must be spiritually enlightened*
2. *one must love Jesus and his teachings with one's whole heart*
3. *one must be able to understand and distinguish his teachings on Ultimate Truth and relative truth.*

Jesus did not concern himself with modification of Judaism, despite similarities of language, themes and respect for the Law, that is God. Neither did he attempt to dissociate himself from past spiritual teachers (called prophets in the Bible) since he quotes them. To perceive Jesus's teachings in terms of either change from, or continuity with an old religion misses the significance of his enlightened realization and the central place that it holds in his message. The Buddha's teachings must be understood in the same light.

The Sermon on the Mount conveyed in unequivocal terms a series of teachings for an ethical and spiritual way of life. It covered such sensitive spiritual areas as unwavering nonviolence, sexual abuse, speech, revenge, generosity, prayer, fasting, money, the Here and Now, the judging mind, the spiritual path and dependency. He tackled issues of daily life, constantly using the relative truth to reveal Ultimate Truth. He used the basis of relative experiences to point out the immediate presence of God. He said that whosoever wishes to save his life will lose it, but whoever loses his life for his sake and that of the teachings will save it. "What profit is there for one to gain the whole world and forfeit his life?" he asked. "No servant can serve two masters. You cannot serve God and mammon." Jesus dismissed attachment to wealth and privilege as incompatible with his teachings. "Everyone of you who does not renounce all his possessions cannot be my disciple."

Both teachers speak of a life free from egotism and the shadow of belief in "self" existence. The Buddha says egolessness reveals:

The feeling that there is nothing that is me
Without worry or doubt that anything might be me
Feeling that nothing is mine
Without worry or doubt that anything might be mine.

Jesus said: "One's life does not consist of possessions. Do not worry about your life. Whoever exalts himself will be humbled. Stay awake for you do not know on which day the Lord will come."

The Sermon on the Mount begins with the 12 Beatitudes, statements connected with the Ultimate Truth. Five of them are:

Blessed are the poor in spirit,
for theirs is the Kingdom of Heaven.
Blessed are the meek,
for they shall inherit the land.
Blessed are the merciful,
for they will be shown mercy.
Blessed are the clean of heart,
for they will see God.
Blessed are the peacemakers,
for they will be called children of God.

Like the Buddha, Jesus called for a life of self-renunciation and dedication to the spirit and letter of the teachings. Authentic spiritual teachers make the same appeal today though Church leaders have frequently ignored these demanding teachings of Jesus. Little wonder that Jesus launched into an invective against Church leaders. He said they were hypocrites since they "preached but did not practice." He condemned them for permitting themselves to be called "Master," he referred to them as "blind fools" for travelling across land and sea to make converts, which meant finding people to identify with their beliefs so that new members expressed a zeal "twice as much as yourselves." He said the religious authorities had "taken away the key of knowledge."

For nearly 2000 years Church leaders have tried to prove the supremacy of Jesus over all people and nations. Their determination to persuade people of the powers of Jesus has produced generations of submissive believers, widespread disillusionment and cynicism and made senior clergymen and missionaries the butt of endless jokes. Thoughtful priests refer to contemporary Church leaders as "the most advanced thinkers of the 5th century!"

During his lifetime, Jesus was a spiritual enigma, a maverick and a ruthlessly independent voice who was neither inside nor outside his religious tradition. He constantly spoke of himself in lowly terms and associated with social failures and the underclass. He was anti-establishment and anti-authority yet spoke with unshakeable conviction and intimate insights about the faith of his upbringing. He used the resources of stories from daily life to communicate spiritual liberation.

Jesus had several intimate friends, both women and men. He was especially close to Mary of Magdala, a prostitute in the area of Galilee, and his mother, Mary. As a teenager, his mother found herself unexpectedly pregnant, unmarried and homeless. She had to leave her home village and gave birth to Jesus in a stable in Bethlehem. Joseph, an old man, befriended her on her journey. Mary, his mother, and Mary of Magdala shared much together, understood each other and remained with Jesus through his final days. Joanna, married to Herod's steward, and Suzanna also travelled with Jesus. These women accompanied him on many of his journeys and provided him with the necessities for daily life. But Jesus had no wish for anyone, either close friends or large crowds, to become dependent on him, and would retreat regularly to the mountains or desert for meditation and silence.

Jesus himself refuted materialist miracles during his 40-day retreat in the desert when he realized that he could not convert stones into bread, jump from the top of a cliff without breaking his body, or assert power and privilege over people and nations. He knew he had no need to test his realization of Truth through some extraordinary show of power. He showed that the authentic miracle was the transformation of people's lives.

The Church appears to have disregarded this public acknowledgement of Jesus that nobody could defy the Law of Dependent Arising. The Church's belief in the literal claim to the miracles, the Virgin birth, the resurrection of Christ's body from the cross into heaven (Apollo space rocket style), original sin and eternal damnation make a parody of Jesus' teachings, yet the orthodox Church has made these beliefs the criteria for being a Christian. Biblical scholars, theologians and the Church hierarchy proclaim such beliefs as though they were the Truth carved in rock. Jesus would wonder what he sacrificed his life for if he witnessed today what the Church has made of his teachings.

Jesus often reminded his close friends that the Kingdom of God was realizable Here and Now. It is "at hand, for you," he said. He told people not to worry about the future. "Look at the ravens: they do not sow or reap, they have neither storehouse nor barn. Even the smallest things are beyond your control." Jesus directed their attention to seeking the Truth and trusting everything will be taken care of. Letting go of material possessions enabled one's life to be shaped by Truth instead of desire. It is a far reaching statement, and a challenge to conventional assumptions and values. Those who follow the teachings of Jesus must be willing to exhaust all interest in the consumer culture for the discovery, he said, of an "inexhaustible treasure."

When his friends climbed the mountain of spirituality, they departed from the area of the known for the unknown. They began to understand the teachings of Moses, Elijah and Jesus yet "they were terrified." Then a "cloud came over them" as they went into the unknown until their faith in Jesus and his teachings lifted their spirits. Jesus shone whenever his authority touched them.

Jesus made plain the Truth of things through his stories. His parables expressed insights into Ultimate Truth. With his lifelong realization and wondrous gifts with language, he communicated the wisdom of a liberated life. Crowds of people came to listen to him wherever he stopped to give teachings, which changed people's lives. Through his message, people found complete renewal spiritually, emotionally and physically. They were born again. Jesus was a liberating breath of fresh air in a religious faith polluted with self-righteous authority. When his close associates asked him why he spoke in parables to his audience, he replied: "Because knowledge of the mysteries of the Kingdom of Heaven has been granted to you, but to them it has not been granted. They look but do not see, and hear but do not listen or understand."

Quoting Isaiah, Jesus said: "Gross is the heart of the people, they will hardly hear with their ears." He then told the parable of the sower, a situation familiar to all spiritual teachers. In this parable, he explained that there were four types of listeners, and compared the teachings to seeds falling on different types of ground. The ground upon which the seeds fall represents the hearts and minds of the listeners. There were those that:

1. *rejected teachings on Ultimate Truth*
2. *expressed interest for a while but dropped away*
3. *were committed but then concerns about money and future took over*
4. *listened and understood and thus embodied the teachings.*

Only one miracle appears in *all* four gospels, that concerning the extraordinary impact he made on a large gathering. The event came to be known as the "feeding of the five thousand." When Jesus disembarked from a boat a huge crowd gathered around him to listen to him, he was able to feed them all, though his close friends thought there was little to offer. There was no need for the crowd to look elsewhere for nourishment when they were more than filled through Jesus. Immediately afterwards, Jesus retreated into a period of solitude for inner renewal. Despite giving much care and attention to those in search of spiritual awakening, he pursued his love of solitude.

His friends left the seashore to cross the sea when a fierce storm blew up in the middle of the night. Then they saw Jesus walking towards them on the water. But they were afraid until they heard the voice of Jesus, of Truth, speak out: "Take courage. It is I. Do not be afraid." Peter climbed out of the boat but when he saw how strong the wind was he became frightened and began to sink. "Why did you doubt?" Jesus asked him. When the storm at sea had no hold over their fearful emotions, it lost its power. In awakening, consciousness has risen above the elements of water, air, earth and temperature. The attempt to make life safe and secure through sitting in a boat inhibits the opportunity for a free and transcendent life. To take risks, as acts of faith, is walking on water.

His parables, stories and metaphors were wide ranging. Jesus told the people that there were two types of gate—one is broad and the other narrow. The gate of ethics, letting go and inner transformation is narrow while the gate that leads to destruction and death is broad. While acknowledging other spiritual teachers, he also warned that there were teachers who appeared humble and gentle like sheep, but the unresolved problems of their inner lives meant they behaved with aggression. Jesus asked: "Do people pick grapes to make wine from thorn bushes? Do people pick figs from thistles? You will know them by their fruits." Those who truly listened to him acted on his teachings—like the "one who builds a home on firm foundations." "The coming of the kingdom cannot be observed. No one will announce "Look, here it is... For behold the Kingdom of God is among you." Again he illuminates the Here and Now, where God is to be discovered. He said the Kingdom of God was like a mustard seed, the smallest of seeds that grows into the largest of plants as a place for birds to dwell. God makes all things possible.

In his teachings, Jesus made clear the significance of actions and the fruits of actions, good and evil, particularly in the field of spirituality. The tree of life may offer sound fruits or rotten ones. Yet, he pointed out, all forms of action, good and evil, belong to the world of conventional experience and expression. "Are not two sparrows sold for a small coin. Yet not one of them falls to the ground without your Father's knowledge." The "Father" embraces all. Jesus himself, as the son of the Earth, of humankind, placed himself in the same position as the rest of the spiritual community. Those who were willing to forget their possessions and their self existence, became disciples, that is, they enjoyed a natural discipline through realization of an enlightened life. "No disciple is above his teacher. When fully trained every disciple will be like his teacher," Jesus reminded them. "Nothing is secret except to come to light." Until his death, Jesus remained a disciple of Ultimate Truth.

Jesus also focused his attention on the world of language because our words pass judgement on us as much as our actions. He reiterated the importance of the spiritual community, of contact with like minded people. Like the Buddha, he placed the family lower in the list of spiritual priorities. When he was told that his mother and brothers were waiting to speak to him, he asked "Who is my mother? Who are my brothers? Whoever does the will of my heavenly Father is my brother and sister and mother." Ultimate Realization rendered meaningless the traditional notions of family since all adults and children matter equally. The poor and the sick were all to be invited to dine, he said.

Jesus criticized the strict Jewish observance of certain dietary restrictions and the sacrifice of animals in the name of religion, a tradition propagated for centuries. "Hear and understand. It is not what enters one's mouth that defiles the person but what comes out of the mouth is what defiles one. Do you not realize that everything that enters the mouth passes into the stomach and is expelled into the latrine? But the things that come out of the mouth come from the defiled heart." He dismissed the teaching authority of the priests because they offered little in the way of Ultimate Truth. Observances of an ancient code were the sum total of their religious life. He reminded them that from a handful of loaves and fishes, he fed thousands.

In one spiritual inquiry after another Jesus kept returning to the theme of Ultimate Truth. The rich young man asked Jesus what he had to do to find Eternal Life. Jesus responded: "Why do you ask me about what is good? There is only One who is good." Jesus told him to follow the precepts of not killing, not stealing, not engaging in sexual abuse, not telling lies and honouring one's mother and father. The young man said he already observed these guidelines. Jesus then told him to let go of his possessions: "It is easier for a camel to pass through the eye of a needle than for one who is rich to enter the Kingdom of God." His friends gasped: "Who then can be saved?" Jesus replied: "For human beings, this is impossible but for God all things are possible." The presence of Ultimate Truth reveals itself as the heart opens. Possessions and possessiveness obstruct the clear vision of Ultimate Truth that is timeless and an unshakeable peace.

Jesus added: "Those who have followed me, in the New Age, when the Son of Man is seated on his throne of glory, will yourselves sit on the 12 thrones judging the 12 tribes of Israel." Jesus meant that those who realize the Truth transcend power, hierarchy, the nation state and the misery and divisiveness that accompanies it. Again Jesus employs vivid language to communicate transcendence of the accepted view of the Earth. All enlightened beings share these same realizations, and for them there is neither past, present nor future.

When Jesus was leaving Jericho, a large crowd followed him. Two blind men sitting by the roadside heard the crowd. They both shouted out to Jesus. He asked the two blind men if they truly wanted to see. The men had to have the motivation to see for the miracle of seeing to take place. The Son of the Earth, who lived to serve and not to be served, spoke to them so they could see the Kingdom of Heaven. Those who had been blind to the Truth realized the New Age was upon them.

Jesus arrived with humility in Jerusalem. He travelled with an ass and a colt, two beasts of burden—symbolic of the world of duality and suffering. He rejected those who had devoted their lives to buying and selling outside the temple, seeing that such dealers excluded themselves from the Temple of God. Simultaneously Jesus challenged not only secular existence but also the Church that supported such activities. He then compared the activities of State and Church to a fig tree that bears leaves but no fruit. His breathtaking authority moved him closer and closer to the Cross.

The priests and senior members of the traditional Church asked him: "By what authority are you doing these things? Who gave you this authority?" The enlightened one then responded with a question using their own dualistic thought to make a point: "Where did John the Baptist gain his authority?" The priests dared not say from Ultimate Truth because John had spoken with awe of Jesus, nor dared refute John because of the reaction of the people. Jesus said: "Neither shall I tell you by what authority I do these things." The priests then plotted further against Jesus. They sent a messenger to entrap him. "You teach the way of God in accordance with the Truth. Tell us then, what is your opinion: Is it lawful to pay the poll tax to Caesar or not?"

Jesus read their minds: "Why are you testing me, you hypocrites? Show me the coin. Whose image and inscription is this? Then repay to Caesar what belongs to Caesar and to God what belongs to God." Such a response could sound like conformity to all the laws of the land, yet it is hardly likely that the man who dismissed the dealers in the financial markets was subservient to images on coins. Jesus placed the focus again on Ultimate Truth. When we understand what belongs to God then everything in the world of relativity, of transactions, is no longer a consideration.

Similarly when the theologians attempted to argue with him about marriage laws, Jesus said that when people have found God they neither marry nor are given in marriage. They are free from such notions and roles. So they tried again to trap him. "What then are the most important laws?" Jesus responded with the Ultimate and then relative truth. "First, you shall love God with all your heart, soul and mind and second, you shall love your neighbour as yourself." The Son of the Earth then lists the failings of the religious authorities. He said they:

do not practice what they preach,
like to control others,
want to be seen,
love places of honour,
love titles,
cannot enter the New Age,
lock others out,
destroy the spiritual lives of others through conversion,
engage in self indulgence and
neglect what is truly significant.

His comments outraged the authorities. Jesus told his close friends that wars, famines and earthquakes, suffering and hatred would continue and false gurus, preachers and prophets would appear. He told people that they did not have to journey to a special person for spiritual satisfaction. "Wherever the corpse is the vultures will fly," he dryly commented but he assured them the teachings of Ultimate Truth will not be destroyed in the world.

The day before his mock trial, torture and death, Jesus and his companions ate together in an upstairs room at the edge of Jerusalem. He took hold of a piece of bread: "Take and eat, this is my body." Then he took a cup and said: "Drink from it. This is my blood." He was speaking neither in a mystical nor transformative sense; he simply expressed the profound nature of Non-Duality, that the world of self and other has no inherent meaning nor inherent existence. In Truth, body and blood, bread and wine, share the same nature but the conventional mind believes in real differences. The notion of the contemporary church that the sacrificial death of Jesus brings forgiveness of sins obscures the deeper truth of the liberating Non-Dual nature of his teachings. Unlike the church, Jesus dismissed the cult of personality. "Notice how the flowers grow. Not even Solomon in all his splendour was dressed like one of them."

St. John's gospel reflects his personal interpretation of the message of Jesus. In this gospel, symbolism and proclamations that Jesus was the Incarnate God express a particular theological position; it alone records Jesus saying: "I am the way and the truth and the life. No one comes to the Father except by me." When misunderstood, this statement condones the zealous activities of Christian missionaries, the dogma to disclaim other historical and contemporary teachings of Ultimate Truth and a brazen degree of self-righteousness.

Is Jesus so egotistical as to demand that all spiritual seekers know and identify themselves with his personal life story? Where is the humility? Or is Jesus referring to the depth of himself—namely love, compassion, humility, awareness, letting go and devotion to Life? This is Jesus. When this "Jesus" is realized within, the Kingdom of God is revealed in the immediacy of things. Placing the historical Jesus as the central person of history offends his teachings and insults the son and servant of humankind.

When Jesus told the priests in metaphorical language that the "Son of Man would sit at the right hand of power" they took it as a claim from Jesus that he blasphemed and thus deserved to die. Jesus had realized and stated the inseparable nature of Ultimate and relative truth. His major task was dissolving people's perceived differences between the Ultimate and the conventional without falling into the trap of self-promotion, duality or theological standpoints. In the realization of Truth, one's world is transformed. The Truth alone sets one free. Those who listened and understood his teachings were not obsessed with the status of Jesus as Son of God, Messiah or Christ. Born of projections onto self existence, the cult of personality distracts the seeker from the Truth: "Blessed are the poor in spirit." "This (bread) is my body and this is my blood (wine)," he reminded his friends.

Like the Buddha, Jesus predicted a future incarnation of Truth. The Buddhist tradition has attempted to generate the conditions for the arising of the next Buddha, whose name is Maitreya (Loving Kindness). I believe there has been a blind spot in the tradition. Buddhists have failed to recognize that Maitreya Buddha incarnated into the world 500 years later in Bethlehem. Jesus is Maitreya Buddha. Jesus, the embodiment of loving kindness, loved others unto death, reminded the world of the Law (that is to love God and love others). Jesus, himself, then predicted a future enlightened one who would announce the cessation of the world.

Jesus said: "All that you see here—the days will come when there will not be left a stone upon another stone that will not be thrown down.... When you see these signs begin to happen stand erect and raise your heads because liberation is at hand.... Be aware at all times."

Church and political authorities plotted to get rid of Jesus. They could not bear his teachings any longer. They persuaded people in Jerusalem to scream for the release of the terrorist, Jesus Barabbas, instead of Jesus of Nazareth. The clergy and the military spat on Jesus, the soldiers beat him with a reed, drove a crown of long thorns into his head, mocked him, stripped him, took him to Golgotha, the Place of the Skull, and crucified him. Priests and soldiers tormented him on the cross. One soldier witnessed the dignity of Jesus while nailed to the cross and expressed a change of heart. Hanging there in tortuous pain, Jesus said in a loud voice: "Eli, eli, lema sabachthani?" "My God, my God why have you forsaken me?"

It might appear that in the last moments of his life Jesus experienced a crippling doubt about his insights and connection with the Ultimate Truth. But his final words were a statement of Truth, itself. Jesus was quoting from a passage of the much loved Psalm 22, which begins with this despairing line and ends in triumph. "Let the coming generation be told of the Lord, that they proclaim to a people yet to be born," reads the psalm's final lines.

Jesus's final shout of Life manifests directly the consciousness of enlightenment. "Eli, eli, lema sabachthani?" testifies to his Non-Dual transcendent and imminent wisdom, his embrace of doubt and triumph. In the Ultimate Truth of things, neither self nor other has control over the unfolding of existence. His last words spelt this out with impassioned dignity.

After Jesus died the two women closest to him, Mary of Magdala and his mother, Mary of Nazareth, sat facing the tomb where the body had been laid. Joseph of Arimethea, a friend and supporter of Jesus, requested Pilate to return the corpse to them. But then Jesus's friends realized the heart of the teachings—Jesus had risen already from the dead. Nobody saw any physical resurrection of Jesus. What they saw came to them "like lightning." They understood his teachings—that the Ultimate Truth embraces all inseparably. "As you do unto others so you do unto me." Within three days of his death, some of his close friends, men and women, had finally realized what he had been telling them day and night for three years. Afterwards they left for Bethany and then returned to Jerusalem "with great joy."

Alienation and
Karl Marx

The victor finds a conqueror
The abuser gets abused
The persecutor gets persecuted
The Wheel of Deeds turns around again
And makes the plundered plunderers.
The Buddha

Karl Marx, born in May, 1818 in Germany, was the first son among the eight children of a relatively prosperous German lawyer. His father, influenced by the ideas of the so-called Enlightenment period and wanting to escape from the ghetto into which German law restricted Jews, had abandoned the faith of his ancestors—who included many rabbis—and become a Protestant. Karl, a somewhat rebellious university student, earned a degree in philosophy and could easily have followed a successful academic career. Instead, under the influence of the radical followers of Hegel, with whom he associated in Berlin, and of his close friend, Karl Koppen, he turned to radical political journalism which was to get him exiled from Germany. It also led him into contact with his life-long friend and benefactor, Frederick Engels.

Inspired by his contact with working class people he engaged in a life long struggle for socialism for which he sacrificed the material wellbeing of himself, his childhood sweetheart, Jenny, who became his wife and their children. In 1861, when Marx was 43 years old, he briefly returned to Germany from London where he again met his friend, Koppen. Koppen had in the meantime written a two-volume study of the Buddha which he gave to Marx as a gift.

In their own way, the teachings of the Buddha and Marx both issue a challenge to selfish, egotistical human behaviour. Whereas the Buddha's emphasis is on the inner forces shaping attitudes and actions, Marx's is on economic, social and political factors in the external world. For Marx, the capitalist economic system both embodies and perpetuates selfishness: capitalists seek out value-creating commodities regardless of any genuine use, with the cost of human labour a primary factor determining the price of goods.

The Buddha and Marx both pursued an understanding of a liberating philosophy of life to uproot selfishness and the institutions born of it. Many of the profound insights of the Buddha and Marx provide inspiration today for the work of the international Green movement, which actively pursues both social and ecological harmony with respect for the Earth and its inhabitants.

Marx's philosophical, political and economic writings on the human condition include *Das Capital*, *Grundrisse* and *Theories of Surplus Value*. He also wrote endless letters, statements and articles for the press dealing with social realities, economic structures and the antagonism arising in society due to the grossly unequal distribution of wealth:

"The right of man to freedom is not based on the union of man with man, but on the separation of man from man. It is the right of the limited individual who is limited to himself. The right of man to property is thus the right to enjoy his possessions and dispose of them arbitrarily without regard for other men. It is the right of selfishness. It leads man to see in other men not the realization, but the limitation of his own freedom."

Whereas the Buddha teaches that the source of suffering is ignorance—the unawakened, unenlightened state in which so many people live—for Marx it is found in the institution of private wealth and property. In Marx's view, the purpose of private wealth is to increase it, maximizing the profits of the owners. Money, as the bearer of profit, becomes the dominant value of all things. "It has therefore robbed the whole world, the human as well as the natural, of its own value. Since human labour is the ultimate source of profit the value money represents is the alienated essence of man's work and being. This alien essence dominates him and he adores it."

Widespread alienation perpetuates the painful condition of millions of workers and the unemployed, i.e. those who do not possess profit-making capital. The freedom that capitalism provides for the few who are able to accumulate property, profit and power destroys community for everyone else; this ideology enriches the minority at the expense of the majority. Those workers who cannot be profitably employed are rejected. Thus the freedom and wealth of the few directly relates to the exploitation of the workers and the misery of the poor and the destitute.

The rich get richer, as Marx wrote, while the poor get poorer. The number of poor will increase through the redundancies of the middle and professional classes, who become unemployable. We are already noticing this trend in our society where more people in the professional classes are unable to secure certain forms of employment because they are considered over qualified. "You will want to move on in a few months," prospective employers tell them. The view of employers is that such people will experience dissatisfaction after a short while and will want to move on as quickly as possible to a more highly paid profession. Many blue collar and white collar jobs are not only dependent upon the decisions of board members, but also on the fluctuating market economy. At any given time, hundreds of workers with large mortgages and bills to be paid, can be permanently laid off with little warning. The cruelty of this system leaves few alternatives for those subject to it. There is not only a financial cost for such methods of employment, but an emotional one as well as unemployment brings hell into the home of once hard-working families.

Large companies act like sharks roaming the waters swallowing up small fish. When initiatives from individuals begin to show success, when imaginative ideas begin to show a profit, when creativity begins to stimulate a public response, the spies of big business begin to move in to take over these small firms or individual enterprises. Or big business reproduces the same commodity for the mass market at a cheaper price to price out the small firm or enterprising individual. This leaves the market in the hands of fewer and fewer people; the self employed and small businesses then struggle often becoming reliant on big businesses for orders to stay afloat. Observing this developing trend, Marx said: "Workers become appendages to machines. Small tradespeople, small farmers, craftsmen and women are gradually swamped by capitalism, partly because their specialized skill is rendered worthless by new methods of production."

The Marxist-Leninist solution to capitalism was nationalization and a centrally planned economy. The ideology of Marx become a "material force" during the 1917 Russian Revolution. Power and privilege then shifted from the hands of wealthy individuals, who owned and controlled production and the land, to the State and the managers of the State. Seventy years later the severe control of the Soviet Union's central committee over people's lives began to fall apart. This ideology of the left failed ignominiously since workers still felt deprived of a full and active role in the direction of their lives at the local level. The central planners dominated their existence as much as the wealthy had before.

After the 1917 Russian Revolution, there was virtual panic in the USA and Europe among the rich and powerful. They were afraid that the workers and millions of unemployed would rise up against the factory and land owners whose capital controlled society. Owned by a handful of news barons, the media, seized with glee on Marx's comment that "religion is the opium of the people." Perhaps through this single statement more than any other, the Establishment attempted to prove that Marxism would destroy religious belief in God and impose a soulless ideology that would seek to negate the spirit of the people. The strategy worked. Powerful business, political and religious leaders persuaded millions to remain loyal to God and country even when that meant continuing in desperate living conditions. The Establishment retained their position of dominance in Western society. The arrival of the brutal face of Communism and the subsequent reign of terror of Stalin ensured that the voice of Karl Marx appealing for social justice and freedom alongside equitable distribution of wealth, would be ignored.

Following the 1989–90 Russian revolution and return to the market economy, many of the former managers of the disgraced Communist system became the new entrepreneurs awarding themselves substantial increases in salaries and power. Like their Western counterparts, millions of workers and the growing army of unemployed in the former Soviet Union now struggle to make ends meet. Since the market economy bases its principles on profit and efficiency, it means workers are treated like products—to be used and discarded according to the fluctuations of capital. Companies engage in the task of producing more and more sophisticated technology and machinery to reduce labour costs thus making workers expendable.

When employees live in fear of losing their jobs, they can spare little thought to changing the economic system that works against their collective interests. The mixed economy, which attempts to act as a buffer against the excesses of the market economy, seems to offer little real protection against the social, spiritual and environmental degradation that haunts our society. Economies of the left, right and centre do nothing for workers in fields and factories in the developing nations when the overdeveloped world takes position as controller overseeing the fate of numerous millions treated as serfs in the Third World.

Marx's realizations about the nature of selfishness directly address this state of affairs. He considered the very roots of capitalism to be founded in what he referred to as "alienated labour." Marx writes: "We have demonstrated that the worker is degraded to the most miserable sort of commodity. The necessary result of competition is the accumulation of capital in a few hands." The suffering and alienation of the worker has four primary aspects.

1. *The worker is unable to relate to what he or she produces since the methods of production of large businesses usually mean machine line assembly where no worker can see the results of his or her work. Such methods destroy creativity. The workers become like robots engaged in monotonous activity*

2. *The worker is alienated from himself or herself, since the work satisfies the owners of production rather than meeting the needs of the worker for creativity, self-expression and job satisfaction*

3. *The worker is alienated from the owners who live and socialize in their own class, separate from the workers*

4. *The worker is alienated from co-workers and the unemployed through having to compete with them for jobs.*

In addition, the growing army of the unemployed are alienated from participation in the market economy. Thus an economic system based on the desire to accumulate capital, amass wealth, private property and luxury goods produces alienated labour, and also prohibits fulfilling genuine human needs—namely the ending of alienation and suffering and finding a fulfilling livelihood.

In the space of a century workers' conditions have improved in advanced Western society. In other countries, however, millions of workers are still experiencing 19th century working conditions or worse. Thus many of Marx's insights, like the Buddha's, have direct relevance today. "Health and safety" for workers now includes awareness of long term damage due to countless toxic emissions, but the law regarding the use of hazardous substances does not provide an adequate margin of safety to workers. Nor do the police understand environmental crime in the way they understand street crime. Pollution of land, water and air has very serious consequences for all people, yet the bosses continue to get away with exposing workers and the public to harmful chemicals and toxins.

Governments and the police turn a blind eye to the abuse of nature and workers by allowing dangerous emissions into the air, seas and land. Companies try to avoid paying compensation to workers, their dependents and local residents for hazardous accidents and neglect of health and safety regulations. The combination of exposure to the range of pollutants in the factory, on the site, in the street and in our diet affects the quality of our lives. The message of Marx in terms of workers' rights world wide still applies today. Yet genuine health and safety for people, creatures and environment continues to take second place to profit, particularly in the Third World.

If the Buddha taught ways of spiritual awakening (both individually and collectively), then Marx taught essential themes dealing with the specific realities of daily life. These include alienation, class struggle, dialectics, historical materialism, criticism of orthodox religion, the use of labour, and surplus value—the means by which the rich become richer and the poor remain poor. His "manifesto" begins with the famous lines: "The history of all hitherto existing society is the history of the class struggle." The sources of human suffering are to be found in the systems that encourage selfishness, egotism and greed. What is essential for both "physicians" is that we can do something about suffering. Both the Buddha and Marx analysed the human condition as it reveals itself in the Here and Now, both engaged in the emancipation of humanity from the forces of greed, violence and the degradation of sections of society and of the world community.

Despite the mutual concerns of the Buddha and Marx, there are also significant differences which, while not contradictory, should not be overlooked. For example, though the Buddha would not have shared Marx's critique of private property per se, he would have shared his concern over the use of property for selfish purposes, ones that run counter to the values of social harmony and justice. Both rejected the notion that orthodox religion could be of any service in ending suffering—acting only as a purveyor of illusory consolation to those who suffer, a service that mostly benefits the rich and the powerful. Marx wrote in his critique of religion that religious belief is the result of alienation from our true nature, hence religion is symptomatic of people's relationship to each other.

In 1844 Marx wrote his famous statement.

"Religion is the sigh of the oppressed creature, the feeling of a heartless world and the soul of soulless circumstances. It is the opium of the people. The first task of philosophy which is in the service of history is to discover self-alienation in its unholy forms. Criticism of heaven is thus transformed into the criticism of Earth, the criticism of religion into the criticism of law and the criticism of theology into the criticism of politics. The immediate task is to unmask human alienation in its secular form."

In a view the Buddha probably would have agreed with Marx saw state religion as an expression of humankind's alienation from itself and the world. "The criticism of religion is the beginning of all criticism," said Marx. Whereas the Buddha criticized dependence on religious forms and traditions, Marx stressed that which supported social and global ills, exploitation alienation and class antagonism. While the Buddha showed how to end suffering through inner investigation, ethical action, profound meditative experiences and liberation, Marx comes across as a fiery prophet possessed of a high degree of moral certitude as he urged social action:

"Man must prove the truth, i.e. reality and power, the this sidedness of his thinking in practice. The dispute about the actuality or non-actuality of thinking—thinking isolated from practice—is purely a scholastic question. Philosophers have interpreted the world in different ways. The point is to change it."

Although Marx aimed to liberate humanity from economic determinism, his main focus is on the poor, both workers and unemployed. He protested about the exploitation of their labour to produce a wealthy class under capitalism. He saw the role of workers as launching social changes to liberate the masses from unjust economics. From his study of the history of social change he believed that, except for a few countries such as the USA, Britain and Holland, force or violent revolution would be necessary if the workers were to be able to take power from the profiteers of production. He criticized the rich for taking far more than they needed, as well as the social and economic conditions which made it possible. Thus one of the main tasks Marx gave himself was to awaken the poor to the nature of their role to instigate a liberation movement.

In contrast, the Buddha sought to address the totality of human existence. Even if there was a society in which there was no economic foundation for distinctions between classes, there would still be suffering arising from blindness to life's inevitable changing circumstances as well as from the influence of personal selfishness and fear. The Buddha would have agreed with features of Marx's economic and social diagnosis of suffering. Nevertheless, with his diagnosis of dependent arising, he would see Marx's analysis as incomplete. He pointed more to widespread ignorance as a cause for suffering rather than focusing on socioeconomic factors. The Buddha spelt out a way of life that inquired into the nature of suffering. Nonviolence, generosity and compassion are fruits of this inquiry as well as remedies for overcoming egotistical values.

In the Dharma of liberation the Buddha did not condemn outright the leaders, the privileged, the religious authorities or the owners of the forces of production. He did not engage directly in the dialect of the haves and the have-nots, pointing out instead the dependently arising nature of all aspects of the human condition. Hardship and deprivation condition and trap the poor; preoccupation with profit and wealth trap the rich. In one of his well known remarks the Buddha emphasized that: "Hatred does not cease with hatred but through nonhatred. This is an eternal truth."

Ferocious debates and hairsplitting arguments influenced Marx in his university days, among members of the Communist League, between Communists and Socialists, and between himself and members of the Establishment. Marx relied on the power of his uncompromising views to cut through those views of the opposition which he perceived gave continued support to market forces. He lacked insight into the psychological and emotional influences on human behaviour, nor did he realize that the acquisition of wealth is as much compensation for a spiritual vacuum as anything else. Though the 19th century environment helped shape Marx's thinking and its limitations, his moral certitude is still a challenge to the glaring economic injustices today at the global level but there is still little sign of a new world order.

The Buddha, in contrast, employed the resources of calm meditative awareness and insights born from clarity and compassion. His teachings took root and spread rapidly in his own lifetime among those for whom the existing religions of northern India had no place. At his death he was revered by thousands, over time his insights spread to neighbouring countries where for more than two millennia they have been one of the most important forces shaping the cultures of Asia.

Marx, by contrast, died largely unknown, except in left wing political circles. He and his family lived in poverty in London. He pawned the family's winter clothes during the summer months; potatoes were sometimes the only daily diet, there was often no wood nor coal for heating or cooking, Marx had to send out begging letters, especially to Engels in Manchester. To a degree, this lifestyle was voluntary since he held qualifications to teach philosophy; thus he and his family lived the life of ascetics.

For 70 years, following the First World War, the world competed between the political and economic systems of Communism and Capitalism. Both sides spent world wide billions of dollars or rubles to promote their model of agrarian and industrial reform. Today, this no longer seems the case. However, the blatant failure of state controlled Communism has little to do with the teachings of Marx, any more than does the relentless propaganda against Marx in the capitalist and liberal press. There is a popular knee-jerk reaction against anything associated with Marx. Few are able to distinguish between the essential message of Marx and that of Stalin, who imposed his distorted version of Marx on Russia and later Eastern Europe. Communist countries have lived for decades in the shadow of control, power, centralized authority and a two class society of communist officials and workers: This, however, is not Marxism.

Our society is obviously unhappy, as can be seen when sociologists examine our widespread social ills. Moreover in the recent past selfishness has had a bright halo of respectability attached to it, at the very time that evidence of impending ecological catastrophe has been increasing. Thus the insights of the Buddha and Marx are still intensely relevant. Both indicate the causes of contemporary suffering, the role of attitudes and institutions, and urge us to do something about it. The rapid decline of the state controlled centralized systems of Eastern Europe is providing thoughtful spiritual and Green movements with the hope that the marriage of selfishness and capitalism also will collapse as speedily. Our miserly response to the desperate suffering in Africa and Asia, as well as at home, reveals the sickness of capitalism.

The Buddha and Marx followed different but largely complementary paths—one stressing spiritual change, the other social action. They certainly could have worked together. It is my belief, that both bodies of teachings will prove to be durable. Even if capitalism as an external source of suffering ended, there would still be individual suffering, egotism and alienation leading to a loss of community. The Buddha's Eightfold Path remains a radical way to preserve the fruits of wisdom, even in a society of Marxist classlessness. And, as long as there is selfishness in our economic and political institutions, then the voice of Marx needs to be heard too.

The Silence
of Wittgenstein

For when all ideas have been abolished,
all ways of saying, too, have been abolished.
The Buddha

Today no Western philosophy student can ignore the writings, and perhaps the life, too, of Ludwig Wittgenstein. International circles of philosophy have granted almost Biblical authority to Wittgenstein's *Tractatus Logico-Philosophicus* and his *Philosophical Investigations*. His ruthless inquiry into the nature of language leaves one in a state of silence as he concludes that one cannot say anything about anything with any final authority.

Wittgenstein is best known for his realization that words derive meaning, not from what they are supposed to refer to, but from how they are used. However, his insights extend much further. He pointed out that it is not possible to step outside all sets of assumptions. He said we keep coming up against *language games* and sets of assumptions to which they correspond. Thus what matters lies not *within* language but *outside* of it, and so there is nothing to explain or deduce. Wittgenstein avoided advancing theories or putting forward a thesis and to imagine he was misses the point. "It does not matter at all if words used are true, false or nonsense," he commented.

Wittgenstein (born April 26, 1889, died April 28, 1951) was the eighth and youngest child of one of the wealthiest families in Vienna. But he took no interest in his inheritance and left it with the rest of the family or gave it away. (Including, incidentally, a donation of 20,000 crowns to the poet, Rainer Maria Rilke, whom he admired). Just as there is austerity of words in Wittgenstein's writings, so there was in his lifestyle. He took no interest in the material world: his room at Cambridge University was virtually bereft of furnishings.

He was a volunteer soldier in the First World War. In a village on the Russian front, he picked up a copy of Tolstoy's writings on the gospels, which had a profound influence on him. His wartime experiences, Tolstoy's book and Wittgenstein's constant reflections on language and the world sparked off insights leading to his *picture theory of reality*. He said that propositions (such as the sky is blue) were a picture of the reality they attempted to describe. To pursue his analysis of the relationship of thought to the world, he often removed himself from any intellectual environment and pursued a solitary existence in Norway, Switzerland, and for a time, as a gardener in a monastery, north of Vienna. In a meeting with the exclusive Vienna Circle of philosophers, Wittgenstein read poems of Rabindranath Tagore to them instead of explaining his ideas. Wittgenstein led a religious life without a religion, as he took no participatory interest in orthodox religion and its forms. "I can well imagine," he wrote, "a religion in which there is thus no talking."

Wittgenstein's life was not easy. Two of his brothers committed suicide and another drowned in the USA in suspicious circumstances. At times he felt suicidal, depressed and painfully misunderstood. He was almost certainly homosexual which left him feeling desperately isolated in an era when "coming out" was unheard of. He spent his career as a Cambridge philosophy lecturer while mostly hating the university environment. He discouraged his students from becoming philosophy lecturers: "If you and I are to live religious lives, it must not be that we talk a lot about religion but that our manner of life is different."

The imposing presence of Wittgenstein in twentieth century philosophy is more than matched by the presence of Nagarjuna, the third century Buddhist saint-philosopher. He founded the Madhyamika School, which offered the most profound commentary on the Buddha's teachings. No other school in the Buddhist tradition has revealed such liberating insights into the nature of things. Nagarjuna was born into the Brahmin caste of South India. As a young man, he ordained as a Buddhist monk, undertook intensive training in calm and insight meditation and recorded his realizations. For the past 1600 years, Buddhism has regarded Nagarjuna as the world's philosopher par excellence. The Buddhist tradition acknowledges him as the foremost commentator on the Buddha's teachings. In his classic text, *Mula-madhyamakarika-karika*, Nagarjuna exposes the pollution of views that hinder realization of the Ultimate Truth:

No existents whatsoever are evident anywhere,
that are arisen from themselves,
from another,
from both
or non-cause.

The self-nature of existents
is not evident in the conditions.
In the absence of self-nature,
other-nature is not evident."

Though the Buddhas have spoken of duration, arising, ceasing, being,
non-being, low, moderate and higher by force of worldly convention, they
have not done so in an ultimate sense.

Designations are insignificant as self, non-self or self-non-self because
all expressible things are, like Nirvana, empty of own being.

Since all things lack substance, either in cause or conditions, or totality
or separately, therefore they are empty.

Without one there are not many. Without many, one is not possible.
Therefore things that arise dependently are indeterminable."

These pithy statements, not unlike Wittgenstein's, are an encouragement to readers to meditate and reflect deeply on these matters. Nagarjuna wanted those committed to mindful inquiry into life to realize that ultimately all *things* and all *views*, are empty of inherent existence. Conflicts, burdens and suffering are negated because they all arise dependent upon a position.

Some academics, such as the late Chris Gudmunsen, author of "Wittgenstein and Buddhism," have noted there are striking parallels between Wittgenstein and Nagarjuna. Nagarjuna revealed that the "mind" has divided the "world" into various "objects." He teaches repeatedly the emptiness of inherent existence of any object or standpoint. Whereas Wittgenstein concentrated his attention on language, Nagarjuna directed his inquiry to the entire field of perceptions, thoughts and activities. Nagarjuna systematically exposed the Emptiness of all experiences, conventional views, suffering, time, action, feelings, self, impermanence and liberation. He revealed the emptiness of Emptiness when he said that to take up Emptiness as a doctrine is to be incurable. "It is as if a drug, administered to cure a patient were to remove all his disorders, but were itself to foul the stomach by remaining therein."

What distinguishes Nagarjuna and Wittgenstein is the impact of their inquiries on their lives. Wittgenstein relied upon the power of his intellect to tackle the "fortress" of logic. Unlike Nagarjuna, he had very little opportunity for living in a healing spiritual environment that could have provided him with sustained joy and insights into his emotional life. His personal suffering and anguish continued life long as he struggled with his thoughts, moods and relationships with others. He spent years in academic circles—a world of words, debate and argument—but often railed against it because it failed to address the whole person. Wittgenstein cared passionately for the quality of people's lives and wanted his philosophy to be regarded as therapeutic. He felt the frustration of having little success since language abuse pervades the academic environment.

Liberation from the suffering wrapped up in "self" existence lay at the heart of Nagarjuna's insights. For this reason he is revered in the Buddhist tradition as a saint, that is, as one who has realized the end of suffering. Unlike Wittgenstein, Nagarjuna abided in a supportive environment of silence, insight meditation and experiential exploration of standpoints with other meditators, all primary features of monastic life. Nagarjuna did not establish anything as inherently existing including pleasure and pain. He spoke from direct insights into ultimate realization.

The teachings of Nagarjuna and Wittgenstein call us to examine the way we take up views, cling to our belief in language games and imagine that any view of our identity and roles has inherent truth. But their insights continue to remain largely inaccessible to many. In one sense their insights appear to be perceived as only obscure and abstract language games, though neither philosopher would have agreed to that position. They wanted their understanding to change people's lives, and their teachings to be taken out of the monastic and university environment. It can appear insuperably difficult to read Wittgenstein, while the painstaking precision of Nagarjuna requires utmost concentration. Nevertheless, what they revealed about the human condition is profoundly valuable and deserves street credibility, otherwise their insights will remain barren in the hands of religious scholars and academics.

In his first book, *Tractatus Logico-Philosophicus*, Wittgenstein tormented himself thinking about the relationship of language to the world. He concluded that there has to be something in common between words and what they are made to represent. He then presented his *picture theory of meaning*, which says that sentences form a picture of the nature of things. Wittgenstein realized that we can learn about the structure of the world of objects from the sentences we employ. He said words only possess meaning through the context of a sentence; for a time he implied that the only sentences that made sense were those that were logical and positive. This means that issues which had troubled philosophers and theologians such as ethics, good and evil, beauty and God could not be meaningfully communicated through language.

In later years, he said that the structure of our sentences determines the way we think the world is. His criticism of other theories and attempts to explain the nature of phenomena have upset certain philosophers and theologians. Thinkers like to establish a firm position for themselves, but Wittgenstein treated language as a descriptive process, ever changing. Nagarjuna, however, held little regard for any contextual view of meaning. He said there is no authentic relationship between words, or between subject and object, since no statements hold any inherent meaning. Both meaning and use lack final verification. Realizing this, the wise surrender all notions of meaning and use. To his credit, Wittgenstein rejected the idea of a "private language" whereas Nagarjuna perceived the Emptiness of both private and public languages. His approach cuts into the ego's desire for a standpoint, and any name and reputation that might accompany it.

In our preoccupation with language we have sometimes grasped key words and formed an ideology around them. This habit perpetuates the notion that these key words have referents; this means that the words refer to some independent "thing." Believing they have a referent we lose interest in the way we use them and imprison ourselves in the words as though they were Ultimate Truth. Wittgenstein wrote: "When we say 'every word in language signifies something' we have so far said *nothing whatever*; unless we have explained *exactly what* distinction we wish to make." Wittgenstein and Nagarjuna both pointed out that there is no essence that defines a word.

For example, we might explore such words as *spiritual, Green* or *Buddhist*. Wittgenstein used the term *family resemblance* to describe a word. A word does not have a meaning in the common sense; there are only lots of patterns of descriptions that make up a word, which means that a word which we may have identified with actually has an endless variety of uses and meanings in different situations, with no inherent truth in any of them. *Spiritual, Green* or *Buddhist* cannot stand for one particular thing. Adopting the language of the Buddha, Nagarjuna said that every word we communicate, every thought we express is "dependently arising."—it has no essence, no particular single thing which it stands for.

The word *spiritual* makes its appearance in all sorts of quarters from presidents of countries who run brutal regimes, to orthodox religious leaders who identify blindly with the status quo, to Greens who care about the Earth. The word is granted meaning through its use. Nagarjuna's concern was that our failure to realize the nature of dependent arising causes conflict and confusion, a breeding ground for narrow or generalized views and divisions within religious and secular life.

The dictionary reminds us that the word *spiritual* has its roots in the Latin word "spirare"—to breathe—with mindfulness and conscious attention. Faced with the pain of the Earth and its people, including our own pain, we remember to breathe rather than react in conditioned ways. To be *spiritual* is to dissolve the patterns of conditioned thought, patterns of greed, hate, fear and confusion. But while this explanation of the word *spiritual* may apply in some circles it has quite a different meaning elsewhere. Other users have equal claim on the word despite the differences in their interpretation of its meaning.

Some environmentalists refute concepts such as *spiritual* so that a managerial response can be implemented to handle global problems. To them, the word *spiritual* indicates a self centred activity which hinders a professional and technological solution to the environmental crisis. These environmentalists rely upon an intellectual and financial commitment to resolve global issues, believing we can then control the use of the Earth's resources in an effective way. This view is common in major political parties; the privatization of *spirituality* has become a feature of secular society. There is a refusal in government and corporations to introduce the issue of a *spiritual* crisis in society into the environmental and economic debate. Prominent environmentalists and their opponents have agreed to exclude the issue of humankind's inner relationship to the Earth.

One school of thought takes a positive stance with regard to the meaning of the word *spiritual*, the other takes a negative one. The language of *spirituality* involves the *environment* for some and remains excluded for others. For some, including many *Greens*, the word *spiritual* implies something immaterial, a deep sensitivity towards the innumerable communications of life. Certain moments of contact with nature, or unusual revelations, elicit certain inner responses which Greens describe as *spiritual*. This notion of *spiritual* is realized through experiences, cultivated or spontaneous.

The Green Party has regular fringe workshops on what *spirituality* means or doesn't mean. Some activists cannot bear such words in political forms of language; to them to be *spiritual* sounds sloppy and unproductive. And, of course, this view has some validity. But one has only to read a single issue of the newsletter *The New Year One* to realize that there is a breathtakingly active wing of *spirituality*. The newsletter gives regular reports of non-violent direct actions on US nuclear bases to stop the production of nuclear weapons. The *spiritual* beliefs of the activists unite in their view of the obscenity of nuclear weapons.

When we examine *spirituality* we see again and again that the word *does not have any inherent meaning*. Its meaning derives from its use. Since it does not have any meaning in itself it begs the question why people make such a fuss about it, either through addiction to its use and repetition, or by aggressively regarding the word as a distraction from what they think really matters. When we hear descriptions of *spiritual* experiences we often assume that the person's real purpose is to bolster their ego.

Similarly, difficulty arises around the question: What does it mean to be *Green*? Presumably it includes not eating animals, birds and fish, and not smoking; perhaps only strict Hindus and New Agers are *Green*. To be *Green* is also said to include living in a sustainable way with the minimum use of resources, regardless of any spiritual dimension. If we use this definition then the homeless and the poor are probably the only ones who qualify. Perhaps to be *Green* is to live in a community with simple, shared resources. Then if we become monks and nuns, or are locked up in prison, would we qualify? Or are *Greens* those who love nature? Then perhaps sunbathers, mountaineers and hikers are *Green*. Surely we would not advocate a whole lifestyle from any single one of these activities? If the world lived as I do (a small mortgage, a 1981 car and a collection of books), the strain on the Earth's limited resources would be greater than it is already. I am grateful that the world isn't turning itself in my direction.

When we examine what *Green* means we recognize the uncomfortable truth that we are unable to claim an authentic *Green* way of life. With a global population of around six billion we may have to acknowledge that to be *Green* primarily fulfils our desire to use a label, to belong. The same principle also applies to other labels we give ourselves as we are mad for identity through language. And yet we *can* contribute to living in a sustainable world; pictures of reality *can* make a difference in the relative world.

At times we like to bring the words together as *Green Spirituality*, but this mixes two concepts; neither has any meaning other than what we think they have. Both belong to a descriptive language with obvious paradoxes: how can spirituality have a colour and how can two descriptions without an obvious referent mean anything? Like everything else language does not hold up to possessing any inherent meaning.

To act with wisdom means not identifying with the Green movement or spirituality, nor regarding the environment as independent of the state of mind, or the state of mind independent of the environment. The environment holds no objective reality and spirituality holds no subjective reality. This dissolves the deeply cherished idea of an independent self existence. Such realizations affect our feelings, perceptions and language in the field of economics, politics and ecology.

Wittgenstein's use of the term *language game* to describe the problems of words has had unfortunate consequences: for many the association with the word *game* is pleasure, a pastime, something unimportant. It is not unusual to hear the accusation that a person is only caught up in a language game, even when the person is inquiring into a word's use and meaning, not just being intellectually clever. It is surprising that Wittgenstein used the word *game* when he approached his work with such seriousness. It needs to be understood that he refers to a *game* in the sense that a *game* only exists as a set of rules or conventions which the players agree to abide by, e.g. poker.

Wittgentstein would have approved of the passages on *Ultimate Truth* written in the Prajnaparamita Sutta, a commentary of the Madhyamika tradition. The Buddha said to Subhuti, a student of his teachings.

"I who do not find anything to correspond to the word Bodhisattva, *or to the words* Perfect Wisdom—*which* Bodhisattva *should I then instruct and admonish in which* Perfect Wisdom?

Subhuti: "As I understand all dharmas cannot be talked about in any proper sense.

The Buddha: "So it is, Subhuti. All dharmas are inexpressible. The inexpressibility of all dharmas is their emptiness. And emptiness cannot be expressed in words.

Subhuti: Can an inexpressible object grow or decline?

The Buddha: No, Subhuti.

Subhuti: Then there can be no growth or decline of the perfections of qualities of mind. Who could fully know the supreme enlightenment?

The Buddha: So it is, Subhuti. But it does not occur to the Bodhisattva "I grow in the perfections of qualities of mind. On the contrary, it occurs

to the bodhisattva "a mere designation is that."
   Subhuti: What is perfect enlightenment?
   The Buddha: It is the suchness of all dharmas.
   Subhuti: What is this suchness of all dharmas?
   The Buddha: It is thus there is no growth nor decline of an inexpressible object. It is thus that the bodhisattva should course in the perfection of wisdom by way of no growth and no decline."

A common religious view claims that life is a temporary phenomenon, a field of woe or a valley of death; while scientists often believe in the theory of evolution. Such views can justify rejection or pursuit of concerns about the state of the Earth. The theory of evolution which commonly claims the ability of certain species to adapt to environmental change or sees evolution as an essential dynamic of self-organization has no inherent truth to it. Such views are bound up with perceptions, views and time. Religious views can encourage forsaking Earthly concerns in order to focus attention on "higher" things with the promise of eternal gratification after death. We often seek to escape from the human condition in this world and from our dependent existence; religion has provided the language of escape. Neither Wittgenstein nor Nagarjuna supported such use of language.

Wittgenstein encouraged thoughtful people to regard language only as a conventional tool. He wanted us to understand that we cannot perceive the world independent of our conceptual framework. Wittgenstein did not claim that words and objects do not correspond at all, but he explained that whenever we refer to objects we are subject to the limitations of language. Like Nagarjuna, he understood that we cannot adopt a metaphysical position that stands above concepts and the conceived. For Nagarjuna, the dualistic world of conceptions and the conceived is relative truth.

The Ultimate Truth reveals the emptiness of inherent existence of all forms of appraisal and all dharmas, including the Buddha's teachings and the Four Noble Truths. The Buddhist traditions make an important distinction between intellectually grasping onto the way things are and realization. Realization dissolves the suffering born of clinging, dependency and belief in inherent existence, whereas intellectual insights may make little difference to emotional pain. The Insight Meditation tradition of Buddhism gives no significance to an intellectual understanding of life.

Only by realizing the Emptiness of labels do we have the opportunity to free the mind from biased judgements. Labels are divisive. Through clinging to our labels we fuel the nightmare of ego identity and "us and them." engaging in a war of words. If we identify with labels, such as *spiritual*, *Green*, *Buddhist* or *English*, we face others who define the same words in a different way. What truly matters is not accessible to us in language or through language. Words mystify us, yet naively we try to discover truth through word games. Ultimately, there are no referents to the nature of things, no pictures, no tools and no guides to the way things are. We have become trapped in a manufactured world of description, criticism and analysis in which language matters due to our blindness and clinging to one interpretation over another.

It is easy to fall back into a materialist perception of the nature of things: if we abandon language it seems that only matter remains, that is, the *environment*, and then the *environment* with all its material components, becomes the only true reality. When the *environment* is perceived independent of language, the *environment* gradually takes second place to language, to the war of words between groups with varying ideological interests. Genuine interest and intimacy with the nature of things becomes insignificant. The ego infects language with the sense of "I know" and "you don't know." Being at loggerheads in language games with others becomes part of our daily life.

We may act with concern for the *environment* as an objective reality, or we may live our lives seeking to secure from it the maximum number of pleasant sensations. Writing and talking about the *environment*, as though it were a true, objective reality is an act of belief, an assumption which requires collaboration and agreement for discussion to proceed. Our sensations matter to us as much as the *environment*. The inseparable nature of *environment*, sensations and mind means that ultimately all three are lacking inherent existence.

Each gains its apparent inherent existence through our *belief* in it. What I realize is that the force of my desires, wholesome or unwholesome, gives the *world* its substance and its meaning. The nature of things humbles my existence. There is nothing in the world of language that I consider worth becoming identified with. *My views* of *the world* are simply that. *I* cannot separate *the world* from *my view*. I realize that *my view* has neither a superior nor inferior existence, nor does any other. The suchness of things, the nature of things, cannot be described since they cannot be made into objects to be described. Truly, there are no objects and thus there is no language. How is this revealed? Through "objects" and "language." Naturally.

In the mystical passages at the end of Wittgenstein's *Tractatus Logico-Philosophicus*, he wrote:

"The world of the happy man is a different one from that of the unhappy man."

"So too at death the world does not alter, but comes to an end. Death is not an event in life; we do not live to experience death...."

"If we take eternity to mean not infinite temporal duration but timelessness, then eternal life belongs to those who live in the present.

"He must transcend these propositions, and then he will see the world aright. What we cannot speak about we must pass over in silence."

The Buddha
and Women

Ananda: *"Are women able, when they have entered*
into homelessness, to experience the
fullness of realizations of the spiritual life?"

The Buddha: *"Yes, they are able. If then Pajapati*
accepts the eight special rules
let that be reckoned as her ordination."

With the above words, reluctantly but nevertheless to his credit, the Buddha triggered the movement for women's spirituality in India. At the time of the Buddha, men enjoyed the exclusive privilege of abandoning the life of the householder with all of it attendant responsibilities, to follow their heart and go on a spiritual quest.

Alienated and anguished, Siddhartha Gautama himself, aged 29, walked out on his wife and child to find the Truth. There was nothing romantic about such a gesture. Years later, after enlightenment, the Buddha gave a full account of his flight from these responsibilities to attend to a duty of a different order. These statements of departing from home to homelessness revealed as much about attitudes to responsibility as about the quest for Truth; he always emphasized disciplines and renunciation for entering into such a form of spiritual life. Yet the urgency of the search must take precedence over the conventional duties of life.

The texts lead us to believe that the Buddha was serious from the start. Whether he was running away from duty, or moving towards Truth or both is something that we can only speculate about. He, himself, may not have known what his underlying motives were though later on in his life, he speaks of his departure from the palace as if it were a very clear decision. It is common enough memory to recall the past in a favourable light forgetting the fears and confusions that took place at the time.

One suspects, however, that his wife, Yashodara or any other woman of the time would not have dared abandon the householders life, particularly their children, to pursue a vague ideal called Truth. So the life of the homeless spiritual seeker remained the domain of men. Women never felt welcomed into such circles of spiritual practitioners, who lived their life under the stars, or spent time in simple dwellings.

Initially, the Buddha declined to invite women to join the homeless sangha. He went along with the accepted conventions of focusing on men for the homeless life. It was Ananda, his trusted attendant, who finally persuaded the Buddha to extend the same invitation to women to join the homeless ones. He challenged the Buddha after listening to Pajapati Gotami, who was to become the founder of the homeless women's sangha.

Pajapati Gotami brought Siddhartha up after the death of his mother when he was a week old. When Siddhartha fled the palace, he made a personal vow that if he realized the Ultimate Truth, he would return as quickly as possible to Kapilavatthu, the capital of the Sakyan kingdom, to tell his family what he had discovered. Upon the Buddha's return to his home city, he met with his family including his wife, his son, Rahula, and Nanda, the son of Pajapati, his foster mother. As a revered older woman, Pajapati saw the potential for women to be accorded the same status as men in the spiritual life so she approached the Buddha to ask him if women could enter the homeless state.

The Buddha replied: "Enough, Gotami. Don't set your heart on women being allowed to do this."

She requested twice again and upon being refused she burst into tears. So later, independently she shaved her head, put on robes and headed for Vasali with other like-minded women to talk to the Buddha again. She stood weeping outside the hall when Ananda approached her wondering why she was crying. So then Ananda approached the Buddha and he also was told three times not to set his heart on such a request. But when the Buddha acknowledged that gender bore no relationship to the potential for an enlightened life, Ananda took the opportunity:

"If women are able to realize enlightenment, and since Pajapati was of great service to you—she was your aunt, nurse, foster mother, when your mother died, even suckled you at her own breast—it would be good if women could be allowed to enter into the sangha."

The women, including Pajapati, had walked 150 miles to Vasali determined to state their case to the Buddha. All of them had set their heart on a different way of life, and thus the Buddha relented:

"If then Pajapati accepts the eight special rules let that be reckoned as her ordination." The Buddha then went on to lay down "Eight special rules for the women, not to be disregarded." Only the women were told to observe these eight rules.

1. *A nun, even of a hundred years standing, shall respectfully greet, rise up in the presence of, bow down before, and perform all proper duties towards a monk ordained even a day.*
2. *A nun is not to spend the rainy season in a district where there is no monk.*
3. *Every half-moon a nun is to await two things from the order of monks— the date of the ordination ceremony and the time the monks will come to give teaching.*
4. *After the rains retreat, the nuns are to inquire as to whether any faults have been committed before both sanghas, of men and women, in respect to what has been seen, heard or suspected.*
5. *A nun guilty of a serious offence must undergo the discipline before both sanghas.*
6. *When a novice has trained for two years in the six precepts (the first five precepts plus the precept of taking one meal a day before noon) she should seek ordination from both sanghas.*
7. *A nun is not to revile or abuse a monk under any circumstances.*
8. *Admonition by nuns of monks is forbidden; admonition of nuns by monks is not forbidden.*

The Buddha added other rules for women: the men in the sangha observed a total of 227 precepts while the women had to accept 311 rules. Each of these extra rules arose as a response to a situation (similar to the British legal system). The five volumes of the Books of the Vinaya explain the rules, the circumstances that gave rise to the rules and the stories involved. In the Theravada tradition, rules are still regarded with the utmost seriousness, whereas other Buddhist traditions have been willing to adapt or abandon many of the minor ones. The Buddha never intended to be an absolute authority on social conventions yet prominent Buddhists still resolutely decline to grant women equal authority in the ordained life. Clinging to the past continues to take precedence over fairness and justice. Established Buddhism often remains reluctant to change preferring to adopt views of conformity rather than challenge.

The additional unnecessary rules upon the women clearly placed them in a secondary position. The texts record that at a later date, Pajapati attempted to change the first rule demanding that a senior ordained woman should not take a secondary role to a newly ordained man. Ananda also tried to persuade the Buddha to drop this rule and the other rules that flowed from it. But the Buddha remained uncompromising—with all the long term consequences of such intransigence. Yet even if the Buddha had granted 100 per cent equality to men and women in the homeless sangha, there is no guarantee that, as time passed, men's need for control would not have led them to reassert priority.

The texts revealed that the Buddha reacted in a rather uncharacteristic and dualistic way when he claimed that the spiritual teachings would be adversely affected through women's ordination. He said: "Women have now received that permission, the teachings will not last so long, the Dharma will now stand for only 500 years. Just as when the disease called mildew falls upon a field of rice in fine condition, that rice does not continue long." It could be argued that it was his prediction and the special rules for women that harmed the future welfare and potential for both men and women in the homeless sangha.

The Buddha lived in an ancient religious culture where for most people one's position remained defined for life. Though the Buddha was unable to dispense totally with gender discrimination, he still launched women's spirituality as a collective force. He had frequently spoken of himself not as a guru but as a "good friend" and his invitation to women to join him in homelessness expressed that quality of friendship. The Buddha's willingness conditionally to accept women into the homeless sangha seems to be an example of three steps forward, one step back. Even with their special rules, there would have been a furore in India at his endorsement of the homeless life for women because it meant that women always had the option to renounce their husbands instead of living behind closed doors supporting family and loved ones. Like men, the homeless women were allowed three robes, a belt, a razor (to shave the head), a bowl, a water filter, thread and needle. In addition, they used a hip-string during menstruation. Nuns went on daily alms rounds in towns and villages.

In a single invitation the Buddha radically challenged this conventional role for women, thus sparking a liberation movement in the culture. No doubt, conservatives would have charged the Buddha with irresponsibility in setting such a precedent. The safety of women, the capacity of women to live in harmony as a community and their ability to realize enlightenment would have become major talking point among traditionalists. The Buddha would have had to have dealt with much of this backlash. In this respect it is to his credit that he provided the same opportunity for a free and enlightened life to women as to men and his decision inspired tremendous love and respect from thousands of women.

His speculation about the future and the imposition of the extra rules have generated centuries of debate in the Buddhist tradition. One of the commonly held views of that period was "Only men can become Buddhas, only women can bear children." This view is still often repeated today among Buddhist traditionalists. One is left wondering whether the Buddha, acted as he did out of need to appease the Hindu traditionalists and Brahmins by providing only a secondary role to homeless women.

There has been speculation that this very rare example of discrimination by the Buddha could have been added to the ancient texts by later generations of monks. The warning about the future outcome and the additional rules for women would deter some women from joining the homeless sangha. But one must take the oral and then recorded texts, written perhaps 300–400 years after the Buddha's life, on face value. For if the monks could make such changes to the texts then they would surely have adapted their own vinaya as well—some of their 227 rules make for an uncomfortable life.

Women featured as an important presence in the Buddha's early life. Being born into royalty, he could choose any woman that he cared for. Many fathers in the Sakyan kingdom brought their daughters to the royal palace hoping that the handsome Siddhartha Gautama would feel attracted to one of them. He lived in a world of sensuality, where the flash of a beautiful woman's eyes could spark his energies. As a young man, he had a harem of beautiful women, who attended to his every whim. (Some of the women, who joined Pajapati in the homeless life, had belonged to Siddhartha's harem several years previously). When Siddhartha married Yashodara, the texts reported that he chose the most beautiful "raven-haired" woman of the land.

On the night of his enlightenment, the Buddha's passion for women rose in his mind as powerful sensual images. Starved of sexual intimacy with a woman for six years, he had to cope with the full force of his sexual fantasies involving three women. Later the Buddha referred to these fantasies as the three daughters of Mara (the tempter). His struggle with his sexual fantasies marked one of the turning points on the night of his enlightenment. If he was going to realize the essential and Ultimate Truth, if he was going to see the emptiness of all projections, then he would have to stay steady as the mind created powerful images of lust and desire.

During the years of his teaching, he recognized the tremendous dedication and determination of women and men to realize an enlightened life. Accounts of women's experiences of enlightenment were recorded in a book known as *Therigatha*, a collection of more than 70 verses or poems. *Theri* means "women elders" and *gatha* means a stanza or verse. The book reveals an extensive collection of insights into women's liberation. The book is unique in that it is perhaps the world's first collection of women's experiences of spiritual insights, there is probably nothing comparable in any other religion. Other religious traditions have tended to marginalize women, except for the occasional woman saint, or worshipped them as the Holy Mother.

The Buddha imparted a practical wisdom, often so self evident that intellectuals and cynics have accused him of offering a banal message. The Buddha intended that people face their life and death and the very nature of their experience on Earth. He never tried to give a comprehensive and intellectually satisfying philosophy of life, rather he shook people out of their complacency, their daydreams, their naivety and the conceit tied up with self existence. "We are all going to die" is an obvious statement but desire and denial obscure the obvious. What sounds banal to the arrogant shakes another person out of his or her indulgence in the belief in the continuity of personal existence.

One of the Buddha's best known encounters with a woman was with Kisagotami, whose baby had recently died. Stricken with grief, she carried the dead baby around looking for someone to perform a miracle to bring the baby back to life. Upon being directed to the Buddha, she appealed to him but he told her: "Go and bring a mustard seed from a house where nobody there has known somebody to die." She could not find such a house, thus realizing that death is common to all. In time, she realizing the essence of the teachings and uttered:

"I have finished with the death of my child
I don't grieve
I don't cry
I'm not afraid of you (death),
The great dark is torn apart
and Death
you too are destroyed."

Since the Buddha placed the highest value on the quest for Truth, he did not concern himself with granting religious significance to marriage, separation or divorce, considering them as social contracts. If a married man or woman left home for homelessness, he or she had to have permission from the partner and the one who remained at home was free to remarry. Some householders complained: "Why has Gautama come here? To take away our sons and make our daughters widows?"

Recognizing that an enlightened mind knows no gender, the Buddha encouraged women in the sangha to express their spiritual authority, offer teachings and establish communities. Their religious insights, expressed in poetic form, stands beside another volume of spiritual poetry, *Theragatha*, stanzas of the male elders. Thus despite the hesitations of the Buddha and his additional precepts, the sangha of men and women engaged in serious spiritual practices, and were equals in ultimate realizations.

Perhaps the major tragedies of the 2500-year-old Buddhist tradition include the Moghuls' desecration of monasteries and destruction of the records of centuries of religious experiences and insight, the colonial and North American governments war against the people of Vietnam, Laos and Kampuchea (formerly Cambodia), and the degenerate force of Western consumerism. Within Buddhism perhaps the major loss is the gradual decline, and virtual elimination, of the order of homeless women of deep spiritual practice. In many monasteries today nuns attend to the needs of the monastery—cooking, cleaning, chanting and a little meditation; lay people turn primarily to monks for spiritual guidance.

In present-day monasteries, monks and nuns know those women with deep spiritual realization. They have always been accorded a special respect, and some nuns are revered as spiritual teachers. But, on the whole, the men receive the bulk of the attention and continue to have the most opportunity for full devotion to deep inner spiritual practices. As violence and sexual abuse increase in Buddhist countries, nuns cannot safely go into solitude—another restriction.

Some of the experiences and realizations recorded in the *Therigatha* include Uttam, who said:

"I have found what is vast and empty,
the unborn.
It is what I longed for.
I am a true daughter of the Awakened One,
always finding joy in peace.
I have ended the hunger
of gods and humans
and I will not wander
birth to birth.
I have no thought of becoming."

In another passage Maitreyi implores her husband for his wisdom. He has seen the futility of accumulating wealth and has decided to go into the homeless sangha. She says to him: "If this whole earth and its treasures were mine could I attain the Deathless through them?" He said "No." She then answered her concern when she asked "So what would I do with that which cannot take me beyond death?"

Mutta, the daughter of a Brahmin family, left her husband to join the women of spiritual practice as she felt trapped by her husband and household tasks.

"Free, I am free
I am free
by means of the three
crooked things,
mortar, pestle, and
my crooked husband.
"I am free
from birth and death
and all that dragged me back."

The Buddha encouraged women and men to reflect on the unpleasant features of bodily life—corpses, excrement, urine, phlegm, spit, sweat etc. The effect of these teachings, along with insights into the nonself, nonpersonal nature of bodily life emptied the mind of embarrassment, pride or shame about the body. The homeless women bathed naked together at the public baths along with the call girls and prostitutes in the area. But the call girls taunted the young women of the sangha: "Why not enjoy pleasure now and renounce the world when you are old. Then you can experience both."

One of the women leading the spiritual life, Vimala, had used her sensuality to attract men. But then she realized the futility of it. In her verses of liberating insight, she said:

"Young,
intoxicated by my own
lovely skin,
my figure
my beautiful looks
and famous too
I despised other women.
And when I stripped for men
I was the woman of their dreams
I laughed as I teased them.
Today, I, my same self,

sit at the tree's foot
no thought,
All ties untied."

These examples of a transformed consciousness reveal some of the many ways that women and men can take responsibility for their situation, the impact they have on others, and understand what it means to relate free from desire and projection. Through insight, patterns of behaviour to each other, such as conforming to social expectations, manipulation of others or taking a subservient position lose all meaning in the discovery of the Ultimate Truth or the Non-Dual. It is these realizations that dissolve the belief in substantial differences between men and women, home and homeless life.

Insight into the Non-Dual, the Deathless, elicits from the depth of being fresh responses to others. There is a natural respect for people, regardless of their conditioning—and people are not divided into the category of the high and the low. In realization of the Ultimate Truth, the prejudices dissolve, yet without reducing everybody to a grey, uniform sameness. Attachment to notions of superiority, inferiority or equality sew the seeds for further conflict and suffering. The primary duty of women is not to gain equality with men, but find the Truth that embraces all dualistic assumptions.

Abhirupa-Nanda understood this well. Insightful women and men will connect with this injunction of hers:

"Get rid of the tendency to judge yourself
as above, below or equal to others
By penetrating deeply into judgement
you will live at peace."

One of the greatest problems among women and men is not seeing that the capacity to accept oneself is an expression of deep understanding. Upbringing, social pressures and demands on oneself exacerbate the common social problem of lack of self acceptance. This lends itself to self rejection, feelings of lack of self worth, and vulnerability when dismissed or ridiculed by others. Lack of self acceptance can drive a person to emphasize ego gratification, profit and gain at the expense of others, towards withdrawal and despair or into a confused and uncertain existence.

Deeply aware of the problems generated through lack of self acceptance and self understanding, the Buddha gave invaluable meditation teachings to negate this problem, to take the problem out of self. Not surprisingly, women and men world wide continue to take a deep interest in the dharma teachings which offer insight into self rejection and self acceptance. Issues around self acceptance feature prominently in religious and secular society. The tendency to lay judgements on ourselves becomes the curse of daily life. The dissolution of investment and belief in the judge, through insight, takes the apparent reality out of projections of being above, below or equal to others. Abhirupa-Nanda found through her experience that the priority for her attention and interest lay elsewhere. She then uttered the immortal words:

"Meditate on the Unconditioned." Her advice summarizes in four words the very essence of the Buddha's teachings.

The Waste Land of
T.S. Eliot

Ajita: *What pollutes the world*
and what threatens it most?

The Buddha: *The hunger of desire pollutes the world*
and fear of pain from suffering (threatens it most).

In the early 1920's when T.S. Eliot was putting together his collection of fragments that formed The Waste Land, he wove into the poem his appreciation of the Buddha's teachings. Eliot frequently turned to the early Buddhist texts, particularly Henry Clarke Warren's "Buddhism in Translation" (Harvard Oriental Series), for insight and inspiration. Warren wrote: "Protestant Christianity teaches salvation by faith while Buddhism places its greatest reliance in meditation."

The Waste Land and the elegant *Four Quartets* are probably Eliot's most revered poems. *The Waste Land* is the most analysed 20th century poem in English. It exposes the soul-destroying forces of a wretched and pained life, a perception expressed in the First Noble Truth of Suffering. This poem established Eliot as one of the greatest English language poets of the 20th century. In 1948, he received the Nobel Prize and the Order of Merit.

Eliot often gave free rendering in his poems to the teachings of the Buddha, the Bhavagad Gita and the Upanishads. The poet Stephen Spender wrote: "If Eliot's own views are to be considered I once heard him say to the Chilean poet Gabriela Mistral that at the time he was writing *The Waste Land* he seriously considered becoming a Buddhist." Eliot said that after three years of study and reflection on Oriental philosophy it left him in a "state of enlightened mystification." Another great poet and Nobel Prize winner, W.B. Yeats (1865-1939), also publicly acknowledged the influence of the Buddha's message on his own life.

Regarded as the Everest of 20th century poetry, *The Waste Land* awakens us to the futile features of daily life in Western civilization, and offers the occasional glimpse of something of a different order. The poem has earned an international reputation for being difficult to understand; this vexed Eliot although he acknowledged that it was not easy to read. He explained: "Genuine poetry can communicate before it is understood." Still, he made his subsequent poems, including *Four Quartets*, easier for readers to comprehend.

The poet Ezra Pound edited whole sections from *The Waste Land* but did nothing to alter its structureless appearance. Following the 433-line poem are 196 lines of Eliot's notes on it but these make only a small contribution to the reader's insights into the messages within the poem. The notes detail the significant influences for each of the five sections of the poem:

1. *The Burial of the Dead*
2. *A Game of Chess*
3. *The Fire Sermon*
4. *Death by Water*
5. *What the Thunder said.*

1. The Burial of the Dead

From the famous opening lines to the end of the poem there is an intensity accompanied by awareness of a painfully harsh existence that compels our attention.

"April is the cruellest month, breeding
Lilacs out of the dead land, mixing
Memory and desire stirring...

...I was neither
Living nor dead, and I knew nothing,
Looking into the heart of light, the silence."

Rooted in the London of dark suits and black umbrellas of the 1920's, the first section of the poem refers to London Bridge across which tens of thousands of office workers march daily, morning and evening, in tedium and conformity. (Between the ages of 15 and 22, I travelled five days a week across this bridge on foot or the number 13 bus. Forty years after Eliot, I can recall occasions when I had similar thoughts until I walked out of the office and wandered to the East for about a decade).

"Unreal City,
Under the brown fog of a winter dawn,
A crowd flowed over London Bridge, so many,
I had not thought death had undone so many.
Sighs, short and infrequent, were exhaled,

And each man fixed his eyes before his feet.
Flowed up the hill and down King William Street,
To where St. Mary Woolnoth kept the hours
With a dead sound on the final stroke of nine."

Office and factory workers in the city who enter the daily tread-mill of the work environment have to undergo, as Eliot himself did, those long, drab winters when cold chills the bone. During his 12 years as a city bank clerk, Eliot witnessed the degree to which he and others remained embroiled in their memories and desires. Amidst the drab conformity and polite veneer of civilization, were a range of inner voices desperately trying to break out—to escape these wastelands and journey to something different. These voices speak in the poem.

Whether Eliot intended it or not, *The Waste Land* has become an incisive and telling indictment of the wretchedness of our society. Degradation of our environment is not only a matter of defilement of land, water and air, it includes a psychological environment reduced to chilling drabness.

2. A Game of Chess

"From satin cases poured in rich profusion.
In vials of ivory and coloured glass
Unstoppered, lurked her strange synthetic perfumes,
Unguent, powdered or liquid-troubled, confused
And drowned the senses in odours; stirred by the air...

'My nerves are bad to-night. Yes, bad. Stay with me.
Speak to me. Why do you never speak? Speak.
What are you thinking of? What thinking? What?
I never know what you are thinking. Think.'

I think we are in rats' alley
Where the dead men lost their bones."

Unlike the Buddha, Eliot declined to pinpoint the remedy for this bleakness of city life but instead highlighted, even accelerated, the reader's confrontation with the First Noble Truth. Eliot said he wrote the poem out of need rather than with any intention to make a comment about 20th century civilization. He told one critic: "I wonder what an 'intention' means! One doesn't know quite what it is that one wants to get off the chest until one's got it off. But I couldn't apply the word 'intention' positively to any of my poems."

The Waste Land has lost none of its authenticity; some would say that its relevance is even greater today. A generation of young men died in the battlefields of Europe from 1914-18. In the post First World War era, when the merciless tyrannies of fascism and communism cast their dark shadows over so-called Western civilization, a pervasive spiritual despair prevailed. Yet Eliot's despair focuses on the city environment rather than any predominantly political ideology. Though fascism and totalitarianism represented the ugly face of civilization of the 1920's, we have as pernicious a threat to our welfare today—the same holocaust of spiritual values and systematic world wide destruction of community life, cultures and environment as that Eliot wrote about.

As the title of the poem implies, a tone of bleak grandeur infuses the reader from one line to another as Eliot conveys his experience of despair and torment. The physical and mental unhappiness of his first wife, his struggles between belief and scepticism, his conversion from "American" to "English" (dress, accent, London residence and citizenship) had a telling impact on his consciousness. *The Waste Land*'s fragmentary rhythm speaks of Eliot himself who acknowledged his "only hope of really penetrating into the heart of the mystery of Indian philosophy would lie in forgetting how to think and feel as an American or an European which for practical as well as sentimental reasons I do not wish to do."

3. The Fire Sermon

Thomas Stearns Eliot, born in 1888 in Missouri, held deep feelings for a religious life, without holding to a religion during his student days at Harvard University. Inspired by the 19th century endorsement of Ralph Waldo Emerson and Henry David Thoreau, the "Brahmin" tradition of Harvard University emphasized the study of Indian philosophies and religion.

It was at this time that he began writing some early pieces that became fragments of the poem. Inspired by saints and spiritual seekers, who shrug off worldly pursuits and the unimaginative conformity of civilization, Eliot devoted much of his studies to reading Buddhist and Hindu texts on the wisdom of the spiritual life. In 1912-13, three of his seven courses were in "Indic philology," two being sections in the original Pali, the language used to record the Buddha's teachings. He regarded his two teachers of Buddhism and Hinduism, Irving Babbit and Paul Elmer More, as the two wisest men he ever met. Eliot had stated that poet's maturity depended upon his or her "range of sensibility... especially in the range of religious feeling."

Perhaps the most damning statement about the Western world is in the third section. In his notes at the end of the poem, Eliot writes:

"The complete text of the Buddha's Fire Sermon (which corresponds in importance to the Sermon on the Mount) from which these words are taken will be found translated in the late Henry Clarke Warren's Buddhism in Translation (Harvard Oriental Series). Mr. Warren was one of the great pioneers of Buddhist studies in the Occident."

Although Eliot overestimates the significance of the Fire Sermon, he recognizes it as a fundamental talk of the Buddha designed to disillusion the listener from all hope of finding any genuine satisfaction through desire and pleasure. The Buddha said that we are burning up with greed, hate and delusion and, as a result, the world is on fire. Due to the overheated mind, we burn up with desire for things of the world. Selfish demands upon each other and the environment generate wars, famines and destruction. The Buddha exposed the unresolved personal problems of human behaviour and our burning desire for gratification regardless of the resultant suffering for everybody and everything, including the Earth.

In a talk given in Gaya, Bihar, India, the Buddha used dramatic language when he said:

"All is burning. And what is All that is burning?"

The eye is burning. Visible forms are burning. Eye consciousness is burning. Eye contact is burning. Also feeling, whether pleasant, painful or neither-painful-nor pleasant, that arises with eye contact as its condition, that too is burning. Burning with what? Burning with the fire of lust, with the fire of anger, with the fire of confusion; it is burning with birth, ageing and death, with sorrow, regret, pain, grief and despair, I say.

The ear is burning. Sounds are burning...

The nose is burning. Smells are burning....

The tongue is burning. Tastes are burning...

The body is burning. Touch is burning...

The mind is burning.

Mental objects are burning.

Mind consciousness is burning.

Mind contact is burning.

Also the feeling, whether pleasant, painful or neither painful- nor-pleasant that arises with mind contact as its condition, that too is burning. Burning with the fire of lust, with the fire of anger and with the fire of confusion; it is burning with birth, ageing and death, with sorrow, regret, pain, grief and despair, I say.

Seeing thus, the wise noble one becomes dispassionate towards the eye, towards visible forms, towards eye consciousness, towards eye contact. Also he becomes dispassionate towards the feeling, whether pleasant, painful or neither-pleasant-nor painful, that arises with eye contact as its condition.

One becomes dispassionate towards the eye, nose, tongue and body and mind....

Being dispassionate his lust fades away; with the fading away of lust his heart is liberated; when the heart is liberated there comes the spiritual insights: it is liberated. One understands: birth is exhausted, the spiritual life has been lived out; what was to be done is done, there is no more of this to come."

Verse after verse of *The Waste Land* conveys the same pointlessness of grasping after pleasure and mediocrity. The "sweet Thames" nourishes the religious voice of Eliot's rebellion against a shadowy existence of daily work rituals and the boredom of the home life, including sex. Eliot communicates our daily struggle with circumstances with only occasional points of light to uplift the spirit—communal feelings found in a pub, or in a sculpture, Magnus Martyr, in a church of Christopher Wren.

In the third section, Eliot writes:

"The river's tent is broken; last fingers of leaf
Clutch and sink into the wet bank. The wind
Crosses the brown land, unheard. The nymphs are departed.

Sweet Thames, run softly, till I end my song.
The river bears no empty bottles, sandwich papers,
Silk handkerchiefs, cardboard boxes, cigarette ends
Or other testimony of summer nights. The nymphs are
departed...

By the waters of Leman, I sat down and wept...
Sweet Thames, run softly till I end my song,
Sweet Thames, run softly, for I speak not loud or long.
But at my back in a cold blast I hear
The rattle of the bones, and chuckle spread from ear to ear.

A rat crept softly through the vegetation
Dragging its slimy belly on the bank
While I was fishing in the dull canal...

O City, city I can sometimes hear
Besides a public bar in lower Thames Street,
The pleasant whining of a mandoline
And a clatter and a chatter from within
Where fishermen lounge at noon: where the walls
Of Magnus Martyr hold
Inexplicable splendour of Ionian white and gold.

The river sweats
Oil and tar..."

Eliot's attention in the final lines of The Fire Sermon turns to the seaside resort of Margate. In the autumn of 1920 Eliot's father-in-law became seriously ill so Eliot and his wife, Vivien, nursed him day and night. Eliot returned the following year: In October, 1921 he went to recuperate at the Albermarle Hotel, Cliftonville, Margate, for the first week of his stay, and two weeks more at a cheaper hotel. He took with him a mandoline that Vivien had given him. While there he wrote much of The Fire Sermon. Eliot was unhappy: his marriage was in a shambles, his mental and physical health were under severe strain. Yet in this section of the poem he expresses a suffering that runs deeper than personal circumstances, becoming impersonal and pervasive in its mode.

4. Death by Water

By the end of the year, Eliot was putting together the final version of the entire poem for Ezra Pound to edit. Vivien and Eliot went to Paris where Pound made changes in the various sections of the poem. Eliot wrote the 10-line Fourth Section, "Death by Water," in Lausanne, Switzerland where he travelled after Paris to seek psychological help. In this section Eliot compares the fine life of fishermen in Nova Scotia with the world of "profit and loss" It speaks as though Eliot had discovered that the city is a lifeless world: he must look windward   otherwise he is spiritually dead.

"Phlebas the Phoenician, a fortnight dead,
Forget the cry of gulls, and the deep sea swell
And the profit and loss.
        A current under sea
Picked his bones in whispers. As he rose and fell
He passed the stages of his age and youth
Entering the whirlpool.

Gentile or Jew
O you who turn the wheel and look to windward,
Consider Phlebas, who was once handsome and tall as you."

5. what the Thunder Said

The fifth and final section "What the Thunder Said," written during his depression of December, 1921, compares a life without spirituality to a life without water. The poem continues to convey religious overtone in the Buddhist sense of a spiritual experience through awareness rather than through metaphysical beliefs.

"If there were water we should stop and drink
Amongst the rock one cannot stop or think
Sweat is dry and feet are in the sand...
There is not even silence in the mountains
But red sullen faces sneer and snarl
From doors of mudcracked houses
                    If there were water
And no rock
If there were rock
And also water....

"Who are those hooded hordes swarming
Over endless plains, stumbling in cracked earth
Ringed by the flat horizon only
What is the city over the mountains
Cracks and reforms and burst in the violet air
Falling towers
Jerusalem Athens Alexandria
Vienna London
Unreal."

To his credit, Eliot did not fall into the oldest stereotype about East and West, namely that the East is spiritual and the West is materialistic. Though some believe that the West has much to learn from Indian spirituality if it is to save its soul, Eliot did not fall into such dualistic standpoints. He regarded wisdom as something common to both. He wrote that the "Christian, the Brahmin, the Buddhist and the Muslim apprehend the same reality. Thus a passage from the New Testament or Thomas à Kempis or Pascal may be juxtaposed with one from the Nikayas or the Upanishads or from some Sufi mystic, *in complete concord.*" But Eliot also warned against dismissing the differences between religions: "No man has ever climbed to the higher stages of the spiritual life, who has not been a believer in a particular religion or at least a particular philosophy."

In the final 40 lines of *The Waste Land*, Eliot turns again to the influence of Indian religion on his poem, and his life. He appears to have given up all hope for cities, past or present, preferring to regard them as unreal, as maya, as belonging to the dead. What is of profound significance is not the daily fortunes of city life but, he declares, "Datta, dayadhvam and damyata"—give, be compassionate and control. To give here means to surrender, to be compassionate means to be receptive and to control means to be a disciplined pilgrim travelling the waters from the known to the unknown.

"Ganga was sunken, and the limp leaves
Waited for rain, while the black clouds
Gathered far distant, over Himavant
The jungle crouched, humped in silence.
Then spoke the thunder (of datta, dayadhrvam and damyatta).

His final verse reads in part:
"I sat upon the shore
Fishing, with arid plains behind me
Shall I at least set my lands in order?
London Bridge is falling down, falling down...
Datta. Dayadhvam. Damyata.
Shantih, shantih, shantih."

Thus one of the most remarkable poems in the English language ends with the Sanskrit words for Peace, Peace, Peace. This is, as Eliot points out in his final footnote to the poem: "A formal ending to an Upanishad. The Peace which passeth understanding is our equivalent to this word."

In 1927, about five years after he completed *The Waste Land*, T.S. Eliot became a member of the Anglican Church and several months later became a British citizen. As he admitted, his religious aspiration had "no longer wings to fly." His new faith brought him simultaneously closer to English life and answered personal needs. It was at some cost in that he sacrificed his earlier faith in silence and a spiritual quest grounded in surrender and discipline. Instead he opted for a Church with solid beliefs. It is not clear whether Eliot entered the Church as a remedy for unhappiness, or out of need for certainty, or both. Years later, he stated: "I am not a Buddhist

but some of the early Buddhist scriptures affect me as parts of the
Old Testament do."

Prince Charles and
Prince Siddhartha

So what of all these titles, names and nations.
They are mere wordly conventions.
They have come into being by common consent.
This false belief has been deeply ingrained in the
minds of the ignorant for a long time.
The Buddha.

At times, Prince Charles, heir apparent to the British throne, breaks out of the stifling royal mould and reveals a genuinely compassionate connection with the real world. Listening to his heart he speaks out on issues that matter to him—spiritual values, community service, the needs of the underprivileged, alternative medicine, architecture, the environment, organic farming, the English language, inner cities. His views endear him to a significant number of thoughtful people working to change the values and institutions of our society. He is a regular talking point in the spiritual and international Green movement.

The spiritually aware Charles (Philip, Arthur, George), the 21st English Prince of Wales, bears considerable authority due to his royal heritage. Whenever the Prince speaks on these issues and on the spiritual decline in society, the media take notice. His international status means that he also incurs the full wrath of the media due to their conventional standpoints. "Royal watchers" target Charles for ridicule; they seek out politicians, doctors, architects, religious leaders and city planners who will undermine Charles' concerns. In the conflict of opinions, the media leaves the British public mystified about the man who will one day be their King. Charles told one journalist: "You know as far as I can make out, I'm about to become a Buddhist monk, or live halfway up a mountain, or only eat grass. I'm not quite as bad as that. Or quite as extreme."

Prince Charles regularly finds himself enmeshed in the pseudo reality of royal protocol, his public image, identification with his role, the superficiality of a pampered lifestyle and various forms of self-indulgence. Constantly involved in public relations, he spends endless days every year dutifully asking the appropriate questions at public functions. "I have had to fight every inch of my life to escape royal protocol. I am determined not to be confined to cutting ribbons," he told a television interviewer. Like his illustrious predecessor, Prince Siddhartha, heir to the Sakyan kingdom 2500 years ago, Charles continues to struggle between the subjugation of himself to orthodox notions of duty to his country and his genuine spiritual concerns for people world wide and their environment.

In 1948, Charles was "born to rule," a situation that has often troubled his life. Advisors, hangers-on, courtiers and private secretaries, whose worlds revolve around maintaining appearances, control and authority, surround him. At times, the future King of England defers to his advisers' views about what he should say and do. Daily exposure to this inner circle as well as a judgemental father, a disappointed mother and a luxurious but tedious lifestyle represses his spirit. Unjustly imprisoned in the royal cage, he endeavours to break out of the extraordinary expectations that he must conform.

Apologists for Charles say that he has no choice in the matter, that he does his best. They say he cannot change his life. But this kind of defensiveness from his supporters damns Charles: it is the worst of all insults of the many that he must endure. With such comments, they treat him as a victim of his birth, upbringing and privileged environment. The example of the Buddha shows that this need not be true.

The Buddha was born Siddhartha Gautama in Lumbini Park to King Suddhodana and Queen Mahamaya in May, 563 BC. He was the son of the ruler of a kingdom in northern India. While en route to her parent's home for the birth, his mother went into labour so she gave birth to Siddhartha in a park named Lumbini. A sage, named Kala Deva, reputed to be a clairvoyant, looked at the baby prince and commented to his father: "I perceive from certain particular signs that this baby is destined to become a fully enlightened one."

Worried that the heir apparent to the Sakyan kingdom might renounce his birthright, King Suddhodhana called in eight leading Brahmin priests. One of them, Kondanna said: "A time will come when Siddhartha will witness four special signs and as a result he will seek enlightenment."

Seven days after the birth of Siddhartha, his mother died. The Queen's sister, Prajapati, brought him up. As children, Siddhartha and his cousin, Devadatta, were exploring the grounds of the palace when Devadatta took his bow and arrow and shot a swan flying overhead. Siddhartha ran to the swan, gently pulled the arrow from its wing and used leaves to stop the blood. Devadatta claimed the bird belonged to him so they went to the Council of the Wise who decided: "A life must belong to him who tries to save it. A life cannot be claimed by one who tries to destroy it." Siddhartha nursed the swan back to health.

The King made every effort to protect his young heir from the signs of suffering in the world. Living a self-indulgent and pampered life, Siddhartha remained apart from genuine contact with suffering humanity, illness, the pain and anguish of old age and even from wandering ascetics. The King built three palaces for Siddhartha, one for each of the Indian seasons, amidst a beautiful environment for hunting and fishing with an abundance of trees, flowers, animals and birds. Siddhartha met many beautiful women in the royal court but he fell in love with Yashodara, a very distant relative. The people of the Sakyan Kingdom rejoiced at the fairy tale marriage of Siddhartha to Yashodara.

Yashodara's pregnancy galvanized the Prince into looking at his life and destiny. Cracks in his fairy tale existence appeared, doubts began to set in his mind. Though, unlike Prince Charles, he had no mass media to contend with, he knew the Sakyan people and his domineering father demanded that he fulfil his duty to the State. Confused and restless, Siddhartha, aged 29, summoned his charioteer, Channa, to take him into the countryside. That trip altered the course of his life; he witnessed an old man with white hair, no teeth, dry skin, bent back and contracted body. "Even I, myself, must one day look like that," he exclaimed to Channa. Siddhartha returned home in despair.

Despite the King's further efforts to hide his son from the real world, Siddhartha saw a sick man writhing in pain, groaning, with blood shot eyes and in terrible agony. "What a wretched plight," Siddhartha said. Then he saw a corpse, cold, stiff and yellowing, carried in a funeral procession en route to cremation. Channa turned to the Prince and said: "There is nothing you can do about death." On the final trip with Channa, Siddhartha met a wandering monk engaged in the pursuit of resolution of the paradoxes of life—life and death, haves and have-nots, good and evil, the profane and the profound. A distressed Siddhartha asked Channa: "Why is this monk so calm amidst the sorrows of the world?" While lost in these thoughts a rider from the palace galloped up to announce that Princess Yashodara had given birth to a son. "Another bond to tie me," Siddhartha sighed. Siddhartha's extremely privileged and sheltered life became meaningless; he now knew he would have to face ageing, sickness and death. His materially secure existence, with its comfortable hereditary and religious values, lost all meaning.

The King called for a sumptuous feast to celebrate the birth of his grandson, named Rahula. After the huge celebration many guests stayed overnight in the palace guest rooms, dining hall and any comfortable spot available. Siddhartha looked at them—some snored, others sniffed in their sleep while others belched—the glamour of the occasion seemed even more trivial than before. He went up to the royal bedroom, took a final look at his sleeping wife but could not bring himself to tuck back the sheet to look at his baby son's face. Hurriedly, he left the room to find his charioteer. He told Channa to saddle his favourite horse Kanthaka. When Siddhartha passed beyond the city gates, he took a quick glance back towards the palace but then rode on with Channa riding besides him. They rode through the night, crossed the River Anoma, and entered the Magadha kingdom.

Siddhartha handed Channa his silk robes, his sword and jewellery, cut off his long hair and changed into ragged clothes. He told Channa that when he had found what he was looking for he would return to the palace to tell his wife, son, adopted mother and the King. There is a poignant story that the horse, Kanthaka, refused to budge when Siddhartha handed the reins to Channa until Siddhartha had walked out of sight in the moonlit night. Tears fell from the eyes of Siddhartha's favourite horse as though he knew his master had abandoned him and all other loved ones.

Siddhartha Gautama (the surname belongs to a subdivision of the warrior caste) set out on a quest for the Ultimate Truth. As Siddhartha pursued his search, people treated him as something of an enigma. Royal attendants told King Bimbisara of Magadha that Siddhartha wandered in the area always "charming and polite." Siddhartha sought out the presence of Kondanna, the priest who had predicted that Siddhartha would renounce his palace responsibilities for a noble calling. At this time, Kondanna shared his spiritual life with four others—Bhaddiya, Vappa, Mahanama and Assaji. The six men became spiritual students of Alara Kalama, a renowned spiritual teacher in Magadha, and later Uddaka Rampautta, glorified for his teaching of mystical experiences.

Still dissatisfied, Siddhartha and his companions formed their own hermitage in Sarnath, near Benares. They gave up hope of finding a teacher of liberation and instead explored severe spiritual practices—fasting, meditating in the heat of the midday sun, bathing in icy water in winter, spending night hours in the mortuary and risking their lives through spending time in places where wild animals marauded. They had a single aim—to transcend fear and to go beyond the duality of life and death.

One day Siddhartha told his companions that he must go his own way. He walked to Bodh Gaya where a young woman, Sujata, the daughter of a wealthy property owner, offered him nutritious milk rice to strengthen his body. He sat beneath a huge tree besides the River Neranjara. There he realized and awakened to the nature of suffering, its causes, its cessation and the way to overcome it. Filled with joy and gladness, he spent seven weeks there meditating and reflecting on forming a spiritual path to enlighten others. His enlightenment filled his heart with compassion for suffering humanity, including spiritual seekers, members of his royal family and all men, women and children. The Buddha analysed the causes and nature of suffering, based on his own experience. "I make known suffering and the cessation of suffering."

He spoke to two merchants, Tapussu and Bahalluka, who offered him food. The Buddha's insights touched them deeply. He then walked more than 100 miles to see his five friends. They saw Siddhartha had put on weight and accused him of falling back into comfort and luxury, but they trusted him enough to listen to what he had to say. He spoke to them for several days, answering their questions until they fully understood his teachings. When the Buddha returned to the capital, his estranged wife Yashordara sent their seven-year-old son to him. With tears in her eyes, Yashodara said to Rahula: "There is your father, the one giving spiritual teachings. Go up to him and say 'I am your son. When I become King I shall become King of Kings. Let me have my property. For what belongs to the father must belong to the son.'" Rahula obeyed and touchingly added: "Father, I love even your shadow."

The Buddha asked Rahula what was the purpose of a mirror. His son said "To look at yourself in." His father said that awareness is like a mirror revealing the acts of body, speech and mind and is a great treasure. It was not long before Rahula, Yashodara and his adopted mother, Prajapati, devoted their lives to awareness, compassion and wisdom. They also turned their back on the supposed glamour of palace life.

For Prince Charles, the signs spurring him to greater awakening also took place while travelling beyond his usual borders to experience a different way of being in the world. In 1977 Prince Charles, aged 29, flew to Kenya on a wildlife trip—an experience that changed his life. Laurens van der Post, the South African explorer and writer, accompanied him on that trip. Van der Post, author of *The Lost World of the Kalahari*, understood the spiritual and cultural heritage of the people native to the region. He also introduced Charles to the writings of Carl Jung, the Swiss psychologist, who emphasised the significance of intuition and dreams. The spiritual life and the wilderness struck a deep chord within Charles. He began the process of awakening to that significant dimension beyond his image makers, conditioned notions of duty and a controlled environment. Van der Post, became Charles' first guru, and later the godfather of Charles' son, William.

Inspired also by his father's concern with conservation, Charles developed a keen interest in the land. With money from his vast estate of 130,000 acres, mostly in Cornwall and Devon, Charles bought himself Highfield House, a country house including a farm with 410 acres, a few miles outside Tetbury, Gloucestershire. It became a refuge from his various public roles, and a place for practical application of his ideas.

Unlike the President of any country, who campaigns for office, Charles was born into his, but the Buddha pointed out that a man does not become noble through birth but through the actions of body, speech and mind. To his credit, Charles has never flinched from controversy. He has earned himself the respect of many who campaign privately and publicly for alternative values that offer a genuine holistic vision connecting health, work, community and environment.

During the 1980's, he became more confident in expressing his views in his public talks. At the 150th anniversary of the British Medical Association, Prince Charles, the outgoing president, spoke to a large gathering of senior members of the medical profession. To their surprise and dismay, Charles spoke highly about unorthodox medicine—stating that Paracelsus inspired him, and that he and other members of the royal family benefit regularly from homeopathy. In what has become a celebrated talk, he told the eminent audience:

"I have often thought that one of the less attractive traits of various professional bodies and institutions is the deeply ingrained suspicion and out right hostility which can exist towards anything unorthodox or unconventional.

"I suppose that human nature is such that we are frequently prevented from seeing that what is taken for today's unorthodoxy is probably going to be tomorrow's convention. Perhaps we just have to accept it is God's will that the unorthodox is doomed to years of frustration, ridicule and failure... I would suggest that the whole imposing edifice of modern medicine for all its breathtaking successes is, like the celebrated tower of Pisa, slightly off balance. It is frightening how dependent upon drugs we are all becoming and how easy it is for doctors to prescribe them as the universal panacea for our ills.... The health of human beings is so often determined by their behaviour, their food and the nature of their environment."

Rather than submit to the outcry of the medical establishment he maintained his support for alternative medicine. The following year Charles visited the acclaimed cancer clinic in Bristol where patients use diet, meditation and group counselling. At the Royal Society of Medicine seminar, he said: "Many, many people in this country are predisposed towards various types of complementary medicine. Increasingly, I think, they are not getting all they want from orthodox medicine."

In 1988, Charles focused his attention on the failings of contemporary architecture. He selected the 150th anniversary dinner of the Royal Institute of British Architects at Hampton Court Palace where, instead of the usual congratulatory speech to British architects, he launched into an unambiguous criticism of modern design and called for the development of "community architecture." He described the extension at Britain's major art museum, the National Gallery in London's Trafalgar Square, as a "a kind of vast municipal fire station... like a monstrous carbuncle on the face of a much loved and elegant friend.

"A large number of us have developed a feeling that architects tend to design houses for the approval of fellow architects and critics—not for the tenants." He then went on to say that a thoughtful architect should be "concerned about the way people live—about the environment they inhabit and the kind of community that is created by that environment."

Charles ought to have severely criticized the developers as well, not just the architects. Architects conform to the wishes of their customers, developers often demand maximum space at minimum cost resulting in narrow, high rise business and apartment blocks. City developers and the land owning gentry escaped the wrath of Charles, although they must be held accountable too for the building projects they finance. (One wonders whether Charles unconsciously protects the rich and the powerful).

Not only is Charles heir to the British throne but he will also become head of the British Commonwealth. Before the collapse of his marriage, he travelled overseas regularly with his wife, Princess Diana. Her exceptional beauty and endless changes of luxurious clothes, a distinctive symbol of privilege, overshadowed Charles' insightful perceptions. To his chagrin, the press overlooked many of his addresses to audiences world wide because they were concentrating on Diana's fashion sense. The media, the public and the royal advisers reduced the Royal Couple to show business personalities, megastars in the megamachine.

The marriage, initially regarded as a romantic fairy tale, became a nightmare, then a sobering lesson to a Prince and Princess about living in a fictional world of self projection and dependency on public acclaim. He and his wife's personal lives filled the front pages and the gossip columns day after day. The media displayed contempt for any request to respect the couple's feelings. Many journalists have their own history of failed marriages, affairs and emotional addictions; yet rather than display compassion for the daily suffering in two other people's lives they haunted them day and night. The press displayed a degree of vulgarity in their pursuit of the royals that is to their everlasting shame. To demand higher moral standards from the monarch is an act of unjustified self-righteousness from the "royal watchers" and their aggressive editors.

The media ignored its duplicity in the public crucifixion of Charles and Diana. The press contributed to the wrecking of the marriage as much as the emotional confusion between the two of them did. For Diana the stress manifested as bulemia and later as substantial withdrawal from all forms of public life. Desperately feeling the need to be understood, Charles sought for years close communication with another woman. Charles's advisers then believed that Charles lost his public credibility. The hardened view of some observers is that the Royal couple and the press deserve each other, but the bottom line must remain compassion. The hope is that Charles can now devote his time fully to the matters that concern him and Diana can find some peace in her life.

Prince Charles continues his annual round of royal duties. The Prince of Wales is Colonel of the Welsh Guards and Colonel-in-Chief of the Parachute Regiment, the Royal Dragoon Guards, the Royal Regiment of Wales, the Gordon Highlanders, the Cheshire Regiment and the 2nd King Edward VII's Own Gurkha Rifles. As a major figure in the military establishment, an historical backbone of the monarchy, Charles never addresses in his public talks the significance of disarmament or nonviolence—though it must have crossed his mind that war causes greater suffering and hardship to people and their environment than any other human activity. His support for the military establishment and for the protection of the environment puts him in two distinct worlds. The former ensures the continuity of the monarchy since the military prefer to fight for Queen and Country rather than the current crop of politicians. Charles wants it both ways—to uphold continuity of his personal lifestyle, and also social and environmental justice.

His love of *Small is Beautiful*, an international best seller on Buddhist economics and other themes, has modestly influenced Charles' perceptions. Written by E.F. Schumacher, regarded as a founding father of the international Green movement, the author explains the necessity for a new form of economics. Schumacher wrote: "While the materialist is mainly interested in goods, the Buddhist is mainly interested in liberation. But Buddhism is the middle way and therefore in no way antagonistic to physical wellbeing. It is not wealth that stands in the way of liberation, but the attachment to wealth; not the enjoyment of pleasurable things, but the craving for them. The keynote of Buddhist economics is simplicity and non-violence. From an economist's point of view the marvel of the Buddhist way of life is the utter rationality of its patterns—amazingly small means leading to extraordinarily satisfactory results."

Many passages from *Small is Beautiful* inspired Charles. He became president of the Intermediate Technology Development Group, a charity that Schumacher founded. Once Charles sent a message to an organic food conference at the Royal Agricultural College in Cirencester. His note demonstrated the influence of Schumacher:

"For some years now modern farming has made tremendous demands on the finite resources of energy which exist on Earth. Maximum production has been the slogan to which we have adhered. In the last few years there has been an increasing realization that many modern production methods are not only very wasteful but probably also unnecessary. The supporters of organic farming, bio-agriculture, alternative agriculture and optimum production are beginning to make themselves heard, and not before time."

In the 1970's Charles established the Prince's Trust aimed to help disadvantaged young people from 14–25 years of age, and later the Youth Business Initiative designed to help the young unemployed set up their own businesses. He became a patron for the Royal Society for Nature Conservation. He regularly advocates support for the plight of the people of the Third World through appropriate technology and education. His projects express the heart of a compassionate man through a genuine willingness to give support to people in need. He has become a spokesperson for their aspirations. Through his empathy with the underprivileged, he once said: "We have managed through our Western arrogance to make at least two generations feel ashamed of their ancient, traditional customs, culture and spiritual values. Now, I suggest, is the time when we should in all humility learn from our Third World neighbours."

In his book, *A Vision of Britain*, Prince Charles wrote on the back jacket: "My chief object has been to try and create discussion about the design of the built environment; to rekindle and alert awareness of our surroundings; inspire a desire to observe; but, most of all to challenge the fashionable theories of a professional establishment...."

Within the same book, he wrote: "Man is much, much more than a mere mechanical object whose sole aim is to produce money. Man is a far more complex creation. Above all, he has a soul, and the soul is irrational, unfathomable, mysterious." It takes a certain courage for the heir to the throne to write and publish such thoughts—an echo of Jung's beliefs. For such statements, Charles deserves our gratitude and not vilification as a "loony" prince.

He told the London Press Club: "Our protection depends, I believe, on the mystical power which from time immemorial has been called God whose relationship to man seems to depend on man's relationship to his inner voice." When he was 26 years old, Charles visited a Buddhist monastery in Kyoto and commented that he felt he had "come home at last." He has found time to spend further days in the Kalahari desert with Laurens Van der Post, and for some relative isolation on a Hebridean Island.

No doubt Charles will continue to include his spiritual, environmental social and global concerns in his public speeches. But I believe his extremely privileged lifestyle, comparable to a tycoon, waters down the authority of his statements. He must introduce personal discipline and wisdom into the way he conducts his life, uses his privileges, prosperity and power. Being a thoughtful person is no substitute for the inner voice which says "NO" to the trappings and gross pursuits of pleasure that run through Charles's life.

The press has noted his use of the royal yacht, helicopters, private planes, flying war planes, lavish holidays, petrol guzzling cars, endless new suits, banquets, indulgence in luxuries and praise for NATO's nuclear defence policy. He receives phenomenal income from his estates yet only began paying income tax as a result of media exposure and public pressure. Charles shows a Victorian attitude to parenting when he gives support to slapping children. Charles takes pleasure in risking serious injury in the pursuit of various sports, whether skiing on dangerous slopes of the Alps, fox hunting or playing polo. Charles uses these sports to prove himself, particularly his sense of self worth. But these sports, which include the pleasure of hunting and killing animals, birds and fish, reveal a displaced sense of risk taking. "I'm not someone overburdened with a sense of self-confidence," he once remarked. Charles must decide whether he will risk total commitment to a life affirming process or engage in duplicity through supporting life denying institutions such as the military, blood sports and a high-flying lifestyle. Every time Charles compromises he turns his back on the fate of the Earth and the depth of his spiritual awareness.

Charles seems pulled between two conflicting values. One is the pressure on him to conform to the stereotyped aims of the royal household and the other is listening to the real world of suffering and its resolution. His first and only duty is listening to his deep inner voice of compassionate action, not to the expectations or pleas of his advisers and private secretary. As long as Charles submits to image makers, he compromises his commitment to the quality of life on Earth. Since the media damns him either way, he must take great risks for the Earth, change his lifestyle and forget his public image. There is no justification for placing personal credibility before Truth.

Unlike Prince Siddhartha, who totally renounced his royal position, Charles has not yet taken such an uncompromising step. Prince Charles belongs to a coterie of power and privilege consisting of the Royal Family, the House of Lords, Senior Civil Servants and the Church. As heir to the throne, Charles Philip Arthur George Windsor embodies the values of wealth and possession. From birth, he has been linked to the hereditary chain which holds together the Establishment in Britain.

Charles is pivotal in this narrow world of wealth and privilege but having let go of the ties of marriage, Charles can bring his deeper yearnings for the underprivileged and the environment to the surface through one simple act of compassion—to renounce the throne, his birth and other associated relics of the Middle Ages. He must cut his tie to his hereditary chains. Such an announcement might rattle the Establishment out of its arrogant complacency and make way for a fair and just society. Then there may be a possibility of freedom in Britain from the rigid control of the Establishment who have always ensured their personal interests come first.

Like Prince Siddhartha, Prince Charles must forget his so-called royal blood, his loyalty to the Queen, his staggering wealth, the expectations of his advisers and the wall of conformity that imprisons him. He must see the emptiness of upholding the charade of believing his national duty is to become King of Britain. Charles must renounce his right to the throne and the suffocating responsibilities that accompany it. In 1936 his great-uncle, King Edward VIII, renounced the throne out of love for Mrs. Wallis Simpson, an American woman. In his message to the nation and the world wide British Commonwealth that then covered a fifth of the Earth, King Edward said he had made an "irrevocable determination to renounce the throne for myself and for my descendents." When his Great-uncle Edward made the decision out of love for a woman, there was a public outcry.

Charles must renounce the throne for himself and his descendents out of love for those causes which touch his heart. He can then give full rein to his intuition and awareness. If he shakes off the curse of his birth, Charles can enter the path to an enlightened life, for which Prince Siddhartha set an historical precedent. Such a step by Prince Charles would free him from the perpetuation of the royal soap opera and the associated morass of lies and deceptions dished out to the public. If Charles renounces the throne and all of his titles, it could become a turning point in the fortunes of Britain with beneficial reverberations for humanity and the Earth.

An Open Letter to the World's Political Leaders

Dear President or Prime Minister,

I appeal to you to examine your political beliefs in the face of the harsh truths of global life. Safeguarding people, the Earth and its protective biosphere are of paramount importance.

People everywhere yearn for peace and justice and to live in safety. It is their right to campaign for food, clothing, a home and medicine. It is also their right to abide in an environment that is free from harmful pollution of land, water and air.

I believe that current political standpoints require a spiritual and ecological basis. Political action has to be grounded in compassion for the sustained welfare of human beings, animals and the environment.

The unrestrained consumption of resources has provided wealth and privilege for a minority of the world's population while the majority live near, on, or far beneath the poverty line. Many policies work at the expense of the deep needs of people locally, nationally and globally. Unless there is dramatic re-evaluation of the influential political ideologies, the remaining years of this millennium will continue to be a time of thoughtless waste, mindless consumption and utterly misguided political and economic views.

I also bring to your awareness the way the ego influences your political judgements. I perceive the main impetus of leaders is the desire to retain power; the will to control becomes the reason for existence. Political beliefs and self interest matter more than the needs of the people, even though decisions are made in their name. Thus you direct your efforts towards controlling others and the natural world rather than implementing wise and compassionate political and economic policies.

The resolution of unsatisfactory patterns in leadership comes through understanding your relationships with political supporters, opponents, the people and the Earth. Characteristics which get a person to pole position can become the model of success. Subordinates achieve a sense of self worth by copying the language and mannerisms of their leader and exuding the same brand of cleverness. They either admire or resent you, imitate you or plot to succeed you. They praise you publicly and undermine you behind closed doors. These concerns become your world at the expense of countless citizens.

Leaders utilize the various powers at their disposal with efficiency to sustain power. But without self knowledge it is impossible to discriminate between wise leadership and the abusive imposition of control over people and the environment. Leaders naively believe they are taking the only course available such as constantly exhorting economic growth, bringing in foreign capital, increasing military exports or imports, and dismissing voices of opposition. All these demonstrate a lack of wisdom and foresight.

Leaders may believe their actions are for the common good but, without realizing it, their decisions may contribute to irreversible harm for the present and future generations. Economic analyses must measure the cost of exploiting resources in the human and natural world. Calculations of economic growth do not measure the rapid depletion of natural capital. Like all such calculations, the result depends on economists' choices: what to include and what to exclude. Ignoring the cost to resources makes economic growth an illusion. I believe you must support a steady economy and oppose an infinite growth economy. A steady economy accords with the reality of the Earth which has finite resources; economic growth is consuming the Earth, soon there will be nothing much left for the world's poor or future generations to live on.

Leaders cannot browbeat ordinary people into becoming workaholics and pawns for economic growth. Leaders think people don't work hard enough when their policies fail. Perhaps you are not working hard enough to look into your political beliefs, particularly around growth. It is vital to look into yourself and explore the underlying motives for your decisions. If you are honest with yourself, you will see your political and economic objectives are not really in the interests of the country, but express your hope to gain respect and a place in history.

Leaders often feel they want an orderly and safe country but perhaps unconsciously pursue a country that has surrendered to their authority. Their relationship to the country becomes a mirror for their mind. While leaders and their opponents undermine each other, the genuine needs of people and the environment become a minor consideration in the struggle of wills and one-line sound bites. Never forget that compassion is the ultimate political ethic, free from prejudice, enabling a leader to act boldly.

I believe political beliefs are reflected in the way we live and act rather than through the words we proclaim. Your use or abuse of power and pressure affect the quality of life in your country and on the international stage. Political leaders make demands for sacrifice on their citizens which they have no intention of observing in their own lives. Many politicians live extravagantly, out of touch with the personal and community hardships of the people they claim to represent. The lavish, self-indulgent lifestyle of the government and official opposition, both at public functions and private gatherings, must stop. Politicians cannot comprehend, emotionally, people's daily struggles and the suffering of trying to make ends meet.

Power is as addictive and dangerous as hard drugs. The desire to hire and fire, approve and condemn takes over at the expense of deep and caring values. Waging a campaign day in and day out to dominate the direction the country will take into the next century is dangerous thinking. Leaders reward those who serve their interests with power, money and titles; yet withdraw support, reduce the benefits and ignore the way of life of the needy. When leaders ignore the poor, hold back financial support for local communities and reject protection of the social and natural environment they expose a depth of insensitivity, a lack of compassion and the absence of wisdom.

People reach the point where they can no longer stomach a leader's policies. They may even rise up and oust their president or prime minister from office. The priority is to relieve suffering Here and Now. How many of your citizens would emigrate tomorrow if it were possible? Those who are not able to be in control of their own lives get neglected or, at best, receive scant attention. Organisations working on behalf of the neglected and dispossessed have to appeal repeatedly for support and assistance, but when finally given, if at all, it is grudgingly.

Modest and reluctant support for global issues is only an exercise in international public relations. If our leaders show a lack of compassion then nothing better can be expected from anyone else. The tendency to direct blame elsewhere, and never to admit to making mistakes fools nobody. When citizens protest nonviolently they are labelled trouble makers or extremists. You feel safe by shutting up the voices of those who think differently. Your identification with power contributes to despising the powerless. The obsession with economic growth damages the fabric of the Earth; people become angry, frustrated aggression and intolerance mounts around the world at the unprincipled values of politicians and the privileged elite. Conflict and tension around money, debts, unemployment and the future run riot. Widespread disillusionment contributes to violence and abuse in the home and on the streets as young people become cynical about the present and even more so about the future.

I urge you to engage in deep political, social and economic analysis of cause and effect relationships, both in the short and long term. The current political ideology of the left, right and centre must change beyond all recognition. There must be the political will to stop the consequences of any political views obsessed with profit and exploitive use of human and environmental resources. You must acknowledge publicly the responsibility to present and future generations; this must be reflected not only in political and economic decisions, but also in modesty and integrity in personal and public life.

Leaders delude themselves when they think truth and vision lie in their hands. You cannot possess the whole picture of political realities for you are only part of the picture. If you acknowledged this then listening would replace attack, generosity would replace arrogance, participation would replace domination and wisdom would replace ideology. Wisdom offers compassionate action to people in need and environmental protection. Wise political leadership expresses personal sacrifice and stimulates the release of insightful initiatives in people, thus offering a genuine opportunity for a safe and fair society with environmental justice.

If you wish to take credit for economic growth then you must also take responsibility for the consequences, namely fragmentation of society, the decline of the local community and the systematic destruction of the Earth. Wise leadership includes providing a pluralistic, tolerant and caring society in a safe and protected environment. The nation's scientific and technological resources must be directed towards the sustained welfare of the field of existence, not to its exploitation. The atmosphere, seas, rivers, forests, landscapes and habitation of people and wildlife, deserve a high degree of care and attention. Applying this vision would encourage others to respond to local, national and global realities.

Wise leadership looks within and far beyond national borders to see the consequences of decisions for the entire biosphere. A spiritual and ecological basis for political life offer a significant contribution to the whole world. By actively acknowledging and respecting the interconnection of the web of life, you participate in a turning point in the life of the nation and the Earth.

Yours faithfully,

Christopher Titmuss.

THE GREEN VISION

A Statement to the Earth and Its Inhabitants

1. Truth makes all things possible. All life is interdependent. Compassionate spiritual, economic and ecological activities arise from and belong to this principle. Our duty is paying respect to all manifestations of life embraced in the ecosystem.

2. This principle is grounded in concern for the sustained welfare of human beings, animals and the environment. The safeguarding of the Earth and the protective biosphere are of paramount significance.

3. I acknowledge the deep human yearning for peace and justice in the world. I support campaigns for the rights of humanity for food, clothing, a home and medicine. I recognize the right for people to abide in an environment that is protected from the abuse of land, water and air. Unlimited consumption of resources has provided wealth and privilege for a small minority of the Earth's population while the vast majority live near, on, or far beneath the poverty line.

4. Spirituality includes a deep analysis of cause and effect relationship, both short and long term. I believe it is vital that we examine the consequences of our way of living and acknowledge the responsibility we share to present and future generations. This responsibility must be reflected not only in our political and social values, but also in our daily lives.

5. I am not opposed to technological and industrial progress but I am concerned with their appropriate use. The concept of progress must be aligned to clearly stated ethics.

6. Ecological wisdom is founded upon an economic analysis that includes the cost of exploiting resources and the damage incurred to the health of people and environment. I am opposed to the current form of indiscriminate economic growth as the Earth's capital is finite and cannot support an infinite growth economy.

7. I believe we ought to direct our considerable scientific and technical knowledge to the sustained welfare of people, animals and environment, not for their exploitation. The atmosphere, oceans, seas, rivers, forests, landscapes and countless forms of habitation for people and wildlife deserve care and attention. Our ecological vision encourages all to act locally, nationally and globally for the welfare and security of the ecosystem.

8. Spiritual awareness includes realization of the Ultimate Truth that remains untarnished by human behaviour; a deep and active reverence for the Earth and a liberating sense of mystery and wonder. It is the right of all to draw upon the diversity of spiritual and religious traditions as well as contemporary expressions of the spiritual impulse. Spiritual life recognizes our deep connection with each other, with all sentient life, the air we breathe, the water we drink and the land we walk on.

9. Spirituality is expressed through support for the local community and inquiry into our own lives in order to free each other from the personal and social forces of selfishness, aggression and fear, and to discover generosity, compassion and wisdom.

10. A joint spiritual, economic and ecological vision offers a precious contribution to the Earth, so join with me in this statement.

Book, Magazine and Newspaper Acknowledgements

I wish to express appreciation to the following authors, editors and translators who have contributed, directly and indirectly, to my inquiry into spiritual, religious and global themes in *The Green Buddha*.

Translated Talks of The Buddha (Pali Text Society, London)
Book of the Discipline (6 vols)
Dhammapada (pub. Buddhist Society)
Elders Verses
Gradual Sayings (5 vols)
Group of Discourses (Sutta Nipata)
Kindred Sayings (5 vols)
Middle Length Sayings (3 vols)
Minor Anthologies
Minor Readings
The Sisters

Translations Of Selected Texts Of The Buddha's Teachings
Large Sutra on Perfect Wisdom, trans E.Conze, Motilal Banarsidas
Life of the Buddha, by Bhikkhi Nanamoli, Buddhist Publication
    Society
Path to Deliverance, Ven. Nyanatiloka, Buddhist Pub. Soc.
Perfect Wisdom, trans. Edward Conze, Buddhist Publishing Group
The Lion's Roar, ed. David Maurice, Citadel
Thus Have I Heard (Longer Length Sayings) trans. M. Walshe,
    Wisdom
Some Sayings of the Buddha, trans. F.L. Woodward, Buddhist
    Society
Sutta Nipata, trans Ven. Saddhatissa, Curzon Press
The Dhammapada (and Notes), trans. Radhakrishnan, Oxford
    Univesity Press
Word of the Buddha, Ven. Nyantiloka, Buddhist Pub Soc.

Buddhism
A Buddhist Vision for Renewing Society, Sulak Sivaraksa, Tienwan
    Pub.

Being Peace, Thich Naht Hanh, Parallax Press
Buddha's Ancient Path, Piyadassi Thera, Buddhist Pub. Society
Buddhism in South-East Asia. R. Lester, Uni of Michigan Press
Buddhist Dictionary, Ven. Nyantiloka, Frewin and Co.
Concept and Reality, Ven. Nnanananda, Buddhist Pub Soc.
Daughters of the Buddha, ed Karma Lekshe Tsomo, Snow Lion
Dharma and Development, Joanna Macy, Kumarian Press
Dharma: The World Saviour, Ajahn Buddhadasa.
Dynamic Psychology of Early Buddhism, Rune Johansson, Curzon
    Press
Emptiness, a study in religious meaning, F.J. Streng. Abingdon
    Press
Faith to Doubt, Stephen Batchelor (Parallax Press)
Handbook for Mankind, Ajahn Buddhadasa, Sublime Life Mission
Heart of Buddhist Meditation, Nyanapoinika Thera, Rider and Co.
Holy Teachings of Vimalakirti, trans R. Thurman. Pennsylvania
    University Press
Kindness, Clarity and Insight, Dalai Lama, Snow Lion
Nagarjuna, Lindtner, Motilal Banarsidas
Nagarjuna, Philosophy of Middle Way, D. Kalupahana, Suny
Path of Compassion, ed Fred Eppsteiner, Parallax
Radical Conservatism,(commentary on Ajahn Buddadasa's
    teachings), INEB
Social Face of Buddhism, Ken Jones, Wisdom
The Buddha, Trevor Ling, Temple Smith.
Theravada Buddhism, Richard Gobrich, Routledge,Keegan Paul
The First Buddhist Women, Susan Murcott, Parallax Press
The Historical Buddha, H.W. Schumann, Arkana Books
The Life of the Buddha, Ven. H. Saddhatissa, Unwin,
The Poetry of Enlightenment. trans. Sheng Yen. Dharma Drum
The Tantric Distinction, Jeffrey Hopkins, Wisdom
Wittgenstein and Buddhism, Chris Gudmensen, Macmillan Press

Psychological, Social, National, Green, Global Issues
A People's History of the United States, Howard Zinn, Longman
A Vision of Britain, Prince Charles, Doubleday
Arguments for Democracy, Tony Benn, Penguin
American Economic Review
Awake, Jehovah Witnesses
Beyond Ego, ed Roger Walsh, Francis Vaughan, J.P.Tarcher
Black Consciousness in South Africa, Steve Biko, Vintage Books
Building the Green Movement, Rudolf Bahro, New Society Pub.

Book, Magazine and Newspaper Acknowledgements

Catholic Study Bible. pub. Oxford Press.
Chomsky Reader, Noam Chomsky, Random House
Collected Poems, T.S. Eliot, Faber and Faber
Critique of Political Economy, Karl Mark. Charles Kerr and Co.
Crossing the Threshold of Hope, Pope John Paul II
Culture of Narcissism, Christopher Lasch, Abacus
Deep Ecology, ed. Devall, Sessions, Perergrine Smith Books
Diet for a New America. J. Robbins, Stillpoint
Freedom from the Known, J. Krishnamurti, K'murti Foundation.
Design for a Livable Planet, Jon Naar, Harper and Row.
Earth in the Balance, Al Gore, Houghton MIfflin Co.
Earth Report, ed. Goldsmith and Hildyard, Price Stern Sloan.
Eliot's New Life, Lyndall Gordon, pub. Oxford University Press.
Fear of Freedom, Erich Fromm, Routledge
Four Arguments for the Elimination of Television, Jerry Mander,
    Quill
Good Neighbour Handbook, Sanford Lewis, National Toxics
    Campaign
Green Line magazine
Health and Survival, Ross Horne, Margaret Gee Publishers
Heart of Religion, R.D. Mehta, Compton Russell
Heroes, John Pilger, Jonathan Cape
Holistic Curriculum, John Miller, OISE Press.
Human Growth, Karen Horney, W.W. Norton
Inquiring Mind
Inside the Third World, Paul Harrison, Penguin
Journey through the Eye of a Needle, Maurice Ash, Green Books
Ludwig Wittgenstein: The Duty of Genius, Ray Monk, Vintage
Lying, a Critical Analysis, Warren Shibles, Language Press
Manifesto for a Sustainable Society, The Green Party.
Manual for a Living Revolution, Coover, Deacon, New Society
Media Sexploitation, Wilson Bryan Key, Prentic-Hall Inc.
New York Times
Owning your Own Shadow, Robert Johnson, Harper Collins
Pedagogies for the Non-Poor, ed Evans, Evans and Kennedy, Orbis
Philosphical Investigations, Ludwig Wittgenstein, Basil Blackwell
Prince Charles, Penny Junor, Guild Publishing
Race to Riches, Jeremy Seabrook, Green Print.
Reality isn't what it used to be. Truett Anderson, Harper and Row.
Republic of Bihar, Arvind Das, Penguin.
Rescuing the Nation's Health, David Gillett, Green Party
Resurgence magazine

Book, Magazine and Newspaper Acknowledgements

San Francisco Chronicle
Seeing Green, Jonathon Porritt, Basil Blackwell
Small is Beautiful, E.F. Schumacher, Abacus
Spilling the Beans, Martin Stott, Fontana
State of the World, ed. Lester R. Brown, W.W. Norton and Co.
The Divided Self, R.D. Laing, Pelican
The Economist magazine
The Guardian newspaper
The Idea of Neighbourhood, Jeremy Seabrook, Pluto Press
The Independent newspaper
The Pocket Green Book, Andrew Rees, Zed Books
The Price of Power, Seymour Hersh, Summit Books.
The Tarnished Crown, Anthony Holden, Bantam Press
The Thirties and After, Stephen Spender, Macmillan Press
The Thought of Karl Marx, David McLellan, Macmillan Press
The Trade Trap, Belinda Coote, OXFAM
The Waste Land, an analytical study, Dr. R.S. Tiwary, Kital Mahal.
Totnes Community newsletter
Towards a History of Needs, Ivan Illich, Heyday Books
Tractatus Logico-Philosophicus, Wittgenstein, pub. Routledge
Utne Reader
Woman Awake, Christina Feldman, Arkana
When the State Kills, Amnesty International
World Bank and the Environment, World Bank
World Military and Social Expenditure, Ruth Sivard, World
    Priorities

Christopher Titmuss is a member of:
Action on Smoking and Health, 5-11 Mortimer Street, London,
    W1N 7RH
Amnesty International, 5 Roberts Place, off Bowling Green Lane,
    London, EC1 DEJ
Animal Aid, 7 Castle Street, Tonbridge, Kent
Buddhist Peace Fellowship, PO Box 4650, Berkeley, CA 94704, USA
Dharmanet International, PO Box 4951, Berkeley, CA94704, USA.
Campaign for Nuclear Dismarmament,22 Underwood
    Street,London N17JG
Friends of the Earth, 26 Underwood Street, London, N17JQ
GreenNet, 23 Bevenden Street, London,N1 6BH
Green Party, 10 Station Parade, Balham High Road, London,
    SW12 9AZ
Greenpeace, 30-31 Islington Green, London, N1 8XE

Insight Meditation Society, 1230 Pleasant Street, Barre, Mass.
01005, USA
International Network of Engaged Buddhists, PO BOX 1,
Onngkhaak, Nakhon Nayok 26120 Bangkok 10401, Thailand
OXFAM (Oxford Committee for Famine Relief) 274 Banbury Road,
Oxford, OX2 7DZ
Prajna Vihar School, c/o Burmese Vihara, Bodh Gaya, district
Gaya, Bihar, India
Self Heal Association, c/o I Redworth Terrace, Totnes. TQ9, Devon
Spirit Rock Insight Meditation Centre, 500 St Francis Drake
Boulevard, PO Box 909, Woodacre CA 94973. USA
Schumacher Society, Ford House, Hartland, Bideford, Devon
EX39 6EE
Survival International, 310 Edgware Road, London, W2 IDY
Vegetarian Society, Parkdale, Altrincham, Cheshire, WA14 4QG
War on Want, 37 Great Guildford Street, London SE1

Index

Index

Index

impermanence 239
imports, military 281
income tax 132
India 51
India at the time of the Buddha 206
individualism 82
industrialists 28
inherent existence 154, 203, 239, 245–246
inner cities 268
inquiry 153
insecurity 133, 135, 138–139
insight 83, 87
insight meditation 155, 159, 162
insurance companies 8
Integrity 139
integrity 134, 138, 283
interconnection 194, 208–209, 215
interdependence 56
international law 23
intolerance 4
investment 132
Iraq 35
Israel, 12 tribes of 223

J
"Japan bashing" 21
Jerusalem 227
Jesus 38, 216–225, 227
jobs 136
Judeo-Christian tradition 159
judgements 194
judging others 150
justice, social and environmental 42

K
Kalama people 149
karma 188–189
Kelly, Petra 143
kindness 132, 134
Kingdom of Heaven 216
Kisagotami 253
knowledge and the environment 29

L
labour 55
land 135
language, nature of 237
law 66, 72
Law, the 216
leaders 139, 208–209, 213
LETS 44
LETS (Local Exchange Trading
   System), 43
liberals 147–149, 151–152

liberation 197–199, 204
liberation theology 4
lifestyle 157–158
literature, decline of 29
livelihood 66
livelihood, right 199
local communities 43
Local Exchange Trading System 43
local government 66
local view 42
logic 239
lotus 84
Love 87
Lovelock, James 40
Loving kindness 87
loyalty to company 21
lust and desire 252
luxury cars 83
lying 210, 212

M
Madhyamika School 238, 244
Maha Ghosananda 213
Mahanth 77
Mahayana 159–160
Maitreya 226
Maitreyi 254
male elders 254
mantra 215
Mara 252
market 230–232
market economy 142, 145, 230–231
market forces 235
Marx, Karl 197, 228–233, 235–236
Marxist-Leninist solution 230
Mary of Magdala 219, 227
Mary of Nazareth 227
McDonalds 16
media 11, 268, 270, 275, 277
media and the environment 27
Medical science 67
medical science 70
Medicine 67
medicine, orthodox 274
meditation 68, 93
megastars 31
membership 31, 33–36
metaphysical category 154
middle way 148, 152, 154, 276
military 28
military and toxic wastes 8
military exports and imports 281
military industry 68

Index

Books by Christopher Titmuss

Available from:
>Insight Books
>c/o Gaia House
>Denbury
>near Newton Abbot
>Devon TQ12 6DY
>England

Spirit for Change (14 interviews on engaged spirituality)	£5.00
Freedom of the Spirit (15 more interviews)	£6.00
Fire Dance and Other Poems*	£3.50
The Profound and the Profane*	£8.00
The Green Buddha*	£11.00

add 20% post and package

* also available from distributors:
>Wisdom Publications
>402 Hoe Street
>London E17 9AA
>England

For selected lists from more than 1000 taped talks by Christopher Titmuss contact Insight Tapes, c/o Gaia House.
Two talks (45 minutes per talk) inland or overseas £5.00
price includes post and package

In the USA contact:
>Dharma Seed Tape Library
>Box 66
>Wendell Depot, MA 01380
>USA

for books and tapes.